D1452399

TRUMAN AND KOREA

TRUMAN AND KOREA

THE POLITICAL CULTURE OF THE EARLY COLD WAR

Paul G. Pierpaoli, Jr.

UNIVERSITY OF MISSOURI PRESS
COLUMBIA AND LONDON

Library of Congress Cataloging-in-Publication Data

Pierpaoli, Paul G., 1962–
    Truman and Korea : the political culture of the early cold war /
    Paul G. Pierpaoli, Jr.
        p.   cm.
    ISBN 0-8262-1206-9
    1. Korean War, 1950–1953—United States.   2. United States—
    Politics and government—1945–1953.   3. Truman, Harry S.,
    1884–1972.   I. Title.
    DS919.P54   1999
    951.904'2373—dc21   98-33326
                                                                     CIP

⊗™ This paper meets the requirements of the
American National Standard for Permanence of Paper
for Printed Library Materials, Z39.48, 1984.

Designer: Stephanie Foley
Typesetter: Bookcomp, Inc.
Printer and Binder: Thomson-Shore
Typefaces: Cheltenham and Palatino

For my loving and understanding family and friends,
and most of all for my mom and dad

CONTENTS

ACKNOWLEDGMENTS

A few brief words here can hardly convey the full depth of my gratitude to the many people and institutions who made this book possible. Nonetheless, I offer my sincerest thanks to all who have helped me over the last several years. Although I sense that they know how important they have been to me, my gratitude knows no bounds. At the Ohio State University, where I began my intellectual odyssey as a professional historian, I wish to thank the following mentors and friends: Michael J. Hogan, William R. Childs, Allan R. Millett, Susan M. Hartmann, Albert J. Churella, and Marianne Holdzkom. Their insights and friendship sustained me and kept this project on track. Financial support from various institutions was also integral to the conclusion of this work, and thus I express my deepest appreciation to: the Ohio State University Alumni Association for its Graduate Research Award; the Harry S. Truman Library Institute for its very generous Dissertation Year Fellowship; and the Department of History at the University of Arizona for its financial support. I also wish to thank my colleagues at the University of Arizona for their patience and collegiality, and I want to especially thank my Department Chair Helen Nader for her unwavering support and encouragement.

The knowledgeable and helpful staffs at the National Archives and the Harry S. Truman Library proved indispensable to my research. I am indebted to them, especially William Creech at the National Archives and Erwin Mueller, Dennis Bilger, and Elizabeth Safly at the Truman Library. I also wish to thank Ruth Dickstein in the Social Sciences/History Division of the University of Arizona Main Library—her expertise and patience made the last leg of this work far more pleasant than it otherwise would have been.

In addition, I offer my steadfast gratitude to my old friend and mentor Alan F. Farrell, who long ago taught me that rigorous thinking, good writing, and unyielding academic integrity are worth fighting for. Further, I am indebted to my old friend Father Joseph H. Metzger Jr., who kept me on an even keel during a storm-tossed period in my career. I am also grateful to my graduate student teaching associates whose excellence and dedication made my own job easier and more enjoyable; they include Megan Taylor-Shockley, George Rising, Peter Alter, Jerry Pierce, and Fabio Pittaluga. Special thanks go to H. Michael Gelfand for his hard work, good teaching, and his invaluable assistance in preparing the final manuscript draft for publication. As well, I would be remiss at this point not to mention another longtime mentor whose personal and intellectual élan has continued to inspire me, even from afar: Josiah Bunting III.

Finally, I thank my extraordinary family, especially my parents, Paul and Arlene Pierpaoli. Their unconditional love, their uncommon wisdom, and their unfailing generosity will always be the guideposts of my life. My brother, Steven, and my "sister," Annie, are all that a sibling could ask for—and more. And the legacy and memories of my grandparents, Gaspare and Olga Pierpaoli and George and Adeline Ottiano, will sustain me always. This book is dedicated to ALL my family, small token that it is for all that has been passed on to me.

ABBREVIATIONS

AFL	American Federation of Labor
BAC	Business Advisory Council
BOB	Bureau of the Budget
CEA	Council of Economic Advisors
CED	Committee for Economic Development
CIO	Congress of Industrial Organizations
CMP	Controlled Materials Plan
DMPA	Defense Materials Procurement Agency
DPA	Defense Production Administration
ECA	Economic Cooperation Administration
ESA	Economic Stabilization Agency
FMCS	Federal Mediation and Conciliation Service
IMC	International Materials Conference
JCS	Joint Chiefs of Staff
NAM	National Association of Manufacturers
NATO	North Atlantic Treaty Organization
NPA	National Production Authority
NRA	National Recovery Administration
NSC	National Security Council
NSRB	National Security Resources Board
ODM	Office of Defense Mobilization
OPA	Office of Price Administration, World War II
OPS	Office of Price Stabilization, Korean War
UAW	United Auto Workers
ULPC	United Labor Policy Committee
UMW	United Mine Workers
UN	United Nations
USCC	United States Chamber of Commerce
WIB	War Industries Board
WPB	War Production Board
WSB	Wage Stabilization Board

TRUMAN AND KOREA

The Trojan Horse of National Security

The primacy of armed conflict in the evolution of the
Western world is the essential tragedy of modern history.
On the one hand, war has helped create the oases of
stability known as states. On the other hand, it has made
the state a potential Frankenstein monster, an instrument
of unconstrained force. The mass state, the regulatory
state, the welfare state—in short, the collectivist state—
is an offspring of total warfare.

Bruce D. Porter, *War and the Rise of the State*[1]

Historians often seek to identify watersheds. These decisive turning points are usually the result of great or ignoble deeds, natural or
man-made cataclysms, momentous decisions, and the like. Historical
watersheds help us to understand the complexities and interconnec-
tions of human motivations and behavior, as well the interrelations of
cause and effect. The twentieth century contains many watersheds: the
coming of World War I in 1914, the onset of the Great Depression of the
early 1930s, the outbreak of World War II in 1939, and the crumbling
of the Berlin Wall in 1989, to name but a few. As this study will show,
the outbreak of the Korean War in 1950—not ordinarily perceived as
a watershed—was one of the great sea changes in postwar American
history. Like the Trojan horse sent into Troy, President Harry S. Truman's
June 1950 decision to intervene in the Korean crisis laid the nation bare
to a bombardment of economic, political, military, and social changes.

1. Bruce D. Porter, *War and the Rise of the State*, 3.

Many of them were completely unanticipated, and they permanently altered the American economic and political landscape.

This book is the first in-depth, scholarly treatment of the Korean War mobilization and the American home front. As it turned out, the Korean mobilization went far beyond preparations for America's first undeclared war; it evolved into the nation's de facto Cold War preparedness program, which came to span nearly forty years. Thus, in its broadest context, this work is about the building of the United States' postwar national security state and the evolution of the political culture of the Cold War. It analyzes the organizational, institutional, and political history of American industrial and economic mobilization for the Korean War within the wider scope of the evolving Cold War. In doing so, it offers new insights into the changing shape of the postwar political economy and political culture by tracing the nation's path from a demobilized peacetime status to an indefinitely mobilized Cold War status.

In the decades following the Korean armistice of 1953, the Korea War experience faded from popular and scholarly concern; it became the "forgotten war." By the early 1980s, however, renewed scholarly interest in the war and the changes it wrought had blossomed into a considerable body of new and important work on the subject. Almost all of these studies have focused on the military, diplomatic, and international aspects of the crisis. None has examined in any detail how the nation mobilized for the war and how that effort affected the economic scene and political culture of the United States.[2] Filling those gaps is the principle endeavor of this work.

2. The literature on the Korean War in general is quite extensive. Following is an abbreviated list of recent monographs dealing with the military and diplomatic-international ramifications of the war: Rosemary Foot, *The Wrong War: American Policy and the Dimensions of the Korean Conflict, 1950–1953;* Bruce Cumings, *The Origins of the Korean War,* vol. 1, *Liberation and the Emergence of Separate Regimes, 1945–1947;* Bruce Cumings, *The Origins of the Korean War,* vol. 2, *The Roaring of the Cataract, 1947–1950;* James Matray, *The Reluctant Crusade: American Foreign Policy in Korea, 1941–1950;* Burton I. Kaufman, *The Korean War: Challenges in Crisis, Credibility, and Command;* Max Hastings, *The Korean War;* Paul G. Pierpaoli Jr., "Corporatist and Voluntarist Approaches to Cold War Rearmament: The Private Side of Industrial and Economic Mobilization."

Some of the more notable works dealing with Korea as a watershed include Nancy B. Tucker, *Patterns in the Dust: Chinese-American Relations and the Recognition Controversy, 1949–1950,* which views Korea as a key turning point in Sino-U.S. relations; Lawrence S. Kaplan, *The United States and NATO: The Formative Years,* especially pp. 149–50, which sees the Korean War as a sea change in U.S.-European relations; Robert Jervis, "The Impact of the Korean War on the Cold War," 563, which lays the responsibility for the militarization of NATO at the feet of Korea; and Robert A. Pollard, *Economic Security and the Origins of the Cold War, 1945–1950,* which identifies Korea as the catalyst that brought American corporate opinion in line with the necessities of high Cold War defense spending and military Keynesianism.

The Korean mobilization that began in July 1950 raised an important issue that had been lying just below the surface since at least 1947. The issue revolved around the capacity and willingness of the United States to match its military capabilities with its newfound superpower status. The overriding concern here was how much the nation could afford to spend on defense without increasing budget deficits, piling up debt, driving up taxes, bankrupting the treasury, slashing social welfare programs, and imposing regimental government controls. In other words, could the nation appropriately arm itself for the Cold War without resorting to the creation of a garrison state? When war unexpectedly broke out on the Korean peninsula, policymakers were faced not only with an international crisis, but also with a domestic one. The Trojan horse had rolled in, unleashing the haunting fears of a garrison state and all the potential nightmares that accompanied it.

Fears of a regimented state originated with the creation of the welfare state in the 1930s, which precipitated acrimonious debates over the role of government in a modern, industrialized society. America's participation in World War II further underscored those fears. By the late 1940s, however, most of these debates had been settled, and a tenuous acceptance of an activist government prevailed among most policymakers. But continued fears of a government run amok and the specter of a garrison state still haunted this fragile consensus. For some, like the conservatives, the apparition was still terrifying.

The image and concerns of the garrison state were the by-products of conceptualizations of modern totalitarianism offered by Austrian economist Friedrich von Hayek and Yale University political scientist Harold D. Lasswell. Viewing the rise of communist and fascist regimes, von Hayek closed the ideological chasm between the two by asserting that they were cut from the same cloth: both based their legitimacy upon collectivism and social welfare "democracy" that exalted government centralization and regimentation. Once established, these governments became mired in thick bureaucracies and stifling regulations, which finally resulted in totalitarianism. Building upon von Hayek's work, Lasswell envisioned totalitarian regimes arising from the national security imperatives inherent in the age of total war. He feared that perpetual military vigilance would lead to a bloated centralized state, the creation of a new, technocratic governing class dominated by the military, the funneling of societal resources from the civilian sector to that of the military, and the subsequent abdication of the civilian governing classes. Again, the final result would be the loss of political and economic liberties and the entrenchment of a totalitarian "garrison state."[3]

It was these fears together with the nation's World War II experience that most directly guided and informed mobilization policy during the Korean War. Only slightly removed from World War II, policymakers in the early 1950s were particularly sensitive to the problems that had arisen during that conflict, and they worked furiously to avoid them during the Korean War. According to some high-ranking World War II mobilization officials, the nightmare of America as garrison state had come perilously close to fruition during that war. The most outspoken of these officials, Donald Nelson, head of the War Production Board (WPB), spelled out these troubles in his book *Arsenal of Democracy* (1946). Nelson and others described how successful the armed forces had been in nearly wresting complete control of the economy from the civilians charged to protect it. They also lamented the creation of huge, overlapping wartime bureaucracies that worked to undermine civilian control and that resulted in massive waste and duplication. Indeed, Korean mobilization planners eyed these admonitions wearily.[4]

Thus the central theme of this study is the tension created by the fears of a garrison state. This very tension was also the most significant undercurrent of concern for Korean mobilization officials. The issue of the garrison state here is not necessarily whether the United States was becoming or did become one, but rather how the *fear* of becoming one influenced and guided strategists' decisions and the public's reactions to those decisions. The garrison state theme was not, of course, an entirely new concept nor could it be easily separated from other issues. It was in fact part of a much larger political and ideological dilemma, one that dated to the founding of the republic. It raised the prickly question of the role and scope of centralized government in a free-market, democratic society. In short, the garrison state directly challenged the nation's traditional ideological trilogy of antistatism, antimilitarism, and isolationism.

3. Freidrich von Hayek, *The Road to Serfdom.* See George H. Nash's *The Conservative Intellectual Movement in America since 1945,* which describes the impact of von Hayek's work in the United States. For Harold D. Lasswell's commentaries see "Sino-Soviet Crisis: The Garrison State versus the Civilian State," 643–49; "The Garrison State," 455–68; "The Garrison State and Specialists on Violence," in *The Analysis of Political Behavior: An Empirical Approach;* and *National Security and Individual Freedom.*

4. Donald M. Nelson, *Arsenal of Democracy: The Story of American War Production;* David Novick et al., *Wartime Production Controls,* 9, 383–85, 401; John Morton Blum, *V Was for Victory: Politics and American Culture during World War II,* 121, 123.

When one examines policymakers' approaches to the Korean mobilization, several phenomena become readily apparent. First, mobilization planners fought valiantly to keep the mobilization from transforming the country into a garrison state. They accomplished this by adhering to decentralization, promoting increased public-private cooperation among functional economic groups, and accepting the advent of civic boosterism as a de facto industrial policy. In doing so, mobilization officials often encouraged a larger role for organized, nonindustrial interest groups in the administration of mobilization policies, something I refer to as "corporative volunteerism." Second, and closely tied to these corporatist strategies, in implementing the postwar national security state, policymakers naturally took their cues from the nation's experiences in World Wars I and II. From those wars, they borrowed not only their organizational and institutional mechanisms, but also their personnel. The majority of high-level mobilization officials and advisers during the Korean War had served in similar posts during World War II, and some had even been involved in the World War I mobilization. The most notable of these officials was Bernard Baruch, head of the War Industries Board (WIB). Third, mobilization planners were required to implement a rearmament program that was commensurate with the nation's resources and its citizens' desire to sacrifice while maintaining and augmenting the civilian economy. The idea was to balance guns and butter through aggregate economic growth and productivity. The result of this balancing act was a modified version of Keynesian economics, sometimes referred to as military Keynesianism.

The continuity in ideology, institutional structure, and personnel between World War I and the Korean War comes as no great surprise. Many scholars have ably demonstrated the pervasiveness of organizational, institutional, and ideological continuity in twentieth-century American history. My work here is heavily influenced by that body of scholarship. I owe much of my broad conceptualization of modern American political and business culture to the organizational approach to historical analysis pioneered by Robert Wiebe, Samuel Hays, James Weinstein, Alfred D. Chandler Jr., William Appleman Williams, and Ellis Hawley, among others.[5] I also owe an intellectual debt to Robert D.

5. Robert H. Wiebe, *Businessmen and Reform: A Study of the Progressive Movement;* Robert H. Wiebe, *The Search for Order, 1877–1920;* Samuel P. Hays, *Conservation and the Gospel of Efficiency: The Progressive Conservation Movement 1890–1920;* James Weinstein,

Cuff, who by himself has produced an extensive body of literature dealing with the evolution of the modern administrative state and the political economy of war mobilization, the most comprehensive single work being his seminal *The War Industries Board*. I am most struck by Cuff's assessment of the World War I mobilization experience, especially that of the War Industries Board, which he notes was one punctuated by "complexity, hesitancy, and ambiguity." These very same attributes may be used to describe the Korean mobilization experience, albeit for somewhat different reasons. In the final analysis, however, I believe that complexity, hesitancy, and ambiguity are traits ingrained in the American system; they certainly are not unique to the nation's wartime experiences. Rather, they are the by-products of America's perpetual search for a "middle way" in political, economic, and diplomatic policymaking and are deeply rooted in the nation's political-economic traditions and its belief in limited government.[6]

Building upon the analyses of organizational and institutional historians, my work has also been guided by scholars of the New Left and by the historians of modern corporatism, who often combine the insights of the New Left with those of the organizational school. Attempting to rationalize, or in some cases even de-emphasize the alleged economic determinism of the New Left, the corporatists have done much to examine the "intersects" between public and private interests and the way in which they organize and often coalesce to affect governmental policymaking. Some corporatists, like Michael J. Hogan for example, have identified the New Deal of the 1930s as the pivotal turning point in the evolution of the modern associative or corporatist state. Noting the changes in the nation's industrial structure during that time, Hogan describes a new coalescence of ascendant liberal internationalists who overpowered their conservative, protectionist opponents in order to

---

The Corporate Ideal in the Liberal State; Alfred D. Chandler, *Strategy and Structure: Chapters in the History of Industrial Enterprise;* Alfred D. Chandler, *The Visible Hand: The Managerial Revolution in American Business;* William Appleman Williams, *The Contours of American History;* Ellis W. Hawley, *The Great War and the Search for a Modern Order: A History of the American People and Their Institutions, 1917–1933.* For good overviews of the sweeping components of the organizational framework see Louis Galambos, "The Emerging Organizational Synthesis in Modern American History," 279–90; and his later and more sophisticated article, "Technology, Political Economy, and Professionalization: Central Themes of the Organizational Synthesis," 471–93.

6. Robert D. Cuff, *The War Industries Board: Business-Government Relations during World War I,* 7; Robert D. Cuff, "An Organizational Perspective on the Military-Industrial Complex," *Business History Review,* 250–67; Robert D. Cuff, "Organizational Capabilities and U.S. War Production: The Controlled Materials Plan of World War II."

expand upon the associative order of the 1920s. The result was the "New Deal Coalition," which carried the nation toward postwar prosperity and internationalism.[7]

The corporatist model has been used to analyze domestic as well as diplomatic developments. Works employing that model have tended to focus almost exclusively upon the post–World War I era, with a particular emphasis on the interwar and post–New Deal periods. There are two chief reasons for this emphasis. First, the organizational impulses inherent in corporative policymaking did not fully mature until the early 1920s, gaining prominence with the advent of associationalism and its early New Deal spin-offs. Second, because corporatism is based upon certain presumptions about the nation's political, industrial, and economic alliances and their ties to governmental policymaking, especially in the areas of trade and international economic policy, to employ this conceptual framework as it currently stands would be more problematic for an era in which the United States lacked the requisite power and stature in the international arena. Thus, corporatist analyses tend to lend themselves to studies that examine the United States *after* 1917, at which time the intersection of foreign and domestic policy became more intertwined as the nation increased its involvement and stature on the international scene. To be sure, I view these corporatist impulses as the sine qua non of policymaking during Korea, working simultaneously from the bottom up and the top down.[8]

My study has been additionally influenced by a number of political and social scientists who deal in the realm of bureaucracies and state building. I have learned much from the analysis of bureaucratic politics, pioneered by Warner R. Schilling and Richard E. Neustadt

7. For good overviews and insights of the corporatist synthesis as it applies to diplomatic history see Michael J. Hogan, "Revival and Reform: America's Search for a New Economic Order Abroad," 287–310; Michael J. Hogan, "Corporatism: A Positive Appraisal," 363–72; Michael J. Hogan, "Corporatism," in Hogan and Paterson, eds., *Explaining the History of American Foreign Relations*, 226–36; Thomas J. McCormick, "Drift or Mastery?: A Corporatist Synthesis for American Diplomatic History," 318–30. For Hogan's conceptualization of the "New Deal Coalition" see *The Marshall Plan: America, Britain, and the Reconstruction of Western Europe, 1947–1952*, 1–25.

8. For samples of the domestic import of associationalism and corporatism see Ellis W. Hawley, "The Discovery and Study of a 'Corporate Liberalism,'" 309–30; Ellis W. Hawley, "Herbert Hoover, The Commerce Secretariat, and the Vision of an 'Associative State,' 1921–1928," 116–40. For a sampling of monographic literature see Joan Hoff-Wilson, *Herbert Hoover: Forgotten Progressive*; Robert M. Collins, *The Business Response to Keynes, 1929–1964*; Kim McQuaid, *Big Business and Presidential Power: From FDR to Reagan*; Kim McQuaid, *Uneasy Partners: Big Business in American Politics, 1945–1990*.

and elaborated by Graham Allison and Morton H. Halperin.[9] I have also found the work of Theda Skocpol, Stephen Skowronek, Thomas Ferguson, and Gregory D. Hooks very helpful in linking the Korean rearmament and the rise of the national security state with the process of modern American state building.[10]

In writing the heretofore untold story of the Korean mobilization and in analyzing the resulting policies and outcomes, I have realized that the Korean experience demonstrated a significant amount of continuity with previous eras in American history while it marked a distinct turning point in the nation's historical and ideological development. Above, I have briefly outlined the themes of continuity both from a practical and a historiographical perspective. And as the story unfolds, I have made a conscious attempt to remind the reader of those continuities when appropriate. I now turn to the other main component of this work—Korea as a multifaceted watershed. By introducing these various turning points, the outcomes can more clearly be identified with the theme of Korea as both watershed and Trojan horse.

The Korean War marked a pivotal turning point in the global execution of the Cold War. To understand the larger context—the Cold War—is to understand how and why Korea fundamentally altered the political and economic scene in the United States. First, Korea marked the militarization of Harry Truman's containment policy. Before June 1950, the United States tended to emphasize the *economic* aspects of containment, during which time it sought to build a strong, free-market–based international order to serve as a bulwark against Soviet communism. Once the war in Korea began, however, the United States emphasized military rearmament—here and abroad—to resist perceived Soviet aggression. Second, by militarizing containment as it did, the Truman administration globalized it as well. After Korea, the nation prepared itself ideologically and militarily to resist the Soviets

9. Richard Neustadt, *Presidential Power: The Politics of Leadership;* Warren R. Schilling, "The H-Bomb Decision: How to Decide without Actually Choosing," 24–26; Graham Allison, *Essence of Decision: Explaining the Cuban Missile Crisis;* Morton H. Halperin, *Bureaucratic Politics and Foreign Policy.* For a good overview of the bureaucratic politics paradigm in a historical context see J. Garry Clifford, "Bureaucratic Politics," in Hogan and Paterson, eds., *Explaining the History,* 141–50.

10. Theda Skocpol et al., eds., *Bringing the State Back In;* Stephen Skowronek, *Building a New American State: The Expansion of National Administrative Capacities, 1877–1920;* Thomas Ferguson, "From Normalcy to New Deal: Industrial Structure, Party Competition, and American Public Policy in the Great Depression," 41–93; Gregory D. Hooks, *Forging the Military-Industrial Complex: World War II's Battle of the Potomac.*

in every corner of the world. Thus, in the final analysis, the Korean mobilization was a mobilization within a mobilization: the nation began arming for the Korean conflict in the short-term while simultaneously mobilizing for the Cold War in the long-term.[11]

Korea also left its indelible mark on the home front. It was a watershed for American economic and mobilization policy. It permanently institutionalized the national security apparatus, in turn fostering the growth of the military-industrial complex and the restructuring of the nation's industrial base. It greatly increased the power of the presidency, mainly at the expense of Congress. And finally, it turned American politics on its head, ushering in the first Republican era in twenty years while forging a new bipartisan consensus based upon internationalism, Soviet containment, and a moderate social welfare state.

It was in the realm of economic policymaking that Korea had its most dramatic and far-reaching effects, some of which are still with us. The quadrupling of the defense budget (from $13.5 billion before the war to more than $52 billion by fiscal year 1952) marked a distinct change in the nation's fiscal ideology and policymaking. That is, instead of determining the aggregate budget and adjusting program spending (like national security) accordingly, the opposite became the rule after 1950: policymakers determined national security requirements first and then adjusted aggregate fiscal policy to meet security demands. This change marked the end of the nation's long-standing dedication to balanced budgets and minimal military expenditures, a dedication so deeply ingrained in its political culture that it had transcended political parties since the founding of the republic.[12]

The results of this fundamental shift formed the essential components of the Trojan horse of postwar national security. The massive increase in defense expenditures unleashed a flurry of short-term and

11. For these developments see John Lewis Gaddis, *Strategies of Containment: A Critical Appraisal of Postwar American National Security Policy;* Hogan, *Marshall Plan,* especially 24–25; Samuel F. Wells Jr., "Sounding the Tocsin: NSC-68 and the Soviet Threat," *International Security,* 116–58; and Melvyn P. Leffler, *A Preponderance of Power: National Security, the Truman Administration, and the Cold War,* especially 312–60.

12. This new way of thinking was explicitly detailed in a 1952 National Security Resources Board (NSRB) report that stated: "expenditures on national security can only be determined by the nature of the threat to national security. They cannot be determined solely on considerations of ability to pay in any normal sense." Record Group 304, Records of the Office of Defense Mobilization and the National Security Resources Board, safe file, box 3, National Archives, Washington, D.C. (hereafter NA). See also David P. Calleo, *The Bankrupting of America: How the Federal Budget Is Impoverishing the Nation,* 11, 19, 48.

long-term implications, most of which were unforeseen. In the short run, the defense buildup badly distorted the economy. It sparked a fire storm of inflation that ultimately forced the Truman administration to issue mandatory wage and price controls. It unbalanced the federal budget and led to across-the-board tax increases and the consequent acrimonious debates between conservatives and liberals over how best to distribute the nation's economic and military resources. And most troubling to policymakers, the great jump in defense spending combined with the imposition of far-flung controls over the economy encouraged the growth of the modern military-industrial complex. As a result, the long-standing bêtes noires of state-sponsored economic concentration and a militarized garrison state loomed ominously over the American body politic.

The economic trends begun in 1950 had long-term implications that were—and still are—deeply troubling. As David P. Calleo has noted, today's budget deficits and massive national debt can be traced back to the fiscal and spending practices initiated during the early Cold War. The abandonment of balanced budgets and minimal military expenditures not only brought about negative economic consequences in the short-term, but it also solidified a new ideology of fiscal policymaking that in the long-term was adapted to programs outside the purview of defense and national security. Indeed, the Korean War began the trend toward increased acceptance of unbalanced budgets, which accelerated rapidly after the 1950s. Deficits thus became increasingly acceptable, long-term debt began to pile up, and federal programs of all kinds proliferated without sufficient income to pay for them. Since Korea, government revenue has generally lagged behind spending; the federal debt mushroomed from $257 billion in 1950 to $3.2 trillion in 1990, an 84 percent increase in constant dollars. In fact, in 1990 the net-interest payments *alone* on the national debt were equal to more than one-half of the total 1951 federal budget. Clearly, the fiscal and monetary policies dating from the Korean era unleashed economic forces that for forty years appeared practically unstoppable. The military Keynesianism of the 1950s devolved into a flawed vision of an ever-expanding economy shackled to a government intent upon continually spending more than it took in.[13]

13. See Calleo, *Bankrupting of America*, 11–20, 48; David P. Calleo, *Beyond American Hegemony: The Future of the Western Alliance*, chap. 3–6; Alan S. Blinder and Robert M. Solow, "Analytical Foundations of Fiscal Policy," in *The Economics of Public Finance*. For

Korea was also a watershed for U.S. mobilization policy. For the first time in its history, the nation established a policy of high war readiness during a period in which no war had been declared. And as the Korean mobilization evolved, war planners conceptualized and implemented the so-called mobilization base. The mobilization base was, for a nation deeply suspicious of the military establishment, a radical departure in defense planning. Implicit in this new approach to mobilization planning was the realization that the United States must create a ready economic, industrial, and military reserve so that it would never again be forced to begin mobilization from scratch. The construction and maintenance of the mobilization base required not only large sums of money and resources—it also bolstered fears of the garrison state and smacked of governmental favoritism toward particular kinds of industries, most notably high-tech, defense-oriented ones. Building a mobilization base was thus predicated upon the construction of excess industrial capacity that could swing into action at the first sign of crisis. The federal government encouraged such construction through a variety of incentives, including government loans and subsidies, relaxation of antitrust laws, industrial pooling, guaranteed markets for specialty items, and accelerated tax amortization. Of course, these arrangements increased the size and scope of the government and tightened the bonds between the public and private spheres. The mobilization base concept helped to draw up the basic blueprints for American defense and national security policies for nearly two generations. In addition, it fanned the flames of the superpower arms race and the concurrent technology race.

While mobilization planners were placing the nation on a permanent war footing, so too were they institutionalizing the national security state. As a result, the military-industrial sector grew inexorably larger and became an entrenched component of the American political economy. The decision to keep the nation partially but permanently mobilized created an entirely new economy within the confines of the existing one. This new economy—the military-industrial complex—accelerated changes already under way in the nation's economy and industrial landscape. These changes included the shifting of population to the South and West, along with the resultant geographical realignment of political power. Consequentially, many of the nation's traditional

---

an excellent overview of postwar fiscal policy and the differing viewpoints on fiscal policy, see Richard J. Cebula, *The Deficit Problem in Perspective*, especially 7–39.

centers of commerce and industry began a long and painful decline. Although these changes were a result of many variables, including Americans' penchant for moving, their love affair with the automobile, and New Dealers' earlier attempts to decentralize industry, Korea most assuredly increased the pace and scope of these developments. Indeed, whole new industries emerged after 1950—industries that were dominated by defense-dependent firms raised in lockstep fashion with the inexorable march of the Cold War and the high-tech weaponry upon which it relied.

Related to the Korean rearmament and the problems it wrought was the growth of the so-called imperial presidency, a term coined by historian and presidential adviser Arthur M. Schlesinger Jr. Most certainly, the expansion of presidential power and prerogative began to most clearly manifest itself under Franklin Roosevelt. But the advent of Korea and other Cold War crises combined with the exigencies of the modern national security state clearly elevated the executive branch to a new level of power. With that power came the inevitable pitfalls. President Truman committed American troops to Korea without formal congressional approval. No act of war was ever declared. Nevertheless, Congress overwhelmingly supported Truman's June 1950 decision. But as the conflict dragged on and the fortunes of war shifted, the president's relations with Congress soured. Truman was then left to shoulder the blame for military reversals and stalemate entirely by himself. And the more frustrated and disillusioned Congress became with the war effort, the less willing it was to support Truman on any issue, foreign or domestic. Furthermore, Truman's foray into an undeclared, limited war set the stage for an even greater struggle a decade or so later in Vietnam. Surely, by 1968, Lyndon Johnson was painfully aware of Truman's 1950 decision to roll in the Trojan horse of undeclared, limited warfare.

Presidential power seemingly unchecked naturally raised concerns about the garrison state. Nothing seemed to better exemplify this than Truman's April 1952 decision to seize the nation's steel mills. Panicked at the prospect of what a steel strike might do to the rearmament program, the president ordered a government takeover of the steel industry under the cover of national security. What resulted was a public and congressional outcry against Truman, couched in the now-familiar terms of the garrison state and dictatorship. A full-blown constitutional crisis ensued that ended in a Supreme Court reversal of the seizure and a humiliating defeat for the president. Clearly, by 1952, presidential usurpation of congressional power coupled with crises like the steel case led many Americans to believe that the executive branch had grown too powerful.

The Korean War also wrought significant political changes, some transitory and some long-lasting. As the war progressed and then stalemated, it became profoundly unpopular. Business and labor chafed under wartime controls and regulations, and the public became disenchanted with and confused by the war effort. The Korean War quickly became "Truman's War," and the president became as unpopular as the war itself. It did not take the Republicans long to capitalize on Truman's misfortunes; they lambasted his conduct of the war and the rearmament program. In doing so, of course, they also implicated the entire Democratic party and its handling of the nation's affairs. As a consequence, the 1952 elections overthrew the New Deal political order, ousting the Democrats from the White House and unseating their majority in Congress. For the first time in twenty years, Republicans controlled Congress *and* the executive branch.

Of course, the Korean conflict profoundly affected the politics of anti-communism, energized ongoing debates surrounding internal security, and fully unleashed the demagoguery of Senator Joseph R. McCarthy (R-WI). Although post–World War II anti-communism and the makings of the Second Red Scare can be traced all the way back to 1946, not until *after* the outbreak of hostilities in Korea and the Chinese intervention did McCarthy reach full fury, hurling wild accusations and contriving a political atmosphere so poisonous that it has since come to bear his name: McCarthyism. Indeed, it would be difficult to imagine McCarthy's four-year reign being so successful—and yet so damaging—without the backdrop of Korea and the vicissitudes engendered by it. McCarthy's direct influence on mobilization and stabilization policy was at best minimal; however, the overall political atmosphere he created certainly affected the parameters within which Truman and his advisers had to operate. Finally, McCarthyism turned the Korean War into an intensely ideological and partisan melee that manifested itself most completely in the Great Debate of late 1950, the firing of General Douglas MacArthur in the spring of 1951, and the political debates surrounding the extension of the Defense Production Act in the summer of that year.[14]

14. For the effects of McCarthyism during Korea see Thomas C. Reeves, *The Life and Times of Joe McCarthy*, 327–29, 347–48; Stephen J. Whitfield, *The Culture of the Cold War*,

At the same time the Korean War fractured the New Deal political coalition, it gave birth to another. By 1952, the waging of the Cold War had formed something of a new political coalition, this one far more loosely organized than that of the New Deal. It comprised a bipartisan group of moderate Republicans and Democrats brought together by one major ideological tenet: Soviet containment. While not exactly a political coalition in the classic sense, this group nonetheless formed a Cold War consensus founded upon Soviet containment, internationalist economic policies, multilateral defense mechanisms, and a limited but activist government designed to execute the Cold War while maintaining existing New Deal social welfare programs. The Cold War consensus once and for all relegated the isolationist and protectionist wings of the far Left and far Right to the margins of the American political scene. For good or evil, the Cold War consensus institutionalized the Cold War and the large, centralized government charged to carry it out.

In the final analysis, however, the Korean era mobilization effort was solidly rooted in the rhetoric and reality of the nation's political and economic traditions. It reflected those traditions while it conjured up ghostly specters of a decidedly undemocratic garrison state. Policymakers tried hard to keep those apparitions under wraps, and to a large extent they succeeded. But the Korean War unleashed, like a genie from a bottle, unforeseen and unwanted consequences. Thus despite the gospel of decentralization that framed the institutional and organizational dynamics of the rearmament program, one cannot escape the fact that the government, in tandem with industry, the applied sciences, and academia, imposed a powerfully centralizing force on the American system. This was not necessarily the result of conscious policymaking. Rather, it was the consequence of allowing national security needs to drive aggregate budget decisions. By concentrating vast amounts of national resources and capital in the hands of national security managers, policymakers in fact vested the federal government with sweeping powers. Part watershed and part Trojan horse, Korea forever changed the trajectory of contemporary American history.

The ideas and themes laid out in this introduction are developed in the chapters that follow. The first half of chapter 1 sketches the domestic and international scene leading up to the Korean War, describing the broad context in which the war was waged. The second half analyzes

---

9–10; and Richard M. Fried, *Nightmare in Red: The McCarthy Era in Perspective*, 128–30, 142, 113–19.

the first five months of the conflict, during which time policymakers envisioned a small war with a quick end. Chapter 2 discusses the second phase of Korea, marked by the American response to the massive Chinese incursion into North Korea in December 1950. This chapter also traces the institutionalization of the Korean mobilization, which by that time became indistinguishable from the much larger Cold War rearmament effort. Chapter 3 deals mostly with the effects of the accelerated and expanded rearmament program, with a particular emphasis on labor-management relations and economic policymaking. Chapter 4 analyzes both the domestic and international political ramifications of rearmament while it traces policymakers' attempts to slow the pace and narrow the scope of mobilization in response to internal and external pressures. Here the garrison state theme is most noticeable.

Chapters 5 and 6 discuss the new equilibrium of the rearmament effort, which was punctuated by numerous crises involving organized labor, management, and the Truman administration. Chapter 5 describes the steel seizure crisis and its import on the rearmament effort and domestic politics. It also traces both the subtle and substantive changes in mobilization planners' attitudes and conceptualization of national security in the nuclear age. Chapter 6 describes the denouement of the Korean mobilization and the ascension of Dwight Eisenhower and the Republicans to political power, during which time the nation moved toward an era of uneasy normalcy.

By February 1953, President Eisenhower decontrolled the economy, dismantled the majority of the wartime agencies, and consolidated the national security apparatus. Most assuredly, however, the nation's newfound "normalcy" was a Cold War normalcy—one marked by perpetual military preparedness, huge military expenditures, and strained government budgets. Superimposed over this chimera of normalcy was the constant threat of nuclear armageddon and a mounting obsession with technological supremacy. Try as he did, Dwight Eisenhower was no more successful than Harry Truman in stanching the forces unleashed by the Trojan horse of Korea.

I

NSC-68 and the Outbreak of the Korean War

Toward a Piecemeal Mobilization, April–November 1950

This first chapter will accomplish two principle tasks. First, it will sketch the background of NSC-68, the National Security Council's blueprint for waging the Cold War, within which the outbreak of the Korean War occurred. Covering the period between 1948 and the spring of 1950, when NSC-68 was first presented to President Truman, this background will provide an overview of the political and economic culture in which the Korean decision was reached. The Korean intervention and the concurrent military buildup begun in July 1950 raised dilemmas of national security and defense that had been simmering just beneath the surface since at least 1947. Korea forced policymakers to come to terms with these issues, ultimately prodding them to decide how much the nation could—and should—spend on defense. Thus, the Trojan horse of national security was unveiled, but the forces inside it were still tightly contained.

The second major task, which constitutes the majority of this chapter, is to analyze the first five months of the Korean War mobilization, from July to December 1950. During these months, which I view as the first phase of the three-year conflict, the United States struggled to implement a coherent military strategy for Korea as well as a broader military and industrial mobilization program designed to follow the prescriptions of NSC-68. During this time, however, these two efforts were often unrelated and uncoordinated. And after General Douglas MacArthur's successful landing at Inchon in September, the Korean mobilization program, which had barely gotten off the ground, lost much of its momentum. The likelihood of a short war with a quick and decisive victory held out the promise of a long-haul Cold War mobilization that could be approached in a relatively casual fashion—free of powerful mobilization agencies and strict governmental controls. But the Chinese intervention in late November changed all that. The second phase of the Korean War began, and in one sudden leap the Truman administration greatly accelerated the pace and scope of mobilization. At that point, the fears of a garrison state contained within the Trojan horse were let loose.

At the end of World War II, the United States engaged in a rapid demobilization, resulting in a great contraction in military spending. It did not, however, revert to the military somnolence that had prevailed during the interwar years because when the war ended the nation found itself thrust into the unfamiliar role of leader of the non-communist world. What is more, hopes for a durable peace withered with the stark realization that the Soviet Union had also emerged from the fighting in a new and more powerful stance, one that directly challenged the United States and its fragile allies. And the nation's traditional security blankets—the Atlantic and Pacific Oceans—began to fray with the explosions at Hiroshima and Nagasaki that ushered in the nuclear age. Simply put, the United States could not stick its head in the sand as it had done in 1919. Although the Truman administration did not return to interwar naiveté, neither did it fully reconcile the nation's military and national security capabilities with its newfound responsibilities as a superpower. Only after the April 1950 appearance of NSC-68 did policy-makers begin to seriously and systematically consider such a reconciliation. And even then it took the shock of Korea to urge them into action.[1]

Even as the Cold War deepened in 1947 and 1948, the prevailing wisdom of the Truman administration and Congress was to hold down defense budgets regardless of the cost to national security. During this time, the nation's limited resources were well recognized and accepted. Many experts argued that excessive military outlays would drain rather than boost the economy. Even the most hawkish of policymakers, like James V. Forrestal, the first secretary of defense, were reluctant to ad-vocate hugely expanded defense budgets. Although Forrestal waged a constant battle for national preparedness and increased military spending after World War II, a battle he ultimately lost to Truman's economiz-ing in 1948, even he later acknowledged that "greatly enlarged military

1. See John Lewis Gaddis, *Strategies of Containment: A Critical Reappraisal of Postwar American National Security Policy*, 58, 91–93, 113; Samuel F. Wells Jr., "Sounding the Tocsin: NSC-68 and the Soviet Threat," 123–31; "NSC-68: United States Objectives and Programs for National Security," 1:237–92; Walter S. Poole, *The History of the Joint Chiefs of Staff, Volume 4, 1950–1952*, iv–v, 38–47.

budgets would wreck the economy."[2] Well into 1949, in fact, the din of those favoring more military spending—emanating mostly from the national security planners in the Pentagon—was muted by economizers within the administration. Thus, the gospel of balanced budgets and manageable military expenditures held through at least early 1949. This holy writ, combined with Truman's distrust of Keynesian economics in any circumstances short of national crisis, substantially limited the size and scope of the national security establishment in the years leading up to 1950.

Truman's reluctance to increase military spending, which in his view would increase the military establishment's clout over the nation's affairs, arose not only from the political culture of the times but also from personal experience and conviction. First, Harry S. Truman was a legendary fiscal conservative. Having to date largely spurned the Keynesian revolution, he fervently believed in a balanced federal budget. Second, the president did not wish to jeopardize his Fair Deal, the social program he unveiled in January 1949, particularly for national security imperatives. Third, Truman exhibited a long-standing fear of "political cliques" in the military establishment and a profound hatred of flashy—and in his mind dangerous—military officers who he feared might lead the nation to military dictatorship. Fourth, his experience as chairman of the Senate committee charged with rooting out procurement waste during World War II had led him to conclude that most military officials were spendthrifts. Finally, Truman disliked and mistrusted the national security establishment and feared losing his power and prerogatives to the likes of the National Security Council and its domestic counterpart, the National Security Resources Board. In sum, many of Truman's beliefs instilled in him a deep fear that any major military buildup during a time of relative peace might create the foundations of a militarized garrison state.[3]

2. Walter Millis, ed., *The Forrestal Diaries*, 421.

3. For Truman's fears of a garrison state, see Millis, *Forrestal Diaries*, 88; Robert J. Donovan, *Conflict and Crisis: The Presidency of Harry S. Truman, 1945–1948*, 141–42; Harry S. Truman, "Our Armed Forces Must Be Unified," 63–64; Harold D. Smith, "Conference with the President," September 19, 1945, President's Secretary's File-Subject File, Truman Papers, box 150, file: "Excerpts of the Diary of Harold D. Smith," HSTL; Harry S. Truman, *Memoirs, Years of Trial and Hope*, vol. 2, 50–51, 53, 422–27.

For the president's views on the budget, fiscal policy, military spending, and economic philosophy in general, see Truman, *Memoirs*, vol. 2, 26–27, 33–38, 40–41.

For Truman's distrust of the national security establishment, especially the National Security Council and the National Security Resources Board, see Robert D. Cuff, "Ferdinand Eberstadt, the National Security Resources Board, and the Search for Integrated

To be sure, both the president's and the nation's trepidations over large military budgets and mobilization in general were far from unfounded. Americans greatly feared a repeat of the pitfalls of World War II, in which centralized civilian control over mobilization was never firmly established. During that war, Franklin Roosevelt, in early 1942, empowered the War Production Board (WPB) to review and control all military procurement. Thus, procurement authority was vested exclusively in civilian hands. However, board chairman Donald Nelson largely abdicated this authority soon after he took over. As a result, the War and Navy departments exercised de facto procurement and allocation powers over large sectors of the economy. Nelson simply found himself unable to compete with the experience and clout of the powerful Army and Navy Munitions Board. The most important lesson to be learned from World War II was that the power to procure is the power to control. So by largely relinquishing its major procurement and contractual powers, the War Production Board was never able to exercise complete control over the mobilization process—some of this power naturally passed onto the military, which was all too eager to accept it. These developments raised not only the possibility of military control over the entire economy, but also the ghostly specter of a garrison state. Naturally, policymakers eyed these developments forebodingly, even as the Cold War deepened in 1948 and 1949. To many, an indefinite Cold War mobilization program still seemed quite unfathomable.[4]

Throughout this period, President Truman enjoyed significant support for his fiscal and military policies from a majority in Congress, including many Republicans. Internally, the Bureau of the Budget (BOB) and the Council of Economic Advisers (CEA) were the president's biggest backers. In 1949, both agencies were headed by fiscal conservatives who insisted on capping military spending—James Webb and then Frank Pace at the BOB and Edwin Nourse at the CEA. Those agencies, along with the Department of the Treasury, made up the powerful cadre of economizers within the Truman administration that were committed to fighting *against* the Pentagon's requests for more money and *for* the president's economic policies, including the Fair

---

Mobilization Planning, 1947–1948," 46–47; Truman, *Memoirs,* vol. 2, 59–60; Alfred D. Sandler, "Truman and the National Security Council: 1945–1947," 369–88; Anna Kasten Nelson, "President Truman and the Evolution of the National Security Council," 360–78.

4. Novick, *Wartime Production Controls,* 9, 383–85, 401; Nelson, *Arsenal of Democracy,* especially pp. 194–242 and 270–73; Blum, *V Was for Victory,* 121, 123.

Deal. The final victory of the economizers seemed assured when in March 1949 Truman replaced the ailing, hawkish defense secretary James Forrestal with the ambitious and acerbic Louis Johnson. Johnson was determined to hold the line on military spending increases and was even more driven to cut military spending whenever possible. In fact, Johnson and the economizers were given a perfect justification for doing just that by an economic downturn that began in 1949. Faced with declining tax revenues, rising budget deficits, and a Congress vehemently opposed to tax hikes, Johnson and Pace began to sharpen their budget axes. Their first victim would be the Pentagon.[5]

In his January 1949 budget message, Truman announced his decision to cap annual defense spending at approximately $14.5 billion. This figure, he said, would apply to FY 1950 and beyond. Truman and the economizers insisted that the cap was necessary to avoid increasing the deficit and sparking inflation. By the spring, with economic forecasts growing gloomier, budget director Pace presented Truman with a proposed 1951 defense budget ceiling of just $13 billion. Truman was pleased with the BOB's budget-cutting zeal and quickly affirmed the new ceiling. Nourse was also gratified with the cut, and the new defense secretary was so elated that he pledged to bring the 1951 defense budget in slightly *under* the $13 billion mark. For Truman and the economizers both in and out of the White House, spring of 1949 marked the apex of their powers over the Pentagon and the national security planners, who had been beating the drums for more money for months.[6]

5. Memo to the President, May 19, 1949, Truman Papers, President's Secretary's Files-Subject Files, box 150, file: "Bureau of the Budget-Misc., 1945–1953 #2," HSTL; Memo for the President, June 22, 1949, and June 30, 1949, Record Group (hereafter RG) 51, Records of the Bureau of the Budget, Series 47.8A, box 51, file: "1951 Budget: Basic Documents," NA; Robert J. Donovan, *Tumultuous Years: The Presidency of Harry S. Truman, 1949–1953*, 53–65; Lester H. Brune, "Guns and Butter: The Pre-Korean War Dispute over Budget Allocations: Nourse's Conservative Keynesianism Loses Favor over Keyserling's Economic Expansion Plan," 358.

6. Harry S. Truman, Annual Budget Message to the Congress: Fiscal Year 1950, January 10, 1949, *Public Papers of the Presidents of the United States: Harry S. Truman, 1949*, 56; Memo to the President, June 22, 1949, and June 30, 1949, RG 51, BOB Records, series 47.8A, box 51, file: "1951 Budget: Basic Documents," NA; Memorandum from Frederick J. Lawton, July 1, 1949, Papers of Frederick J. Lawton, box 6, file: "Truman, President Harry S., Meetings with the President—Agendas and Memorandums, 7/49–7/52," HSTL; "NSC 52/1, Report to the National Security Council by the Acting Executive Secretary Lay, with Enclosures A and B," July 8, 1949, *FRUS, 1949*, 1:352–57; Memorandum from Edwin Nourse, July 6, 1949, Papers of Edwin G. Nourse, box 6, file: "Daily Diary," HSTL.

Beginning in 1949, while Truman was still basking in his budget victories over the Pentagon and the national security operatives, domestic and international events converged to turn the tide against the president and the economizers. First, Dean Acheson replaced General George C. Marshall as secretary of state early in the year. Although Truman and Acheson enjoyed a close personal and professional relationship, the two men parted company over issues of national security and military spending. Simply put, Acheson did not believe that Truman's defense budgets were commensurate with the nation's responsibilities and commitments. And unlike his predecessor, he was unwilling to see defense needs subordinated to Truman's domestic economic agenda. Thus, as soon as he took over the State Department, Acheson began lobbying for higher military spending and a thorough reassessment of the nation's security commitments and capabilities. Before long, Acheson had assembled within the State Department an impressive clique of policymakers whose views on defense and national security matters were more in line with those of the Pentagon and other national security managers. One of Acheson's most influential new lieutenants was Paul Nitze, who in January 1950 had edged out George Kennan to direct the prestigious Policy Planning Staff. To be sure, administration economizers like Frank Pace and Edwin Nourse were no match for the imposing secretary of state and his corps of young turks bent on augmenting the nation's military capabilities.[7]

At the same time, another chink in the economizers' armor appeared. Edwin Nourse began to lose control over the CEA, as he became embroiled in an increasingly vitriolic debate with his vice chairman, Leon Keyserling. During 1949, Nourse lost more and more battles with Keyserling, who was becoming the darling of the national security planners, especially those in the State Department. Nourse and Keyserling parted company on economic philosophy as well as on more practical matters. Nourse believed that the CEA should operate above politics, remaining strictly as a behind-the-scenes advisory group to the president. Keyserling saw the council's role very differently. He believed it should be an *activist* advisory group, willing to engage in the political process freely and to advocate the president's policies whenever possible. Keyserling's viewpoint was shared by other council members. By the end of 1949, Nourse had lost the confidence and support of his team

7. Donovan, *Tumultuous Years*, 158–60; McCoy, *Presidency of Truman*, 191–216; William E. Pemberton, *Harry S. Truman: Fair Dealer and Cold Warrior*, 128–31.

and thus became totally ineffectual in the economizers' waning efforts to hold the line on budget increases.[8]

The biggest schism within the CEA occurred over philosophical and substantive approaches to economic policymaking. Keyserling and Nourse had little in common in this regard. Keyserling's economic philosophy revolved around one basic tenet: sustained economic growth. Concomitant to his expansionary policies was the belief that the American economy could best meet the needs for increased government spending by limited and controlled deficit spending. Keyserling did not advocate deficit spending as a long-term strategy, nor did he necessarily promote deficits as a way to "prime the pump" of the economy. Rather, he saw limited, short-term deficits as a way to meet unforeseen expenditures. In the long-term, Keyserling believed that increased production, employment, and aggregate economic growth would generate more than enough revenue to offset short-term budget deficits. Nourse could not have disagreed more. He simply did not believe in deficit spending, even in the most controlled and planned situation; either expenditures had to be limited, or revenues had to be increased sufficiently to offset any shortfall. In other words, Nourse's world was one of choices—more guns, less butter. In Keyserling's world, these choices were deemed unnecessary, so long as economic growth continued apace.[9]

Keyserling also thought that the best way to assure economic growth was through a policy of close business-government cooperation. In fact, in early 1949 he advocated the establishment of a "National Economic Cooperation Board" through which business and government would work together to generate sustained and balanced economic growth. At the time, Nourse ignored Keyserling's advocacy, questioning his affinity for government planning through public-private cooperation. In the broadest sense, Keyserling's views were not so much classically Keynesian as they were refined continuations of classic economic liberalism, which maintained that an ever-expanding economy would provide for the general welfare. Economic growth would also provide an enlarged economic base through which increased defense expenditures

8. Bertram M. Gross and John P. Lewis, "The President's Economic Staff during the Truman Administration," 114–30.
9. Leon Keyserling, "Prospects for Economic Growth," September 18, 1949, Official File (hereafter, OF) Truman Papers, box 1564, HSTL; Brune, "Guns and Butter," 357–63; D. K. Pickens, "Truman's Council of Economic Advisers and the Legacy of New Deal Liberalism," 2–12, Paper given at the Harry S. Truman Conference, Hofstra University, April 15, 1983, copy found in the Papers of Leon Keyserling, box 1, HSTL.

could be absorbed. To Keyserling's way of thinking, this expansion should be promoted by the government in close cooperation with private enterprise. His views on the political economy clearly reflect the mid-twentieth-century quest for an American-style corporatism, which refers to a political economy "founded on self-governing economic groups, integrated by institutional coordinators and normal market mechanisms, led by cooperating public and private elites, nourished by limited but positive government power, and geared to an economic growth in which all could share."[10]

By 1950, this was the prevailing philosophy among an increasing number of policymakers in the administration, most notably those who favored increased defense expenditures. Those not sharing this viewpoint were sooner or later cast aside. Indeed, Edwin Nourse resigned his post in September 1949, and Keyserling assumed the helm of the CEA. Thus by 1950, just as the United States began to debate how to redistribute its economic and military resources to meet the demands of large military budgets prescribed in NSC-68, corporatist ideas had become the hallmark of the CEA. By then, the economizers were on the ropes. Policymakers like Keyserling, Acheson, and Nitze viewed corporatist mechanisms in two ways. First, they viewed the structural and functional implications of public-private cooperation as the sine qua non of efficient, responsible government. Second, and perhaps more important, they believed that such cooperation would mitigate fears that a large rearmament program would lead to military and economic tyranny. In other words, public-private cooperation would help them in their quest for expanding the military establishment while keeping the Trojan horse tightly sealed.[11]

At the same time the economizers were under siege by the national security planners, they were rocked by a series of international crises in 1949 and early 1950. First came the stunning September 1949 announcement that the Soviet Union had successfully detonated its first atomic bomb, thus ending the United States' atomic monopoly. Next came the early October victory of Mao Tse-tung's Communist forces in the Chinese civil war. The People's Republic of China was formally established, forcing the American-supported Nationalists into a hasty retreat to Formosa—China was now "lost" to the Communists. A few days

10. Alonzo M. Hamby, *Beyond the New Deal: Harry S. Truman and American Liberalism,* 182, 295, 330; Pickens, "Truman's Council," 13–14, 17.
 For quotation on corporatism, see Hogan, *Marshall Plan,* 2–3.
 11. Brune, "Guns and Butter," 362.

later, on October 7, the Soviet Union created the German Democratic Republic, all but sealing the fate of a permanently divided Germany. And as if these setbacks were not enough, the new year dawned with more bad news.[12]

In January 1950, the Soviet delegate to the United Nations stormed out of a Security Council meeting to protest its refusal to seat the new People's Republic representative, and in February, the USSR signed the Treaty of Friendship, Alliance, and Mutual Assistance with the new Chinese government. In the meantime, Americans were shocked by the audacity of Russian espionage when British officials arrested Klaus Fuchs on February 3 for spying on the Manhattan Project and passing nuclear secrets to the Soviets. This relentless procession of events slashed the American psyche like repeated thrusts of a dagger. The coup de grace was delivered a few days later in Wheeling, West Virginia, when Senator Joseph R. McCarthy, taking advantage of the supercharged atmosphere, unleashed his first barrage against alleged communist infiltration into the highest levels of the federal government.[13]

To be sure, McCarthy took advantage of an already supercharged political atmosphere, combined with the recent international crises, and by doing so created a full-blown domestic crisis. His February speech not only marked the beginning of his national political ascendancy, it also laid the groundwork for vitriolic anti-communist attacks on President Truman, Secretary of State Dean Acheson, and later Dwight D. Eisenhower. Certainly not coincidentally, the Wisconsin senator's Wheeling harangue occurred only two weeks after Alger Hiss's conviction in the famous Whittaker Chambers–Alger Hiss case. Although Hiss's conviction on perjury charges would not under ordinary circumstances have precipitated a political crisis, the *implications* of the case were enormous. Hiss's presumed involvement in a Soviet spy ring in the 1930s may have gone technically unpunished, but McCarthy seemed to single-handedly try and convict for treason not only Alger Hiss, but also every person who fit his general description. And because Hiss had been a Democrat and a New Dealer, this made *all* Democrats and New Dealers suspect. Thus, as historian Stephen J. Whitfield explains, "the

12. Gaddis, *Strategies*, 89–91; Wells, "Sounding the Tocsin," 117–18; Walter LaFeber, *America, Russia, and the Cold War, 1945–1984*, 84–89.
13. Wells, "Sounding the Tocsin," 117; Dean Acheson, *Present at the Creation: My Years in the State Department*, 321, 355; Charles E. Bohlen, *Witness to History, 1929–1969*, 237.

political fallout for the Democratic party—and for the fate of liberals—was immediate."[14]

In this atmosphere, policymakers began to formulate the ideas contained in NSC-68. By January 1950, Truman was sufficiently moved by recent events and the ascension of the national security planners that he reluctantly agreed to a systematic reappraisal of the nation's military capacities. In doing so, he gave the green light to the building of the hydrogen bomb as well as a directive to the Departments of State and Defense to review the nation's military commitments and capabilities. The results of this review appeared as NSC-68, which was, in the words of Dean Acheson, designed "to so bludgeon the mass mind of 'top government' that not only could the President make a decision but that the decision could be carried out." As it turned out, NSC-68 was a decisive victory for the national security planners. The economy-minded Louis Johnson was left completely out of the writing process of NSC-68. Dean Acheson and Paul Nitze won the day, with the considerable backing of Leon Keyserling, upon whose economic philosophy the report was based. Although Truman was still skeptical about the import of such developments, it was clear that the national security planners were poised to push aside the economizers and had caught the attention of the president.[15]

On April 14, 1950, the National Security Council released to President Truman *A Report to the National Security Council by the Executive Secretary on United States Objectives and Programs for National Security* (NSC-68). This document established the intellectual and psychological underpinnings of American defense and national security policies for more than a generation. The basic thrust of the report was that the Soviets had developed a workable fission bomb and certainly would attain thermonuclear capability in a relatively short period of time. It followed from this premise that by 1954 the Soviets would be able to launch a devastating preemptive attack against the United States. The United States could not preclude such a strike, according to the report, without a significant increase in its military and economic capacity. The Soviet threat to American interests, the report concluded, was "more

14. Whitfield, *Culture of the Cold War*, 28.
15. Arthur A. Stein, "Domestic Constraints, Extended Deterrence, and the Incoherence of Grand Strategy: The United States, 1938–1950," 114–18; Seyom Brown, *The Faces of Power: Constancy and Change in United States Foreign Policy from Truman to Clinton*, 36–38. For Acheson quotation see *Present at the Creation*, 374.

immediate than had previously been estimated." In reality, NSC-68 was more than a call to arms—it called for more foreign economic aid, greater military assistance for the nation's allies, more investment in propaganda and information campaigns, increased intelligence capabilities, and a massive expansion of the nuclear stockpile.[16]

One of the most significant presumptions of NSC-68 was the year of maximum danger: 1954. By then, policymakers presumed that the Soviet Union would possess enough nuclear force to deal a crippling blow to the United States, thus leaving Western Europe completely open to a massive Soviet advance. Thus, national security planners set 1954 as the target date for the completion of the massive buildup prescribed in NSC-68. But how would the bold and far-reaching initiatives set forth in NSC-68 be carried out? The report was conspicuously vague on this crucial question.

Selling President Truman on the concepts put forward by NSC-68 was no easy task. NSC-68 struck a raw nerve with him because it challenged, among other things, his fundamentally conservative fiscal outlook. It also conjured up haunting specters of a Cold War garrison state. Despite the report's sometimes alarming language and baleful predictions, Truman refused to be taken in by it, knowing full well that its implementation would be prohibitively expensive and would thus force a complete turnabout in his economic policies. A few days after receiving the report, Truman referred it to the National Security Council, asking for further study of its major premises and for additional information on "estimates of the probable cost of such programs." In the meantime, NSC-68 was shelved. Truman simply would not accede to the recommendations of the report until he had an idea of the scope and cost of the programs involved. In the end, the president reluctantly agreed to most of the prescriptions in NSC-68 only *after* the outbreak of the Korean War, and he did so without fully thinking about how they would be fulfilled.[17]

Compiling the information Truman had requested was difficult because, as the National Security Resources Board (NSRB) admitted in late

16. NSC-68, April 14, 1950, U.S. Department of State, *Foreign Relations of the United States (FRUS)*, 1950, 1:237–92; quotation p. 287.

17. Gaddis, *Strategies*, 91–93, 113; Millis, ed., *Forrestal Diaries*, 438; Walter S. Poole, *The History of the Joint Chiefs of Staff*, vol. 4, 1950–1952, iv–v, 38–47; Wells, "Sounding the Tocsin," 123–31; Memorandum for the President, no date, RG 304, Records of the National Security Resources Board and the Office of Defense Mobilization, Office of the Chairman, box 17, file: "National Security Council," NA.

April, "the Defense Department has(n't) the slightest intention of giving us substantial figures upon which we might base mobilization planning before August 1." Even worse, in early May, the NSRB discovered that the two current JCS war plans failed to offer any guidance for actual mobilization purposes. "In other words," wrote an NSRB staffer, "there is no proper strategic plan for the defense of the United States. . . . At (the) current Pentagon rate of planning there will be no plan upon which to base mobilization programs until December." Thus, the fate of NSC-68 was very much up in the air. Truman's suspicions of the report, combined with the lack of firm requirements data and painfully slow planning, rendered the report largely moot.[18]

There were other reasons why the fate of NSC-68 hung in the balance during the spring of 1950. Some of Truman's advisers shared his concerns. Some openly challenged the predictions and premises upon which the report was based. Not surprisingly, the Bureau of the Budget was most critical of NSC-68 on both analytical and substantive grounds. First, the budget office was skeptical of predictions that the USSR was approaching the point of military superiority over the United States. Citing the vast superiority of America's naval and air forces and the fact that "our supply of fission bombs is much greater than Russia['s], as is our thermonuclear potential," the bureau refused to accept the need for a military buildup commensurate with the one envisioned in NSC-68. Furthermore, budget officials knew that the kind of defense program prescribed by the national security planners would greatly inflate the budget deficit, increase the pressure on the nation's economy, raise the need for more taxes, and increase the demand for stifling economic controls. In short, although the national security planners had won some important battles with the economizers, they had not yet won the war.[19]

In the meantime, others in the Truman administration were still concerned with the economy, which was just beginning to show signs of recovery from the 1949 recession. In 1950 the economy was just recuperating from a recession that originated in 1948. Late that year, inflation and the consumer price index (CPI) had hit all-time peaks, and as a result, the economy had begun to overheat. In the first half of 1949 there

18. Memorandum for Mr. Symington, May 17, 1950, RG 304, Office of the Chairman, box 17, file: "National Security Council," NA; Memorandum for Record, May 5, 1950, Rg 304, Office of the Chairman, box 17, file: "National Security Council," NA.
19. Memorandum for the President, no date, RG 304, Records of the National Security Resources Board and the Office of Defense Mobilization, Office of the Chairman, box 17, file: "National Security Council," NA.

was a mild recessionary "adjustment." The CEA saw the adjustment as beneficial because it eradicated "a major inflation without falling into a severe recession."[20] Truman agreed. His economic report to Congress in January 1950 was upbeat. The economy was in recovery, it said, and it "can and must continue to grow." The president even asked for modest tax increases in order to dampen inflationary pressures and to begin liquidating the national debt accumulated during World War II.[21]

At that point, however, Truman did not ask Congress to increase defense expenditures, despite growing international tensions and the ascension of the national security planners. The huge increases that took place later that year were completely unforeseen. On the contrary, Keyserling actually warned in January 1950 that the economic upturn might be threatened by the overall tapering off of "war-accrued backlogs," by which he meant the pent-up consumer demand left over from the Second World War. "To maintain reasonably full employment and reasonably high business opportunities," he said, "we will have to create new types of demands in the economy." Little did he know that six months later the Korean War would create those demands.[22]

The economy continued to expand in the first quarter of 1950, although there were lingering doubts as to how healthy this expansion actually was. Inflationary pressures again began to build, unemployment still remained at nearly 7 percent, and the rate of employment was not expanding as quickly as the labor force. What is more, the economy was not growing fast enough to eliminate the persistent problem of budget deficits. According to Frederick J. Lawton, Truman's new budget director, it was "highly questionable that a balanced budget [could] be achieved in the foreseeable future." Lawton also asserted that the economy "is not growing in accordance with its full potential." Of course, critics of the Truman administration pointed out the folly of continued budget shortfalls. Conservative columnist Henry Hazlitt lambasted Truman's January 1950 tax message to Congress, terming it simply "irresponsible."[23]

20. "The Economic Situation at Midyear 1949, A Report to the President by the Council of Economic Advisers," *Midyear Economic Report of the President* (July 1949), 3.

21. *The Economic Report of the President, Together with a Report to the President: The Annual Economic Review by the Council of Economic Advisers, 1950* (January 6, 1950), 6.

22. Leon Keyserling, "A Look into the 1950s: Its Promises and Pitfalls," speech given to the Institute of Scrap Iron and Steel, Annual Convention, January 23, 1950, Papers of Leon Keyserling, box 18, file: "Speeches, 1950," HSTL; *Economic Report of the President*, 16.

23. The subject of new inflationary pressures was raised several times during the nomination of Roy Blough to the Council of Economic Advisers in May 1950. See

The economy began to expand more rapidly in the second quarter of the year, and by June 18, doubts about the state of the economy had begun to disappear in the midst of what appeared to be a major boom. The economy, in fact, was nearing the finish of its most prosperous period since the end of the Second World War. In March, the economy had begun to gain momentum, and it continued unabated. Productivity and consumer demand were up sharply. Unemployment stood at 5 percent and was heading downward. Sales of automobiles and televisions were so frenzied that the food and clothing industries initiated a major cost-cutting campaign to lure consumers away from car and TV showrooms. But just as earlier concerns about the economy began to fade, new ones surfaced on Sunday, June 25, 1950, when reports of the North Korean invasion of South Korea hit the news wires.[24]

Truman was first notified of the massive North Korean assault by a grim and shaken Dean Acheson late on the evening of June 24. The news stunned the president, but in characteristic fashion, he acted decisively. Cutting short a long weekend in Missouri, Truman flew back to the capital on Sunday to confer with his top advisers. By Sunday evening, less than twenty-four hours into the crisis, Truman had decided to intervene in the Korean War, sending U.S. troops into combat for the first time since 1945. As a precaution, the president also ordered the Seventh Fleet to the Straits of Formosa, and directed the Air Force to prepare plans for destroying all Soviet airfields in the Far East. Convinced that the surprise attack was Moscow-inspired or worse yet, a Soviet ruse to distract the West while it invaded Europe or attacked the United States, the nation panicked. According to a Gallup poll taken during the last week of June, 57 percent of Americans feared that World War III had begun. Over the next several days, as Truman committed more and more military assistance to the beleaguered South Koreans, Americans lauded his actions. His approval ratings soared, and the populace appeared to hunker down for what would be a long struggle.[25]

The Korean crisis served Dean Acheson and the national security operatives very well. Here was proof of the Soviets' evil intentions of

---

Nomination of Roy Blough: Hearings before the Committee on Banking and Currency, United States Senate, 81st Cong., 2nd Sess., May 23, 1950. See also Bert G. Hickman, *Growth and Stability of the Postwar Economy,* 76; Memo for the President, April 19, 1950, President's Secretary's Files (PSF)-Bureau of the Budget, box 151, HSTL. For Hazlitt's quotation see *Newsweek* 34 (February 6, 1950): 12.

24. John Edward Wiltz, "The Korean War and American Society," in Francis H. Heller ed., *The Korean War: A 25-Year Perspective,* 112.

25. Ibid., 113–15; Donovan, *Tumultuous Years,* 189–99.

world domination. The economizers within the Truman administration were then completely discredited, and Truman reluctantly agreed to begin rearming the nation along the lines envisioned in NSC-68. Although it can be assumed that the president would have more than likely authorized some strengthening of American and European military strength had the Korean crisis not occurred, it is very doubtful that he would have acceded to anything like the rearmament prescribed by NSC-68. He was simply too determined to balance the budget and curb inflation. Korea changed all that. By September 1950, Truman had pushed the last of the economizers—Secretary of Defense Louis Johnson—out of his administration. He replaced Johnson with George Marshall. In the same month, he formally approved NSC-68. For the first time, the United States was prepared to match its military capacity with its defense commitments, here and abroad.

The immediate and enduring impact of the Korean War on the American political economy was stunning. The president's decision to intervene provided a powerful stimulus to the economy. Income and employment levels reached new heights, thus sustaining the economic recovery well into 1953. On the negative side, the huge jump in defense expenditures from $13 billion in 1949–1950 to more than $52 billion by 1952 rekindled inflation and forced the Truman administration in January 1951 to issue a mandatory wage-and-price freeze. The war also led to increased taxes and acrimonious debates between conservatives and liberals over how best to redistribute America's economic and military resources. Finally, the imposition of far-flung government controls over the economy promoted an increase in bureaucratization, greater government intrusion into the affairs of private enterprise, and most critically, brought to the fore fears of America as garrison state.

Without a doubt, the Korean War called for new measures of economic control. It forced prices up sharply as consumers and producers alike engaged in panic buying and hoarding in anticipation of shortages. Retail sales soared by 8 percent in July 1950 alone, five times as much as the rise in personal income. Production neared capacity, and unemployment plummeted; the economy now had very little excess capacity to cope with a national emergency. The Truman administration tried to calm the speculation by asserting that the Korean crisis would not result in a derailment of the economy or a dangerous new round of inflationary pressures. Nevertheless, prices continued to surge upward, especially for basic raw materials. A feverish round of speculative buying and hoarding of raw materials catapulted the price of rubber from $.34 to $.86 per pound, while tin prices soared from $.76 to $1.84 per pound in the last two quarters of 1950. These drastic price surges resulted in severe shortages of critical raw materials that threatened to halt production of both civilian and military goods. Only two weeks into the crisis, the NSRB, the Treasury Department, and even the Budget Bureau began lobbying for the imposition of economic controls, especially for raw materials in short supply.[26]

Publicly, the administration tried to allay growing alarm in the first weeks of the crisis; privately, however, officials expressed deep concern. Some panicked; Stuart Symington, Truman's new chairman of the NSRB and former Air Force secretary, was one of the first to do so. He complained of a serious shortfall of U.S. military forces and of the lack of a long-term defense strategy. Symington bluntly informed the president that the Soviets appeared ready to strike at any moment and most certainly would try by 1954, the target year set in NSC-68. He also warned that the nation lacked sufficient air power to engage in any other crisis besides the one currently under way in Korea without jeopardizing minimum defense requirements for the continental United States. The United States, he said, must "embark promptly on whatever program is necessary" to support the president's new position.[27]

Symington was certainly not the only one sounding the alarm. In a particularly somber cabinet meeting on July 8, Secretary of the Treasury John Snyder wanted to let it be known that "we mean business"; he pushed for tighter controls over the economy but tempered his remarks by warning that such a statement might induce even more panic. A representative of the Munitions Board complained about "drastic" shortages of copper and manganese, and Truman instructed the attorney general to prepare for a government takeover of the strike-ridden Rock Island Railroad, which was holding up shipments of raw materials.[28]

As the second full week of the Korean crisis unfolded, the Truman administration knew that it would have to act quickly to reorient

26. Hickman, *Growth and Stability*, 81; Leon H. Keyserling, "The United States Economy and World Events," speech before the Seagram International Business Conference, July 3, 1950, Papers of Leon Keyserling, box 18, file: "Speeches, 1950," HSTL; Memorandum for the Chairman, NSRB, July 7, 1950, RG 304, Office of the Chairman, box 17, NA; Memorandum for the Chairman, NSRB, July 11, 1950, box 17, NA; Alfred E. Eckes, *The United States and the Global Struggle for Minerals*, 166–68.

27. Letter from Symington to Truman plus attached memorandum of July 6, 1950, President's Secretary's Files, subject file, box 146, file: "National Security Resources Board—Miscellaneous," HSTL; *Newsweek* 35 (March 6, 1950): 17.

28. Notes on Cabinet Meeting, July 8, 1950, Papers of Matthew J. Connelly, box 2, file: "Notes on cabinet meetings 1950 (1/6–12/29)," HSTL.

the economy to meet the rapidly increasing needs of the military. At that point, however, there was little agreement as to how this was to be accomplished. The Departments of State and the Interior argued that economic controls would soon be needed to contain inflation. The secretary of the interior especially worried about the steel supply and thought that controls were needed to bolster production and inventories. The Commerce Department suggested that Truman ask Congress to invoke standby controls if voluntary measures failed. The Departments of Agriculture and Labor concurred. The National Security Resources Board stressed the importance of controls but stopped short of advocating even standby controls. The secretary of defense also shied away from economic controls, stating that his department was receiving without difficulty the materials it had ordered. Policymakers in the White House and on the CEA were likewise reticent to ask for control legislation. Truman's advisers, including Keyserling, believed that any such request would have a negative psychological effect. In essence, they feared that the mere mention of controls would make them a self-fulfilling prophesy.[29]

It was against this background that President Truman sent a message to Congress on July 19 reporting on the Korean situation. The United States' commitment in Korea, he warned, would have serious repercussions at home, especially in the form of shortages and inflation. Truman went on to recommend legislation that would give the president the power to assure adequate supplies for military and civilian use and the means to increase production of strategic materials and services. In short, he was asking for specific wartime powers to facilitate mobilization and rearmament. His message set in motion a process that resulted in the Defense Production Act of 1950. Congress immediately commenced work on Truman's proposals. Most members of Congress wanted to empower the president with appropriate legislation. But they were not of one mind as to the extent of the powers to be granted. Ultimately, what the president had called for, according to *Newsweek* magazine, was "something about half way between full war mobilization and peacetime business as usual."[30]

29. On July 7, the White House held an interdepartmental discussion on the Midyear Economic Review draft in which the subject of controls became a focal point. Memo from Roy Blough, Council of Economic Advisers, July 10, 1950, Papers of Roy Blough, box 9, file: "CEA June–July 1950," HSTL.

30. *Defense Production Act of 1950, Hearings before the Committee on Banking and Currency House of Representatives*, 81st Cong., 2nd sess., July 24–25, 1950, 1–8; *Newsweek* 36

Undoubtedly, with important congressional off-year elections less than four months away, Truman did not want to overemphasize an issue like economic controls, which might play right into the hands of conservatives. He also must have realized that a draconian mobilization act might send the wrong message to the Soviets, forcing them to conclude that the United States was arming for a general war. Furthermore, Truman limited his controls request to Congress because he still lacked firm requirements data from the armed forces and wanted to avoid, in his words, "putting any more money than necessary at this time in the hands of the Military." Finally, no one, including Truman, knew how long the war would last, so it was difficult to determine how expansive the control legislation should be. If the Korean War ended quickly, the need for strict controls would be minimal, and the nation could proceed with its long-term rearmament program gradually, without assembling large and costly mobilization agencies. Given Truman's aversion to disruptive military spending, this scenario was obviously much preferred.[31]

Not surprisingly, both the White House and the Congress looked back to the last war in formulating Korean-era mobilization procedures. In that conflict, the United States employed what John Kenneth Galbraith has termed the "disequilibrium system," which relied very heavily on direct controls to stabilize the economy and assigned only a limited role to tax and credit policies. The White House made it clear from the beginning that it did not want to impose blanket controls on the economy. Neither did it want to superimpose new war-related deficits on the already existing ones, especially because the Korean War mobilization was only one part of a long-term rearmament effort. Instead, the White House strategy emphasized pay-as-you-go taxes and an overall restrictive credit policy. In other words, it urged tax and credit policies that would curb inflation, keep supplies steady, prevent deficits from increasing, and hold economic controls to a minimum. At that point, many in Congress were prepared to raise taxes significantly to pay for the new mobilization effort. The Congressional Joint Committee on the Economic Report, for example, informed the White House on July 18

(July 24, 1950): 24; Note from Dick Neustadt, July 14, 1950, Papers of Harry S. Truman-Files of Stephen Spingarn, box 1, HSTL.

31. Memorandum for the Record, by Frederick J. Lawton, July 22, 1950, Papers of Frederick J. Lawton, box 6, file: "Truman, President Harry S., Meetings with the President-Agendas and Memorandums, 7/49–7/52," HSTL. Truman was quoted in Lawton's memo.

that "increased military expenditures" must be "accompanied by a tax bill which will finance the expense without increasing the debt."[32]

The congressional hearings surrounding the Defense Production Act, which began in late July, predictably encompassed a whole host of opinions as to how far the legislation should actually go. Taking their lead from Senator Robert A. Taft (R-OH), conservative Republicans in Congress generally favored a voluntary approach to mobilization controls. In a speech on the floor of the Senate on July 24, the very day that hearings on the subject were slated to begin, Taft dramatically stated the conservatives' opposition to the pending mobilization legislation. "I am not at all confident," said Taft, "that the Russians contemplate an all-out military attack at any time, or that there is a certainty of a third world war." "It is unnecessary," he added, "to grant . . . dictatorial powers over industry as is proposed in the bill recently introduced. The President's message is comparatively mild. This bill itself goes far beyond the message." But this was not the majority opinion. A few hawkish Republicans thought that Truman's proposal did not go far enough, insisting that mandatory rationing and consumer price controls be instituted immediately. Moderate Republicans and Democrats preferred measures in between these two extremes. Congress was under extraordinary pressure from the public, which seemed to be leaning toward more of an all-out mobilization effort than even Truman had wanted. In this case, the fires of public opinion, fanned by runaway inflation and panic buying, seemed to be outpacing both Congress and the president.[33]

On July 26, Bernard Baruch appeared before the Senate Committee on Banking and Currency, which was conducting hearings on the Defense Production Act. Baruch, a wealthy Wall Street financier and frequent presidential emissary, had headed the nation's World War I mobilization effort as chairman of the War Industries Board. He made an impassioned statement before the committee in which he urged full-scale mobilization. "Events have left us no choice," Baruch said.

32. "A Tax Program to Support the Policy of Containment," October 19, 1950, Papers of L. Laszlo Ecker-Racz, Director-Tax Advisory Staff, Department of the Treasury, box 4, p. 1, HSTL; Memo from the Joint Committee on the Economic Report, July 18, 1950, Papers of Stephen J. Spingarn, box 1, HSTL (quotation); John Kenneth Galbraith, "The Disequilbrium System," 287–302; Tibor Scitovsky et al., *Mobilizing Resources for War: The Economic Alternatives*, 103–6, 141.

33. *Defense Production Act of 1950, Hearings*, 81st Cong., 2nd sess., 12; *Newsweek* 36 (July 31, 1950): 22, 24–25; "The Economic Situation Produced by the Korean Crisis," Speech of Robert A. Taft in the Senate of the United States, July 24, 1950, 2, 4.

"We have to mobilize." Baruch went on to assert that the situation was sufficiently grave to warrant immediate blanket wage and price controls, a comprehensive system of strict allocations, and taxes high enough to prevent profiteering and to cover increased defense costs. Such a dramatic plea by a well-regarded elder statesman and mobilization expert was apparently enough to force a sizable number of congressmen and senators to begin considering controls beyond even those that the president had requested.[34]

In August, Congress began formal floor debates on the Defense Production Act. Ideologically, the debates generally followed partisan political lines. Conservative Republicans and conservative southern Democrats were most cautious in their willingness to enact comprehensive wartime powers. They feared creeping governmental "socialization," regimental government controls, and a centralized government with sweeping powers; in short, they feared the creation of a garrison state. Many more in Congress, however, were willing to grant the president the powers he sought *plus* additional standby powers, including controls over prices and wages. New York Representative Jacob Javits summed up this viewpoint best: "We have got to have not only what this bill provides, but we have got to have more. . . . We have got to give the power to effect rationing and price control . . . not to mention wage controls." Javits added, "I think the American people are way ahead of their leaders in the things they are willing to do to defeat this communist menace as we see it in Korea." Indeed, the public's clamor for action to arrest inflation and control material shortages was pushing Congress to invoke a war powers act that was considerably more expansive than the one Truman had proposed.[35]

By the middle of August, a majority in Congress was convinced that the Defense Production Act should include standby control powers over prices and wages, something that Truman had not originally requested. Once more, however, Republicans and moderate Democrats split over how best to administer standby controls. For example, some Republicans wanted to provide the president with inflexible standby

---

34. *Defense Production Act of 1950, Hearings*, 81st Cong., 2nd sess., 97–103. For quotation, see p. 97.

35. For Jacob Javits' remarks on the House floor see *Congressional Record*, 82nd. Cong., 1st sess., 1950, 96: 11519–11520. For congressional debates in general on the Defense Production Act see *Congressional Record*, 1950, 96: 11506–35, 11591–92, 11609–37, 11726–69, 11830–48, 11853–68 (House) and 12150–77, 12197–12225, 12397–12412, 12910–11 (Senate).

controls over prices and wages. By doing so, they hoped to paint Truman into a corner. Under this scenario, the president could not selectively establish controls. He would have to make a painful choice between clamping down with blanket economic controls or continuing a voluntary program. The White House interpreted this move as a purely political one and was not about to play the game. Truman made it clear that he would veto the Defense Production Act if the agreed-upon standby controls were not flexible. As it turned out, the forces behind inflexible controls were subdued, and Congress presented Truman with virtually all of the powers he had originally requested, plus standby flexible rationing and wage and price controls.[36]

Although Truman had initially opposed price and wage controls, he had little choice but to accept them on a standby basis in the face of strong public demand and a bipartisan call for action in Congress. In fact, during late July and August, the White House was inundated with telegrams and letters urging the president to invoke or at least accept standby controls. These messages came from all sectors of society; even organized labor called on the president to control prices and profiteering.[37]

Finally, in the first week of September, Congress passed the Defense Production Act, and President Truman signed it on September 8. It granted the president considerable power to place the nation on a war footing. Included in those powers was the authority to establish priorities and allocations systems; to requisition personal property for defense purposes; to expand productive capacity and the extraction of strategic materials; and to invoke wage, price, and credit controls. While not as sweeping as the executive powers granted during World War II, the Defense Production Act was nonetheless an unprecedented foray into government planning and control during a time in which no formal war had been declared. With the passage of the Defense Production Act, Congress and the executive branch had taken the first substantive step toward the institutionalization of the Cold War.[38]

36. *Newsweek* 36 (August 21, 1950): 69; Memo re "Worries: The Defense Production Act and the November Elections," August 21, 1950, Papers of Harold L. Enarson, box 2, HSTL.
37. See Papers of Harry S. Truman-OF, box 1737, which contains hundreds of letters urging the President to accept stricter controls. See also Letter to the President from the Cleveland District of the United Steelworkers, August 17, 1950, Papers of Harry S. Truman-OF, box 1736, File: "U," HSTL.
38. "Third Annual Report of the Activities of the Joint Committee on Defense Production," Joint Committee on Defense Production, October 20, 1953, 227–28, 278–302.

Over the next three months the Truman administration moved slowly and steadily to implement the Defense Production Act. On September 9, the day after Truman signed the legislation, the White House issued an executive order creating two stabilization agencies: the Economic Stabilization Agency (ESA) and the Wage Stabilization Board (WSB). This same order also provided for a director of price stabilization, who would work under the aegis of the ESA. Truman named Alan Valentine, an English professor and president of the University of Rochester, to head the ESA on the same day, although he would not be put up for Senate confirmation until December. The president also chose Cyrus S. Ching, director of the Federal Mediation and Conciliation Service, to chair the WSB. The position of director of price stabilization would not be filled until December. It seemed that few competent individuals wanted to take on the post because of the highly divisive nature of price stabilization during the last war.[39]

Truman's approach to industrial and production controls during the late summer and early fall was even more casual than his approach to economic stabilization. Weeks before the Defense Production Act was passed, the NSRB began jockeying for position to take control of mobilization activities. And many of Truman's advisers backed the idea of having the NSRB serve as the overall coordinating agency for the mobilization effort. But at the time, the president was reluctant to extend such broad authority to the Resources Board. Truman believed that the situation was not yet critical enough to do so and furthermore made it clear that he wished to move cautiously toward mobilization before the November elections. His fears of creating a garrison state and the bureaucratic behemoths that accompanied it also resulted in this initial reluctance. The NSRB continued to talk gloom and doom, however, asserting in early August that "a chaotic situation is in the making—one which could seriously sap our productive power—one which only the Chairman of NSRB seems in a position to prevent." Symington's strategy worked; on September 9, Truman put him at the head of the controls setup. The president authorized Symington to settle

39. Memorandum re Economic Stabilization-Defense Production Act of 1950, undated, President's Secretary's Files, box 228, HSTL; National Security Resources Board, "Calendar of Formal Actions by Federal Departments to Implement Defense Production Act of 1950 and Executive Order 10161," October 25, 1950, RG 296, Records of the Economic Stabilization Agency, Records Maintained by the Administrator, Classified General Files, box 2, file: "NSRB/Interagency Controls," NA; Heller, *The Korean War*, 119–20.

interagency disputes, establish policy, issue program directives, and take whatever measures might be needed to guarantee the coordination of the mobilization program. So the NSRB was essentially charged with policy development and coordination of the mobilization effort; it would not be involved in day-to-day operations—those functions would be assigned to various cabinet-level agencies and other already existing government bodies.[40]

The operational functions of other industrial control measures were assigned to various cabinet members. Truman charged Commerce Secretary Charles Sawyer with handling priorities and allocations of materials and manufacturing facilities. To accomplish this task, on September 11, Sawyer established the National Production Authority (NPA) within the Department of Commerce. The director of the NPA was William H. Harrison, president of ITT and a former staffer on the War Production Board of World War II. Immediately thereafter, the NPA began establishing a series of industrial advisory committees comprising various corporate leaders representing different industries and sectors of the economy. The committees served two chief functions: they provided needed personnel and statistical data to the NPA for purposes of targeting and increasing defense production; and they formed the nexus of the public-private cooperation that would hold the military's role in the mobilization program to a minimum while simultaneously keeping key elements of the private sector working cooperatively on matters of materials allocation and production. Later on, the NPA industrial committees became a model for public-private cooperation in the administration of wage and price controls.[41]

Mandated by Congress in the Defense Production Act and embraced fully by Department of Commerce and NPA administrators,

40. Confidential Memo from NSRB, August 3, 1950, Papers of Harry S. Truman, White House Confidential File (WHCF), box 16, file: "Defense Production Act," HSTL; Memorandum for the President, with attached F. J. Lawton Memo to the President, July 28, 1950, Papers of Harry S. Truman, President's Secretary's Files, Subject File, box 144, file: "Defense Production Act," HSTL; Memorandum for the President with attached Recommendations from F. J. Lawton, August 10, 1950, President's Secretary's Files, Subject File, box 144, file: "Defense Production Act," HSTL.

41. Memorandum for the President (undated), with attached F. J. Lawton Memo to the President, July 28, 1950, Papers of Harry S. Truman, President's Secretary's Files, Subject File, box 144, file: "Defense Production Act," HSTL; Memorandum for the President with attached letter to the Commerce Secretary, RG 304, Office of the Chairman, box 13, file: "Commerce," NA; "Interagency Collaboration in the Establishment and Use of Industry Advisory Committees," November 14, 1950, RG 296, Records Maintained by the Administrator, Classified General Files, box 2, file: "NSRB-Interagency Controls," NA; *Newsweek* 36 (September 18, 1950): 65.

industry advisory committees proved invaluable in the execution of NPA rules, regulations, and orders pertaining to industrial expansion and materials allocation. In fact, according to George R. Lunn, a government attorney assigned to the NPA, these committees provided "the most important organized method of consulting with industry representatives."[42] By mid-June 1951, the NPA would include in its management setup 397 separate industrial advisory committees working in tandem with the NPA industry divisions. The vast majority of these committees worked with NPA officials at the local or regional level through 105 existing field offices of the Department of Commerce. Each Commerce-NPA field office would then forward the various suggestions and findings emanating from its advisory committees to Washington, where the appropriate industry division would set the final policy for the nation as a whole using the information gleaned from the advisory committees. This close, public-private partnership, decentralized as it was, went a long way toward ensuring that NPA guidelines were as fair as possible and were responsive to individual industry's needs and the geographical market differences of the diverse economy.[43]

Throughout the mobilization period, the conduct and functions of the NPA industrial advisory committees underwent continuous review and adjustment, at once demonstrating the Truman administration's willingness to experiment with varying managerial forms while attempting to mitigate growing unease among American industries toward the unprecedented Korean-era rearmament. The overall coordination of the NPA advisory committees was charged to Lyle G. Belsley, formerly the executive secretary of the War Production Board of World War II and an industrialist himself. Belsley supervised the establishment and membership of the committees and in addition supervised a staff of industry specialists who regularly attended advisory committee meetings and who advised and aided regular NPA personnel. Belsley's job was also to ensure that advisory committee recommendations to NPA industry divisions properly adhered to antitrust laws, which he accomplished rather successfully by maintaining continuous contact with the Antitrust Division of the Department of Justice.[44]

42. George R. Lunn Jr., "Voluntary Cooperative Action between Industry and Government under the Defense Production Act of 1950," 40.

43. "Material for Inclusion in Annual Report of the Secretary of Commerce," October 18, 1951, RG 277, Reference Materials, 1951–1953, box 38, file: "Congress, Report to," NA.

44. Letter to Charles E. Wilson, June 29, 1951, RG 277, Official Correspondence, box 14, file: "Correspondence with General Agencies," NA.

The particular concerns and needs of small business were also addressed through the NPA-Commerce network of advisory committees. Another mandate of the Defense Production Act stipulated that small businesses be allowed to maintain or improve their competitive position through the mobilization period and to garner as many government defense contracts as practical. This mandate became critical to small firms that were threatened with closure as a result of metal curtailments later in the defense period. As a result, the NPA, the Commerce Department, and later, the Small Defense Plants Administration (SDPA) began to conduct industry-assistance programs and seminars that brought together military procurement officials and small-business specialists, representatives of prime defense contractors, and large civilian manufacturers and educated them on the character and availability of prime contracting and subcontract production for defense purposes. By January 1952, prime contractor-subcontractor clinics sponsored by the NPA, the SDPA, and the Armed Services were being held throughout the country to help bring together large contractors and small-business operators. By then, there were more than four hundred small-business specialists, enough to work with every major procurement agency to ensure that small firms enjoyed equal opportunity to bid on government contracts that could be fulfilled by them.[45]

At this particular point, the mobilization structure was decentralized to the point of being fragmented. This setup reflected Truman's belief that mobilization programs should be administered through existing agencies whenever possible; clearly, the president wished to avoid the bureaucratic behemoths of the World War II mobilization and the specters of a garrison state that they evoked. Also, by placing operational responsibilities in existing agencies, the administration felt that the new mobilization programs could be administered faster and more efficiently. Truman was also worried about the possibility of a conservative backlash to "government pork" and inefficiency should a whole host of new agencies be established. These attitudes thus resulted in the relatively unstructured and highly decentralized style of the early mobilization effort.[46]

45. Fourth Quarterly Report to the President by the Director of Defense Mobilization, "The Battle for Production," p. 40, RG 277, Policy Coordinating Bureau, box 2, file: "ODM-The Battle for Production," NA.

46. News Release, Statement of W. Stuart Symington before the Committee on Banking and Currency, July 24, 1950, Papers of Harry S. Truman-Files of Stephen J. Spingarn, box 1, file: "DPA of 1950 Volume 2, Tabs 44–113," HSTL.

The relatively slow progression toward mobilization during the summer and early fall also seemed to reflect the lack of clear-cut goals for the new defense effort. This is not surprising given the fact that the Korean-era mobilization was quite unlike any past war mobilizations. The Korean War was a limited war, and Truman meant to keep it that way. The United States had never fought a limited war, let alone mobilized for one, so there were no precedents to follow other than those from World War II. And a mobilization effort modeled after the total war effort of World War II threatened to impose a garrison state over the long haul of the Cold War. The Truman administration viewed the Korean mobilization as only part of a much larger and more protracted defense effort. The United States was preparing itself not only for the Korean War but also for the Cold War. Neither the military establishment nor the NSRB had any firm requirements figures upon which to base the mobilization effort. As Stuart Symington stated in October, "(T)he first and biggest task is to get from the military . . . their needs in terms of military end products scheduled out on some kind of time basis into the future for the next two years or thereabouts." At that time, no such data existed. Given these ambiguous circumstances, the Truman administration had little choice but to move slowly and cautiously with mobilization.[47]

Not surprisingly, the Korean mobilization effort also closely followed the tide of military events. Although American-led UN forces in Korea had taken a beating since the end of June, by mid-September the fortunes of war had changed dramatically. General Douglas MacArthur's daring amphibious landing at Inchon on September 15 had changed the entire scenario. Suddenly, the Korean crisis did not look so bad. *Newsweek* gushed that "the news from Korea suddenly changed from the blood and sweat of retreat to the triumph of audacious advance."[48] Such euphoria spread throughout the nation, and Americans believed MacArthur when he promised that the boys would be home by Christmas. In early October, with the North Koreans on the run, MacArthur had already begun plans for the ill-fated reunification of the Korean peninsula.[49]

In response to the apparent military successes in September, the fever of panic-inspired buying that had gripped the nation since June

47. Summary of Interagency Coordinating Committee, Meeting No. 2, October 18, 1950, RG 296, Records Maintained by the Administrator, Classified General Files, box 2, file: "Coordinating Committee, NSRB," NA.
48. *Newsweek* 36 (September 25, 1950): 29.
49. Heller, *The Korean War*, 127–28; David Rees, *Korea: The Limited War*, 85–107.

broke. Retail sales dropped sharply in the last week of September and continued to fall through November. Although prices continued to rise during this same period, the problem was not caused by a shortage of goods. In a cabinet meeting on September 29, Secretary of Agriculture Charles Brannan asserted that there was absolutely no justification for consumer price increases for foodstuffs. Commerce Secretary Sawyer concurred, blaming wholesalers and retailers for the markups. So the administration perceived that the situation was easing. No severe shortages at the civilian level existed, and the increase in military procurement had not yet caused significant dislocation of the economy. As a result, there seemed to be no good reason for speeding up the process of mobilization or economic stabilization. It actually looked as if the war might be over in a few months, so policymakers continued to move cautiously toward a gradual buildup geared to the long pull—namely the 1954 target date set in NSC-68.[50]

In late November, however, America's hopes for a short war and a gradual mobilization effort were dashed when the Chinese entered the war. On November 25, 1950, Chinese Communist forces, numbering over two hundred thousand, lunged southward in a devastating attack against UN forces, pushing them into a humiliating and hasty retreat. On November 28, Douglas MacArthur declared to the United Nations that "we face an entirely new war." The stunning reversal shocked Americans and the Truman administration. If UN forces faced "an entirely new war," then Americans faced an entirely new mobilization effort. In reaction to the news, many Americans embarked upon another wave of buying and hoarding. Inflation soared, and public approval for the war dropped precipitously; Gallup polls indicated that support for the Korean War effort had fallen nearly 25 percentage points since October. The president's approval rating plummeted as well, and many Americans began calling for the ouster of Secretary of State Dean Acheson, who was still viewed as the symbol of the administration's failures in East Asia.[51]

As the situation deteriorated, the White House was inundated with letters and telegrams from every corner of the nation urging the president to invoke full mobilization for war. One citizen from Lubbock,

---

50. Hickman, *Growth and Stability*, 81–83; Cabinet Meeting, September 29, 1950, Papers of Matthew J. Connelly, box 2, file: "Notes on Cabinet Meetings (1/6–12/29)," HSTL.
51. Rees, *Korea*, 157; Heller, *The Korean War*, 128–29; John E. Mueller, *War, Presidents and Public Opinion*, 50–51.

Texas, wrote: "I suggest that all auto factories be converted to war material plants," while a small-businessman from California conceded that "my partner and I expect to lose our small business as the result of the defense effort. . . . That is not important. Our only concern is the safety of our country, and of free people everywhere." Some citizens urged the president to launch a preemptive war against the Soviet Union while still others demanded that he use the atomic bomb against the Chinese.[52]

The events of late November and early December pushed the administration to accelerate appreciably mobilization and stabilization efforts. The United States, in other words, entered the second phase of the Korean War and the concomitant mobilization effort. On December 3, John D. Clark, vice chairman of the CEA, broke ranks with Keyserling and urged Stuart Symington to call for an immediate price-and-wage freeze. Leon Keyserling politely disagreed with Clark and counseled the president not to impose controls in one fell swoop because the necessary administrative mechanisms were not in place. He was also concerned about the public reaction to a sudden price-and- wage freeze. This time, however, Keyserling's cautious approach was the minority position in the White House. On December 5, Secretary of Defense George C. Marshall urged the president to declare a national emergency. In a December 8 cabinet meeting, Truman announced that he was leaning toward a "proclamation for total mobilization." Acheson and Marshall asked him to issue the proclamation in a nationally televised address to the nation.[53]

By December 12, Truman had made up his mind to do just that. He had already spoken with Charles E. Wilson, president of General Electric, about heading up a new mobilization agency. The president also stated that he realized a national emergency would mean the imposition of wage and price controls. He was not, however, sure when

52. Letter to Harry S. Truman, December 18, 1950, Papers of Harry S. Truman, OF, box 1735, file: "P," HSTL; Letter to Harry S. Truman, December 19, 1950, Papers of Harry S. Truman, OF, box 1732, file: "B #1," HSTL. See Papers of Harry S. Truman, OF, boxes 1732–1735 for many more examples of public support for an all-out mobilization effort and the imposition of wage and price controls.

53. Letter to W. Stuart Symington, December 3, 1950, Papers of Leon Keyserling, box 5, file: "Roy Blough, 1948–69," HSTL; Memo to the President, December 7, 1950, President's Secretary's Files, box 143, file: "Council of Economic Advisers," HSTL; Notes on Cabinet Meetings, December 5, and December 8, 1950, Papers of Matthew J. Connelly, box 2, file: "Notes on Cabinet Meetings (1/6–12/29)," HSTL; Notes for Meeting with the President, December 5, 1950, Papers of Harry S. Truman, President's Secretary's Files, Subject File, box 142, file: "Advisory Committee on Management," HSTL.

this should happen. So by mid-December, the Truman administration had been forced to move toward a greatly expanded mobilization effort. The unexpected military reversals in Korea raised the possibility of a much larger and more protracted war effort, and the internal and external constraints placed upon the administration had prevented it from acting more forcefully from the beginning, which, in turn, necessitated a rapid buildup almost overnight.[54]

On the evening of December 15, 1950, President Truman addressed Americans on national television and radio, solemnly explaining the new and dangerous turn of events. The next day, he formally proclaimed a national emergency. To carry out the added exigencies of mobilization, Truman announced the creation of a new mobilization agency—the Office of Defense Mobilization (ODM). Charles E. Wilson would direct the ODM and was given unprecedented powers to coordinate the overall mobilization program. In fact, Wilson's statutory mobilization authority far exceeded that of Bernard Baruch during World War I and, as Truman's presidential assistant wrote, Wilson was given "the broadest grant of power ever held by anyone other than the president." In luring Wilson to head up the ODM, Truman promised the GE executive "a completely free hand" in organizing and administering the new stepped-up mobilization effort.[55]

Clearly, by creating the ODM and by giving Wilson such vast powers, Truman had radically altered his approach to the mobilization effort. First, the White House understood that the creation of the Office of Defense Mobilization carried with it certain psychological imperatives. Americans would now know that they had entered a new game—with the attendant sacrifices that a substantial mobilization effort required—and the Office of Defense Mobilization would serve as a "symbol of unity" for the mobilization program. Policymakers viewed this type of psychological symbolism as critically important during a partial mobilization of indefinite duration. In a Cold War setting, during the engagement of a "limited war," positive public relations were paramount to success. Unlike World War I or World War II, the

54. Cabinet meeting, December 12, 1950, Papers of Matthew J. Connelly, box 2, file: "Notes on Cabinet Meetings (1/6–12/29)," HSTL.
55. Defense Mobilization Board, Meeting No. 1, December 28, 1950, RG 296, Records Maintained by the Administrator, Classified General Files, box 2, file: "Defense Mobilization Board Meetings," NA; *Newsweek* 36 (December 25, 1950): 14–15; *Newsweek* 37 (January 15, 1951): 67–69; Heller, *The Korean War,* 133; John R. Steelman and DeWayne H. Kreager, "The Executive Office as Administrative Coordinator," 704.

Korean War had rather vague goals; this time, there were no Huns or Hitlers to defeat.[56]

Second, the creation of the ODM sent a strong signal to Stuart Symington; the president did not have faith in his ability to lead the stepped-up mobilization effort that began in December. After Wilson took over at ODM, the NSRB once again became an advisory group to the president, and its function reverted to long-term planning exclusively. Before Symington took over the NSRB, it had proven unable to adequately coordinate national security programs among the various departments involved. And even after Truman had empowered the NSRB to coordinate the mobilization effort, Symington had been unable to unify the mobilization process. Truman had also grown tired of Symington's constantly gloomy forecasts about the nation's level of military and economic preparedness. During a time of national crisis, Truman did not need words and warnings—he needed action. The statuesque Wilson simply delivered what Symington and the Resources Board could not. By 1951, "the NSRB had become 'a laughing-stock around town,'" according to a White House aide, and by 1953 it had been reorganized out of existence.[57]

Third, with the establishment of the ODM came the realization that the fighting in Korea had become indistinguishable from the much larger Cold War struggle. Thus, mobilization planning had to take

56. "An Analysis of the Central Management Elements of the Defense Mobilization Programs," October 23, 1952, Papers of David H. Stowe, box 3, file: "Organizational Study, ODM-NSRB-NPA-ESA (1952)," HSTL.

57. Oral History Interview Collection, Harry S. Truman Library: Oral History Interview with Leon Keyserling, May 3, 10, and 19, 1971, Washington, D.C., 142–43; Cuff, "Ferdinand Eberstadt," 50–51.

Even as Secretary of the Air Force, Symington continually warned that the United States was losing ground to the Soviets militarily and economically. He publicly argued with his former boss, Defense Secretary Louis Johnson, asserting that the United States could not "even hope to match Red Russia man for man, gun for gun, and plane for plane . . . to attempt it would wreck the national economy." See *Newsweek* 35 (March 13, 1950): 17 and *Newsweek* 35 (March 6, 1950): 17. As NSRB chairman, Symington continued his litany, which culminated in a January 1951 report to the President in which Symington lambasted the administration's containment efforts and asserted that "until recently the United States has made little real effort to integrate its political, military, and economic plans and programs." Truman sent the report back to Symington with a handwritten message: "My Dear Stu, this is big [*sic*] a lot of Top Secret malarkey as I've ever read. Your time is wasted on such bunk as this. H.S.T." See top secret report entitled "Current History of National Planning . . . Diplomatic, Economic, and Military; and Reasons Why It Is Essential That These Three Segments of National Security Be Further Integrated," Papers of Harry S. Truman, President's Secretary's Files-Subject File, box 147, file: "Agencies," HSTL.

into account far more than the just the tide of military events on the Korean peninsula. The Chinese intervention forced mobilization planners to think beyond Korea, and to speed up the mobilization effort prescribed in NSC-68 lest the nation find itself facing another crisis with insufficient military capabilities. The problem was, however, that although administration officials had reconciled the "Korean" mobilization with the larger Cold War mobilization, the public was generally unaware of this shift. It continued to tie the military events in Korea to the mobilization program as a whole. This would prove to be a significant dilemma throughout the three-year conflict.

The reverses in the Korean theater led the Truman administration to realize that the Korean War would *not* be a short war and, further, that the United States had to prepare for any eventuality, including fighting another war simultaneously. The shock of the Chinese intervention and the creation of the Office of Defense Mobilization in December 1950 reflected new thinking on and new approaches to the rearmament effort. By creating the ODM and relegating the NSRB to long-term defense planning, the Truman administration decided that immediate and short-term planning had to be separated from medium- and long-term planning. Implicit in this policy shift was the recognition that besides creating organizational structures for the immediate crisis, the United States had to provide policies and programs for the development and maintenance of a "mobilization base." The mobilization base strategy would create a ready reserve capacity in terms of industrial capacity, raw materials inventories, manpower, and other items critical to national defense. Reserve capacities would be built up so that the United States would never again have to begin a full mobilization program from scratch. The conceptualization of an ongoing mobilization base actually dates back to 1947 and was vigorously pursued by James Forrestal during the deliberations surrounding the National Security Act of 1947. At that time, the Truman administration quietly swept the concept under the carpet because it simply was unwilling to commit itself to any regimentation of the economy for the purposes of national security. By December 1950, however, the administration had moved full circle and was moving rapidly toward the development of a mobilization base. From then on, this approach to national preparedness would became a hallmark of American national security policy.[58]

58. "An Analysis of the Central Management Elements of the Mobilization Programs," October 23, 1952, Papers of David H. Stowe, box 3, file: "Organizational Study,

The decisive actions taken by the Truman administration in December 1950 certainly marked a change in strategy. They did not, however, indicate any radical departures in the goals the administration had set six months earlier. Truman continued to stress the need for economic growth. Realizing that America's industrial might was the true force behind the nation's ability to project power abroad, the administration knew that industrial and economic expansion had to continue apace. Furthermore, sustained economic growth might preclude the necessity for strict, ongoing economic controls and would mitigate fears that the nation was moving down the road toward a garrison state. If wage and price controls *were* invoked, they would be used with great caution, be as flexible as possible, and be invoked only as a last resort. And a tax policy emphasizing the pay-as-you-go philosophy would be pursued as vigorously as possible. The defense effort would continue to be predicated upon close consultation and cooperation between government and the major functional and economic groups in society. In doing so, mobilization officials combined managerial decentralization with corporatist linkages at every level. Thus, cooperation between the private and public sectors would continue to be the keystone of the mobilization program. In the words of the CEA, "[T]his will help not only in the formulation of policy, but also in its execution. It is superficial and dangerous to conclude that a defense emergency must convert us into a totalitarian state."[59]

Despite the Truman administration's use of a new tack in the last weeks of 1950, many questions remained unanswered regarding how the government would respond to the new challenges of the Cold War. How deeply could the defense effort cut into the civilian economy without wrecking it? How many more sacrifices would the American people tolerate without some kind of backlash? And, most critically, would the United State evolve into a garrison state, a mirror image of

---

ODM-NSRB-NPA-ESA (1952)," HSTL, pp. 4, 49–51; Vawter, *Industrial Mobilization,* 1–2, 30–31, 69–95; Cuff, "Ferdinand Eberstadt," 38–40; see also Paul Y. Hammond, *Organizing for Defense,* especially chap. 2–3.

59. For a fascinating discussion of how the concept of national economic power and productivity has evolved into de facto deterrence against war, see John Mueller, *Retreat from Doomsday: The Obsolescence of Major War.* Mueller argues that the Soviet Union would not have preemptively attacked the United States even in a nuclear free world because the United States "would *still* have possessed an effective deterrent: Detroit." p. 122.; For quotation see "The Economics of National Defense," Fifth Annual Report to the President by the Council of Economic Advisers, December 1950, Papers of Leon Keyserling, box 3, HSTL.

its nemesis in the East? These were difficult questions for policymakers in the dark days of December 1950; the answers would come slowly, sometimes painfully, and always with much experimentation.

In fact, as the second phase of Korea gave birth to a new mobilization program, it also unleashed many of the forces Truman and his advisors had tried so hard to keep constrained. The creation of myriad mobilization agencies and the imposition of wage, price, and materials controls in 1951 resulted in a huge array of government bureaucracies. The federal budget strained under the weight of billions of dollars of additional defense expenditures, taxes rose dramatically, and inflation threatened to derail the economy and add billions to the cost of rearmament. Finally, defense industries increased in number as well as influence. The second phase of the Korean conflict forced the modern national security state into adulthood, bringing with it all of the fears that encompassed America as garrison state.

II

"An Entirely New War"

*The Chinese Intervention and the Institutionalization
of Rearmament, December–January 1951*

By the time President Truman declared a national emergency on December 16, 1950, the nation was bracing itself for any eventuality, including full-scale war with the Soviet Union. Consumers and producers alike, sensing the impending price and wage controls, bought at record levels, pushing inflation to new heights. The press was rife with talk of World War III, and the continued gloomy reports of military reverses in Korea dimmed the brightest of holiday spirits. Above all, an air of confusion and uncertainty pervaded society, seeming to paralyze the country from the top down. The angst of the period and of the war itself was ominously illustrated in *Life* magazine, which warned amidst a barrage of Christmas ads that "the news is of disaster; World War III moves ever closer . . . our leaders are frightened, befuddled, and caught in a great and inexcusable failure to marshal the strength of America as quickly and as strongly as they ought to have done in recent months."[1]

The period from mid-December 1950 to February 1951 witnessed a flurry of activity aimed at stabilizing the overheating economy while heightening the nation's war readiness. In short, the nation was entering the second phase of the Korean mobilization, which became subsumed within the administration's drive to significantly increase the pace and breadth of the nation's broader Cold War rearmament effort. During this time, the Truman administration concentrated on building organizational and bureaucratic structures to carry out the new exigencies of the stepped-up mobilization process. At the same

---

1. *Life* (December 11, 1950): 46.

time, Truman called for substantial troop reinforcements to be sent to Europe, under the new command of General Dwight D. Eisenhower. This action precipitated the three-month-long Great Debate in the Senate, which fractured the Republican party, splintered heretofore foreign policy bipartisanship, and further strained the administration's already shaky mobilization program. The administration also finally moved the nation to an across-the-board wage-and-price freeze, and began to implement industrial controls designed to increase production and lessen the severity of raw materials shortages. Thus, mobilization planners tried to accomplish in six weeks what they had been unable to do during the preceding six months: put the nation on a credible yet partial war footing. In the attempt, mobilization and stabilization officials clashed, nearly causing a derailment of the entire rearmament effort.

Charles E. Wilson, chosen by Truman to head the newly created Office of Defense Mobilization (ODM), was charged with directing and coordinating the intensified mobilization effort. In this regard, Wilson's delegated powers were enormous; the press termed his position a "co-presidency." *Business Week* likened the new mobilization chief to World War II's "Jimmy Byrnes, Donald Nelson, Leon Henderson, and Jesse Jones—all in one bundle, and then some."[2] In fact, the hard-driving, pugnacious Wilson saw to it that his powers were commensurate with the job he was given. Before agreeing to take the position, Wilson reminded Truman of what he perceived as the pitfalls of the last mobilization, during which centralized control was realized too late; as a result, bureaucratic inertia slowed the process considerably, and civilian planners ceded far too much authority to the better-organized military establishment. Apparently Truman agreed, for he extended to Wilson sweeping authority to mobilize the nation for war. The president had even agreed to allow Wilson to review the Executive Order establishing the ODM before he signed it. Before he agreed to accept the ODM job, Wilson changed the wording of the Executive Order, giving to himself even more power than the administration had originally intended. But neither the president nor any of his advisors quibbled—the Order was signed, and Wilson, at least on paper, became the most powerful man in Washington next to the president himself. Wilson's insistence on the delegation of sweeping powers, along with his strong personality, sowed the seeds for continual

2. *Business Week* (December 23, 1950): 19.

difficulties between his staff, those of subordinate operating agencies, and the White House.[3]

Charles Wilson was no stranger to the Washington scene, nor was he inexperienced in mobilization policy. Wilson had gained national recognition during his meteoric rise from office boy to the presidency of General Electric. His reputation caught the eye of New Dealers, who had lured the rising star into serving as an administrator in the NRA during the 1930s. He then reappeared in the capital during World War II to become first a vice chairman and then the executive vice chairman of the War Production Board (WPB)—the number-two spot under Chairman Donald Nelson. It was during his tenure at the WPB that his knack for getting things done, along with his legendary temper and impatience, became nationally known. One apocryphal story illustrative of Wilson's demeanor recounts his lunging at an Army general during an argument over the WPB's authority. Wilson, a "big, bull-necked Irishman from New York's Hell's Kitchen," grabbed the general by his lapels, thrust him into the air, and shook him violently. From then on, the two were known to get along fine.[4]

Despite his sometimes less-than-gracious behavior, Wilson was certainly no slouch when it came to business management and production methods. His genius for production techniques was legendary at GE. And quite naturally, he adapted this know-how to the NRA and WPB before going to the ODM. Wilson brought to the ODM the knowledge gained from wide experience and the procedures he had mastered during his previous government service, thus acting as a link between the Second World War and the emerging postwar order. Although he was a moderate, progressive Republican, Wilson's philosophy and modus operandi in many ways reflected those of his liberal business contemporaries. Like many of them, he came of age during the heyday of Taylorism and the advent of moving assembly lines in the early years of the century. He also took his cues from the Republican New Era, having actively participated in the associationalism of the 1920s. Wilson's experiences and background had instilled in him a strong

3. Ibid.; "Bloodless Coup Scored by Wilson," *Washington Evening Star,* January 22, 1951; *U.S. News and World Report* 29 (December 29, 1950): 20; Oral History Interview with David H. Stowe, by Charles T. Morrissey, Harry S. Truman Library, Independence, Missouri, November 1987. Stowe was administrative assistant to the president from 1949 to 1953 and was actively involved in the mobilization setup in the early stages.

4. Nelson, *Arsenal of Democracy,* 194–242; Millis, *Forrestal Diaries,* 3–5; *Newsweek* 37 (January 29, 1951): 17–21.

commitment to efficiency and productivity. Yet he was also cognizant of industry's responsibilities to raise living standards and provide for the general welfare of the nation. A tough, inner-city kid at heart, Wilson knew how to get a job done, but he also expected certain things in return: unconditional loyalty, hard work, and concern for the greater good.[5]

As the new production czar, Wilson's first order of business was to organize—quickly and decisively—the new mobilization setup. To help him do this, in December 1950, he named long-time acquaintance and Wall Street financier Sidney Weinberg as a special assistant. Weinberg, a vice chairman to Donald Nelson's War Production Board during World War II, was charged with recruiting businessmen for the new mobilization program. Wilson also asked General Lucius D. Clay to be his number-two man in charge of policy formulation and coordination of industrial production and procurement. Clay had performed a similar function for World War II mobilizer James F. Byrnes.[6]

Wilson clearly wished to keep the ODM staff small but powerful, reflecting the administration's desire to avoid the unwieldy bureaucratic agencies of the last war and the resultant interagency squabbling that accompanied them. Furthermore, Wilson believed that the Office of Defense Mobilization should be a policymaking and coordinating agency only. He never envisioned its becoming involved in day-to-day operations unless it became necessary to arbitrate disputes between constituent agencies. The maintenance of a small ODM staff also ensured that most of the operational responsibilities involved with mobilization would remain with already existing mobilization agencies in the departments of Commerce, Interior, and Agriculture. So the mobilization program now began to resemble the management structure of many industrial corporations of the day, including Charles Wilson's General Electric: centralized management and policymaking combined with decentralized implementation and operations. Broadly speaking, as Wilson moved to intensify the mobilization effort, the resulting organizational structures came to resemble vertically integrated, multidivisional firms like General Motors and General Electric.[7]

5. The 64-year-old Wilson began his career with GE in 1899 at the age of thirteen. He started out as an office boy with the Sprague Electrical Company, which was eventually consolidated with General Electric. *Newsweek* 37 (January 29, 1951): 17–21; Blum, *V Was for Victory,* 122–30; Nelson, *Arsenal of Democracy,* 342.
6. *Business Week* (December 23, 1950): 20; *Business Week* (January 6, 1951): 25–26; *Newsweek* 37 (January 1, 1951): 41.
7. Rodolfo A. Correa, "The Organization for Defense Mobilization," *Federal Bar Journal* 13 (September 1952): 1–4 (Correa served as General Counsel to the Office of

The decision to keep the ODM and other mobilization agencies decentralized also arose from policymakers' fears of the garrison state associated with the bureaucratic behemoths of the last war. In the minds of Korean-era mobilization planners, one way to avoid such monstrosities was through the use of decentralized management structures tied together with functional advisory committees from the private and public sector. Thus by keeping Wilson's office as a planning and coordinating agency exclusively, and by entrusting those operational functions to already well-established government agencies, the administration hoped to keep the specter of a militarized garrison state at bay. In addition, it hoped to keep all of the key elements in the private sector—including organized labor—working cooperatively on matters of wages, prices, and materials allocations. This task was to be accomplished through industry advisory committees and tripartite advisory bodies like the Wage Stabilization Board.

On December 28, only twelve days after the pronouncement of the national emergency, Wilson moved toward a permanent organizational setup. First, he convened the newly created Defense Mobilization Board. In that meeting Wilson proposed that the board, designed to be the top governmental advisory committee for mobilization, comprising all officials involved in the mobilization effort, would meet periodically to evaluate the progress of the mobilization effort. The board would also discuss and debate major policy decisions and recommend courses of action designed to expedite those policies.

It was at this meeting that Wilson unveiled his organizational plan to deal with production operations of the mobilization program. The principal component of the plan was the creation of a Defense Production Administration (DPA), which would operate in a similar fashion to the War Production Board of World War II. The new agency superseded the authority of the National Production Authority (NPA), which was

---

Defense Mobilization); *Newsweek* 37 (January 1, 1951): 41; see Novick, *Wartime Production Controls* for an excellent analysis of the problems that befell the World War II mobilization agencies.

For a good example of the governmental adoption of corporate management techniques during World War II, see Cuff, "Organizational Capabilities." See also Alfred P. Sloan Jr., *My Years with General Motors;* Alfred D. Chandler Jr. and Fritz Redlich, "Recent Developments in American Business Administration and Their Conceptualization [1961]," in Thomas K. McCraw, ed., *The Essential Alfred Chandler, Essays Toward a Historical Theory of Big Business,* pp. 117–39; and Chandler, *Strategy and Structure,* all of which describe the evolution and implementation of centralized/decentralized multidivisional management forms and their applicability to noncorporate entities including governmental wartime control agencies.

established in September 1950 under the auspices of the Commerce Department. The DPA would handle all industrial requirements and allocation responsibilities but was expected to redelegate most of those tasks to already existing agencies. The basic functions of the DPA were broken into several categories: the establishment of aggregate production priorities; the determination of program feasibility; the setting of production quotas; and the determination of the scope of industrial expansion. Wilson impressed upon his colleagues the need for quick implementation of the plan, likely including the Controlled Materials Plan to deal with materials shortages.[8]

By delegating to the Defense Production Administration overall policy formation with mandatory redelegation of operational procedures to already established agencies, the ODM was keeping to Wilson's overall centralized/decentralized approach. The DPA would thus provide centralized decision making and coordination while old-line agencies (like the NPA) would administer day-to-day operations. In addition, officials believed that in the case of materials allocations, basic policy-making should be vested in an independent agency over and above both claimant and allocation agencies.[9]

Not surprisingly, the creation of the Office of Defense Mobilization and Charles Wilson's vast array of powers sounded the death knell for the National Security Resources Board. The president directly informed NSRB chief Stuart Symington that the board's emergency functions would be immediately transferred to the newly established mobilization agencies. Although Symington seemed generally to escape personal blame for the agency's failure to respond to the Korean crisis, the NSRB as a component of national security planning had obviously lost much of its power and prestige. It remained in a strictly advisory capacity to the president and the National Security Council, and the board busied itself with long-term defense planning and civilian defense coordination until 1953, when it was folded into the Office of Defense Mobilization. Symington himself left the NSRB in April 1951 to head the Reconstruction Finance Corporation. In the final analysis,

8. Minutes, Defense Mobilization Board, Meeting No. 1, Wednesday, December 28, 1950, RG 296, Records of the Economic Stabilization Agency (hereafter RG 296, National Archives [NA], Washington, DC, with filing information), Records Maintained by Administrator—Classified General Files, box 2, file: "Defense Mobilization Board Meetings," NA; "Executive Order Establishing the Defense Production Administration," President's Secretary's Files, box 144, HSTL; *Business Week* (January 6, 1951): 25.
9. Correa, "Defense Mobilization," 5.

the NSRB was never able to establish itself as *the* central mobilization agency, even after Truman had given it specific authority to do so in September. Ultimately, it took the emergency of the Chinese intervention to push the administration toward creating such an agency. And even then, the NSRB was quickly cast aside in favor of Wilson's more powerful ODM.[10]

In late December, Wilson named William Henry Harrison, former president of the International Telephone and Telegraph Company (ITT) and current NPA director to head the new DPA. Manly Fleischmann, general counsel for the NPA, was in turn tapped to take Harrison's place at the NPA. Like the other top administrators of the new setup, Harrison was an old hand at mobilization issues, having served as an administrator under Wilson on the War Production Board. And like Wilson himself, Harrison was a successful corporate executive cut from the same cloth: a results-oriented, hard-driving man who repeatedly straddled the corporate world and government service. He was, in fact, a permanent member of what by that time had become a cadre of "dollar-a-year" men whose service dated back to, in some cases, the First World War. Like the two mobilizations before it, the Korean mobilization tended to recruit corporate, internationally minded men for top administrative posts.[11]

Between December 15 and February 1, the Truman administration created a whole host of agencies to formalize the new mobilization effort. By the first of February, nineteen government agencies had been established to carry out the Korean rearmament program, most of which had been set up since the Chinese intervention. Many of these new alphabet agencies were created under the auspices of old-line, cabinet-level departments. Nevertheless, their creation marked a critical turning point in the mobilization process. By establishing so many new agencies, the administration was committing itself to a far greater and more protracted defense effort than it had envisioned only a few months earlier. With this development, of course, came renewed fears of America as militarized garrison state.

10. Letter to Symington from Truman, January 3, 1951, White House Confidential File, box 28, file: "1295–1951–August 1952," HSTL; *Business Week* (December 23, 1950): 19–23; Cuff, "Ferdinand Eberstadt," 37–52 (especially 50–52); "Will RFC Fade Away?" *Washington Daily News*, April 30, 1951; Oral History Interview—Leon H. Keyserling, by Jerry N. Hess, HSTL, May 3, 10, and 19, 1971.
11. *U.S. News and World Report*, 29 (December 29, 1950): 20; *Newsweek* 37 (January 29, 1951): 19; *Business Week* (January 6, 1951): 25–26.

In addition to the ODM, ESA, and WSB, the administration also formed the Defense Transportation Administration (DTA) within the Interstate Commerce Commission. The DTA's job was to ensure that the nation's transportation network continued to provide the defense effort with the needed materials to boost production. Meanwhile, under the Department of the Interior, the Truman administration established five new wartime agencies: the Petroleum Administration for Defense (PAD); the Solid Fuels Administration for Defense (SFAD); the Defense Fisheries Administration (DFA); the Defense Power Administration (DPA), to handle electric power generation; and the Defense Minerals Administration (DMA). The Agriculture Department created three new offices to deal with defense-related concerns and agricultural production. Maurice Tobin, secretary of labor, created the Office of Defense Manpower to analyze the nation's manpower needs and help locate workers for defense work. Also set up to handle defense-related needs were the Division of Selective Credit Regulations (part of the Federal Reserve) and the Emergency Procurement Service (under the guidance of the General Services Administration).[12]

As if the new crisis in Korea and the attendant bureaucratic proliferations were not enough for the Truman administration to handle, ex-president and quasi-isolationist Herbert C. Hoover began a brief but contentious national debate over foreign policy and national security in a nationally broadcast speech on December 20. Hoover was reacting to—and criticizing—Truman's December 19 decision to reinforce American ground forces in Western Europe as the bulwark of NATO forces, to be led by General of the Army and first Supreme Allied Commander of NATO Dwight D. Eisenhower. In his speech entitled "Our National Policies in This Crisis," Hoover pessimistically stated that "it is obvious that the United Nations have been defeated in Korea by the aggression of Communist China. There are no available

---

12. "19 Alphabet Agencies Spring Up under Defense Production Act," *Washington Evening Star*, January 20, 1951. In addition to the agencies mentioned here, several already-existing agencies were also directly involved in the mobilization program including: the Munitions Board (under chairman John Small), which determined the overall needs of the production and defense program and ordered the appropriate amounts of strategic materials to meet those needs; the Reconstruction Finance Corporation, which loaned money for building and expanding defense plants; the Housing and Home Financing Agency, which regulated civilian-oriented government loan guarantees (like GI Guarantees); and the Federal Civil Defense Administration, which prepared the nation against possible enemy bombing attacks and other forms of wartime violence.

forces in the world to repel them."[13] Continuing his litany, Hoover asserted that America's financial and economic strength would be ruined by the administration's policies, charging that "if we continued long on this road the one center of resistance in the world will collapse in economic disaster."[14] Hoover's "solution" to the nation's dilemma was a retreat from America's global military and political commitments; he urged America to "arm (the) nation's air and naval forces to the teeth" and to abandon the stationing of ground troops in Asia and Europe.[15] Finally, he called for national unity behind a policy that put America's continental defense and national interests first by the creation of a "Western Hemisphere Gibraltar of Western Civilization."[16]

Hoover's remarks created quite a stir, especially among conservative Republicans, who were already eyeing suspiciously the administration's new approach to mobilization. Above all, the ex-president's speech ignited renewed isolationist sentiments, with the likes of Joseph P. Kennedy leading the charge. It also opened the Truman administration to new criticism over its military strategies in Korea and its larger mobilization program. Thus, the speech by Hoover began the "Great Debate." Although the conservative opposition in Congress wanted desperately to wrest power from the president and his Democratic supporters, their initiatives generated more heat than light. The Great Debate produced a short-lived but vituperative war of words in the Senate and the national media over the president's power to deploy troops to Europe without congressional consent and over the critical issue of the importance of Europe's security to the United States during a crisis in which American forces were involved in Korea. Fiscal conservatives who were opposed to the administration's stepped-up defense spending also joined in the fray, arguing that Truman's new commitments to NATO combined with the Korean mobilization effort would bankrupt the nation. As well, the Great Debate played right into the hands of McCarthy and his supporters, who renewed their attacks on Truman, Acheson, and their conduct of foreign and military affairs. The Great Debate lasted only about four months, but its timing could not have been worse for an administration struggling to

---

13. Herbert Hoover, *Addresses upon the American Road, 1950–1955,* 5.
14. Ibid., 6.
15. Ibid., 7.
16. Ibid.

formulate new defense strategies while placing the country on a war footing.[17]

The substantive issues that lay behind the Great Debate were the status of civilian-military relations, presidential prerogative in the conduct of foreign affairs, and most important, fears that the evolving Cold War was ruining the American system and paving the way for the creation of a garrison state. In short, the debate can be viewed as a last-ditch effort by congressional conservatives to reverse the decision to implement the prescriptions of NSC-68. Truman too fretted over these issues; however, the gravity of the situation and the clamor of popular support for increasing the defense effort overshadowed the president's reservations. Furthermore, nobody, including the president himself, knew what lay ahead; the United States had to prepare itself for every contingency, including the possibility of an escalated Asian war or a general war with the Soviet Union. The Great Debate's lasting legacy was to provide added grist for those who doubted the wisdom and efficacy of the administration's foreign and domestic policies. Time and again, these foes of Truman would resurrect the arguments made in the debate to defeat or dilute his administration's mobilization and stabilization initiatives.[18]

At the same time the administration was organizing the production side of the mobilization program, it was also moving toward greater economic stabilization efforts, including full wage and price controls. Economic stabilization proved to be quite a difficult task, however. Staffing the stabilization agencies had been a problem since their inception in September. The Director of the Economic Stabilization Agency (ESA), Alan Valentine, had not been confirmed by the Senate until early December; thus, when the president declared a national emergency, the ESA lacked the requisite staff to handle a full stabilization program. And the key position of price administrator remained vacant until the first week of December. Furthermore, the three top men in

17. *Life* 30 (January 1, 1951): 18; *New Leader* 34 (January 8, 1951): 2–4; D. Clayton James, "Harry S. Truman: The Two-War Chief," in Joseph G. Dawson III, ed., *Commander in Chief: Presidential Leadership in Modern Wars*, 124; Walter Millis, with Harvey Mansfield and Harold Stein, *Arms and the State: Civil-Military Elements in National Policy*, 345–46; Ronald J. Caridi, *The Korean War and American Politics: The Republican Party as a Case Study*, 108–40.

18. Harry S. Truman, *Memoirs of Harry S. Truman, 1946–52: Years of Trial and Hope*, vol. 2, 414, 416–17, 419–27; James T. Patterson, *Mr. Republican: A Biography of Robert A. Taft*, 474–86; *U.S. News and World Report* 30 (January 5, 1951): 27; *Business Week* (January 6, 1951): 120.

the stabilization effort—Valentine, Michael DiSalle (director of price stabilization), and Cyrus Ching (Wage Stabilization Board chairman)— had little in common and differed considerably over the tempo and extent of the economic stabilization program.

However reluctant the administration had been to move toward full controls, by the end of December, it was fully committed to a complete wage-and-price freeze. Despite the waning rate of inflation in October and early November, the price index of basic commodities rose by 35 percent in the last six months of 1950, while wholesale and retail prices rose by 11 percent and 5 percent, respectively. Strong public and congressional calls for the immediate implementation of economic controls grew louder still. And the administration knew that if it did not act quickly to stem the tide of inflation, the stepped-up rearmament effort would end up costing far more than projected— effectively dashing any hope of a pay-as-you-go program.[19]

Besides the logistical and staffing concerns facing the stabilization program, the mechanics of a wage-and-price freeze were daunting. The unavoidable inequities involved with the freeze caused economic hardship for some and political turmoil for many. A general price freeze following a brief period of high inflation like the one that had occurred between December and January almost always catches prices in badly distorted relationships. First, because wholesale prices had risen faster than retail prices, many retailers were caught in a price squeeze: They were forced to restock their inventories at higher prices while their selling prices remained fixed, and they were unable to cover all of their costs. Second, the many manufacturers who had diligently tried to hold down their prices during the voluntary effort found themselves at a comparative disadvantage to those less-cooperative producers who had ignored voluntary price restraints and charged all that the market would bear. The imposition of a wage freeze presented additional challenges to stabilization officials. A wage freeze, like a price freeze, also resulted in inequities: Workers who had just received a pay raise prior to the freeze were better off than those who had not received recent pay increases. Wage contracts that had built-in cost-of-living adjustments might be negated, thus guaranteed fringe benefits and productivity bonuses had to be somehow included in the total

---

19. *Building America's Might: A Report to the President by the Director of Defense Mobilization*, no. 1, 30; Hugh Rockoff, *Drastic Measures: A History of Wage and Price Controls in the United States*, 177–78.

wage-freeze package. Finally, only a portion of the nation's wages had kept pace with increased living costs since the outbreak of the war. Thus, stabilization officials knew that a price freeze had to be quickly followed by price adjustments—forward and backward. They also realized that a wage freeze had to give way to some sort of "catch-up" formula that would mitigate the inequities of wage controls.[20]

The man charged with overseeing the economic stabilization program, Dr. Alan Valentine, seemed from the very beginning singularly ill suited for the position. Valentine came to the Economic Stabilization Agency from the academic world, having taught English and history at Swarthmore College and Yale University before serving as president of the University of Rochester for more than fifteen years. The only government work Valentine had engaged in was a one-year stint as chief of the Economic Cooperation Agency's (ECA) mission to the Netherlands in 1948–1949. While at the ECA, he directed the $500 million recovery program for Holland—certainly a far cry from controlling the world's largest industrial economy. Valentine, a tall, handsome former star fullback and Phi Beta Kappa, had held no positions in industry or business prior to his nomination as ESA director; he had, however, served on several corporate boards, including the Rochester and Pittsburgh Railway and the Bausch & Lomb Optical Company. Why President Truman chose the bookish Valentine for such a position had been a mystery in the capital since the announcement was made in late September. Rumor had it that Truman purposefully chose him because the "initial holder of a position such as Economic Stabilization Administrator should be regarded as expendable, in the opinion of some who remember the [ill] fate of Leon Henderson, who guided (World War II's) OPA through its early days."[21] Valentine was unknown in Washington circles, although he and Stuart Symington had been friends for many years. Acquaintances and colleagues described him to the press as quiet and unassuming, yet tenacious. He showed little inclination to back down from a given position and was highly principled.[22]

From the start, Valentine demonstrated a cautious side that came to haunt him as the stabilization program evolved. He was reluctant to

20. Rockoff, *Drastic Measures*, 180; *Building America's Might*, 33–34.
21. "Alan Valentine, The Man Nobody Knows," *Washington Evening Star*, October 14, 1950.
22. Ibid.; U.S. Congress, Senate Committee on Banking and Currency, *Confirmation of Dr. Alan Valentine: Hearing before the Committee on Banking and Currency*, 81st Cong., 2d sess., December 4, 1950, 1–2.

delegate authority and seemed to distrust those around him, especially businessmen and politicians. The ESA director continually shied away from press conferences and interviews, which certainly did little to help him sell his ideas or ingratiate himself with the public. Valentine had gone on record, both to the president and Congress, stating that he did not believe wage and price controls were the preferred way to deal with inflation; instead, he argued that credit controls and taxation were better because they attacked the inflationary virus at the source: the money supply. Beyond that, Valentine believed strongly that "a sincere and thoroughgoing attempt at voluntary controls" should be tried before price controls were mandated.[23] After the Chinese intervention and the proclamation of the national emergency, Valentine stuck to his go-slow approach toward price and wage controls even in the face of stiff public and congressional opposition. He refused to be pushed into a control program with which he did not fully agree. Furthermore, the ESA, in Valentine's view, had neither the staff nor the organization to administer mandatory wage and price controls much before March or April 1951.[24]

Michael V. DiSalle, mayor of Toledo, Ohio, and President Truman's nominee for the Director of the Office of Price Stabilization (OPS), was grouped from the start with those officials proposing vigorous price-control action. DiSalle's views toward stabilization were markedly different from those of his boss, Alan Valentine. He reportedly confided to the president just prior to his appointment that "I'm just five hours removed from the people of my town, and I know what they are thinking. It is no different from the thinking of people in all the other towns across the county, and frankly, Mr. President, they are so far ahead of Washington in this crisis that you'll have to hustle to catch up."[25] Thus, the stage was now set for repeated conflict between the new price-stabilization director, who favored a rapidly instituted wage-and-price-control program, and the ESA administrator, who continued to preach a cautious, conservative approach to economic stabilization.

In most respects, in fact, DiSalle was quite the opposite of his bookish, retiring boss. Forty-two years old at the time of his appointment,

---

23. *Confirmation of Dr. Alan Valentine: Hearing*, 8–9.

24. "Price-Wage Split Undermines Valentine in Stabilization Job," *Washington Post*, January 12, 1951; *U.S. News and World Report* 30 (January 12, 1951): 23–30; David Ginsburg, "Price Stabilization, 1950–52: Retrospect and Prospect," 523–24.

25. Felix Belair Jr., "The Amiable 'Mike'—Policeman of Prices," *New York Times Magazine* (February 18, 1951): 13.

DiSalle was a born politician; he had graduated from Georgetown Law School and practiced law for five years before being elected to the Ohio legislature. From there he went on to serve five consecutive terms on the Toledo City Council and then served two terms as mayor. The rotund and jovial DiSalle was well liked, outgoing, and a real fighter. His personality—as much as his philosophy toward wage and price controls—set him on a collision course with ESA director Valentine.[26]

The third member of the stabilization triumvirate, Cyrus S. Ching, had been tapped by Truman in October 1950 to chair the tripartite Wage Stabilization Board, which was charged with advising the ESA director on wage and salary stabilization measures. Ching, a lugubrious-looking but effective businessman left his post as head of the Federal Mediation and Conciliation Service (FMCS) to preside over the WSB. In addition to his other varied experience in the field of personnel and labor relations, he had served a brief stint as a staffer for the National War Labor Board of World War II. His experiences in the business world along with his acclaimed work with management and organized labor as director of the FMCS would serve him well as the head of the WSB.[27]

As the crisis in Korea deepened in December, the WSB found itself in the same position as the other stabilization agencies: unprepared. The board's full membership had not been sworn in until November 28; thus, it was not ready to institute a full wage freeze only four weeks later. Nor had the nine-person, tripartite board clearly delineated its functions and responsibilities vis à vis the stabilization effort. The Defense Production Act, which authorized the establishment of the WSB, was loosely worded—apparently leaving the determination of the board's precise role in the hands of the ESA administrator. Alan Valentine in turn took the position that the board was to be strictly an advisory body with no operational authority. This interpretation was not shared by the majority of the board's members, which insisted that it should not only be entrusted to make wage stabilization policy, but also empowered to administer it. Despite this difference of opinion, the easygoing Ching maintained cordial, if businesslike, relations with the ESA director.[28]

26. Ibid., 13–14; Bernstein, "Administrative History of the ESA," 23–25; U.S. Congress, Senate Committee on Banking and Currency, *Confirmation of Michael V. DiSalle: Hearing before the Committee on Banking and Currency*, 81st Cong., 2d sess., December 5, 1950, 1–13; *Newsweek* 36 (December 18, 1950): 69.
    27. *Newsweek* 36 (December 11, 1950): 68; "Wage Stabilization Program, 1950–53," vol. 1, p. 4, RG 293, box 1, file: "WSB-ESA 6/30/53," NA.
    28. "Wage Stabilization Program, 1950–53," vol. 1, 4–7; Bernstein, "Administrative History of the ESA," 17–18.

Other board members were not as charitable to Valentine. The three labor representatives were especially rankled by their mere advisory status under Valentine's control. Ching patiently tried to assuage their concerns while repeatedly and delicately pointing out to Valentine that "a tri-partite board could not survive if its decisions were merely recommendations which might or might not be approved by the Administrator."[29] Labor did not buy Ching's diplomatic maneuvering, however. Board members, led by the labor bloc, threatened to quit unless Valentine agreed to delegate more direct authority to the board for administering wage stabilization guidelines. On December 12, the board went so far as to draw up a proposed order delegating it the powers it believed necessary to carry out the stabilization program. Valentine was frustrated with what he perceived as the board's intransigence. On December 16, he wrote to Stuart Symington in exasperation, stating that one of his biggest headaches was the difficulty he was encountering with the WSB. Valentine's differences with the WSB over jurisdictional powers helped engender labor's wrath toward the entire mobilization program, which ultimately led to a showdown with Charles Wilson in February 1951.[30]

Ching and the WSB faced another hurdle as 1950 drew to a close: inflation was growing. The Labor Department's economic overview for December warned that the latest Consumer Price Index had hit an all-time high, surpassing the "great inflation" of 1948. Wage adjustments began to spread quickly throughout the economy, and wage settlements for November and December were averaging more than 10 percent. And for the more than one million workers covered by automatic cost-of-living contracts, this meant that their wages went up commensurately, resulting in ever-increasing inflation. Of course, the many laborers not working under such contracts fell further behind as aggregate prices continued to surge forward.[31]

While Ching shared Valentine's cautious approach to the imposition of wage and price controls, his reasons were very different from Valentine's. Ching feared that rushing toward a wage stabilization policy without first considering the effect such a program might have on

29. Bernstein, "Administrative History of the ESA," 17.
30. Ibid.; "Wage Stabilization Program, 1950–53," vol. 1, 4; Second Draft to Alan Valentine from Cyrus Ching (undated), Papers of Harold L. Enarson, box 3, file: "labor disputes machinery, 1950–52," HSTL.
31. *Newsweek* 36 (December 11, 1950): 68; "Wage Stabilization Program, 1950–53," vol. 1, 3.

labor-industrial relations would be foolhardy. He especially feared that a hastily implemented wage policy might trigger a backlash from workers operating under long-term labor contracts. "No sound wage stabilization policy . . . can be framed," Ching wrote to Valentine, "without giving the most careful consideration to the effect on those [contract] clauses and without studying the consequences of action inconsistent with the anticipations of those who negotiated them."[32] At the heart of Ching's concern lay the fact that labor disruptions and restrictions on the movement of labor might derail the defense effort by hampering production. Furthermore, he believed that the implementation and administration of wage controls without the full cooperation of industry and labor would be folly; the result would be an untenable situation over which no one would have control.[33]

The Wage Stabilization Board also doubted the efficacy of wage and price controls in the fight against inflation. The board made known to Valentine its belief that inflation control could be ensured only by a multifaceted attack on the basic causes of inflation. Thus, the WSB advocated increased production, the curtailment of credit and currency expansion, and increased taxes as the sine qua non of inflation fighting. Wage and price controls should be reserved as the last alternative and, if invoked, should be implemented simultaneously and across-the-board. "Selective wage control is impossible; it simply won't work," wrote Ching to Harold L. Enarson, a White House aide.[34] Ching also told Valentine that should controls become necessary, a general wage freeze should be invoked—under no circumstances would the board tolerate selective controls on specific industries.[35]

No doubt, part of Ching's caution stemmed from the December 15 formation of the United Labor Policy Committee (ULPC), which promised to monitor closely the government's policies toward mobilization and stabilization and to "take united action" with government agencies on "important policy matters."[36] The ULPC boasted an influential and

32. Memo to Valentine from Ching (undated), Papers of Harold L. Enarson, box 3, file: "labor disputes machinery, 1950–52," HSTL.
33. Ibid.
34. Memorandum to Mr. Murphy from Enarson, December 15, 1950, White House Confidential Files, box 34, file: "Wage Stabilization Agency," HSTL.
35. Ibid.; Diary of Roy Blough (Council of Economic Advisors), entry: December 14, 1950, Papers of Roy Blough, box 13, file: "Diary of Roy Blough, CEA 6/29–12/31/50," HSTL.
36. Statement release from the American Federation of Labor, December 15, 1950, Papers of Harold L. Enarson, box 6, file: "Wage and Stabilization Board Policies, 1950–52," HSTL.

powerful membership, including the top brass of the American Federation of Labor, the Congress of Industrial Organizations, the International Association of Machinists, and the Railway Labor Executives Association. As an old hand at labor mediation, Ching took the ULPC very seriously: He knew the power that men like George Meany, Philip Murray, and Walter Reuther wielded. In the absence of a World War II–style "no-strike pledge," these men and their organizations had to be properly courted. Unfortunately, Ching was one of the few mobilization officials who fully realized this.[37]

The first month of the new year was indeed a busy one for the Truman administration. In the span of four weeks in January 1951, the administration finally laid out the essential blueprints of the stepped-up mobilization program. Amidst this monumental task arose partisan and bureaucratic bickering that oftentimes threatened the entire mobilization and stabilization effort. Despite all of the turmoil, however, Congress and the American people generally rallied behind the new defense effort and came to accept the sacrifices asked of them, including increased taxes (both personal and corporate), unprecedented "peacetime" military expenditures, tighter controls over materials allocations and industrial production, and finally, across-the-board wage and price controls initiated by the general wage-and-price freeze of January 26, 1951.

In addition to the problems officials encountered with the economic stabilization program, mobilization planners faced challenges in industrial output and defense procurement. First there were the continuing raw materials shortages that had first appeared during the preceding June and July and had worsened considerably with the military reverses of November and December. Some of the most spectacular price increases of December and early January were in the commodities market, which catapulted the prices of such critical materials as rubber, tin, copper, and alloys to new heights. Mobilization officials feared that these price increases would continue to fuel inflation and would lead ultimately to shortages. Some administration officials went so far as to advocate the creation of a government-controlled central purchasing agency to act as the sole buyer of critical materials. Most officials, however, preferred to deal with the raw materials crisis at a cooperative international level through such mechanisms as the State Department–sponsored International Materials Conference, which was

37. Ibid.

formally chartered on January 12. The Munitions Board, under the new leadership of John D. Small, advocated a swift upward adjustment of the nation's stockpile goals as well as an accelerated procurement level to meet those new goals. The NSRB urged the Munitions Board to undertake an immediate "re-examination of the stockpile objectives," promising that "the stockpile program will continue to receive appropriate consideration as a claimant for materials in short supply."[38] In addition, the National Production Authority advised members of its Consumer Durable Goods Committee that the continued scarcity of critical raw materials would necessitate the use of substitute materials, especially for the home appliance industry, which competed most directly with defense production.[39]

Congress also voiced its concern over the materials crunch. On December 20 the Joint Committee on Defense Production, the "watchdog" committee of the mobilization program, held a special hearing to gather information on what it considered an untenable situation in the commodities market. Senator Homer Capehart (R-IN) pointedly asked NPA general counsel Manly Fleischmann whether a significant amount of materials hoarding was occurring. Fleischmann answered in the affirmative, and Secretary of Commerce Charles Sawyer concurred, adding, "I doubt if there is much hoarding on the part of the housewife, but . . . there is much . . . hoarding on the part of certain organizations and institutions."[40] As for Capehart's allegations that the Commerce Department was imprudently authorizing the export of critical materials to other countries to the detriment of the war effort, Sawyer emphatically replied that rumors to that effect were entirely false. The sharp exchanges during the hearing illustrated not only the severity of

38. Letter to J. D. Small, from Stuart Symington, January 15, 1950, RG 304, National Security Resources Board Office of the Chairman, box 16, file: "Munitions Board," NA.

39. Letter to W. Stuart Symington from J. D. Small, December 15, 1950, RG 304, NSRB Office of the Chairman, box 16, file: "Munitions Board," NA; Council on Foreign Relations, *The United States in World Affairs—1950*, 426; *Public Papers of the Presidents of the United States, Harry S. Truman—1950*, 738–40; Letter to John C. Houston Jr. from Willard Thorp, January 26, 1951, White House Confidential Files, box 28, file: "National Security Resources Board (7 of 10)," HSTL; Letter to Symington from Alan Valentine, December 12, 1950, RG 304, NSRB Office of the Chairman, box 14, file: "Economic Stabilization Agency to W. Stuart Symington," NA; National Production Authority Daily Information Digest, January 30, 1951, RG 296, Economic Stabilization Agency, box 17, NA.

40. U.S. Congress, Joint Committee on Defense Production, *Defense Production Act, Hoarding and Strategic Materials: Hearing before the Joint Committee on Defense Production on Hoarding of Scarce Materials and Restrictions upon Shipments of Strategic Materials*, 81st Cong., 2d sess., December 20, 1950, 4.

the materials shortages, but also Congress's insistence that it be kept abreast of the mobilization program.[41]

The second major hurdle with which mobilization officials had to deal was the strengthening of the industrial base and the expansion in defense procurement. Secretary of Defense George C. Marshall ordered the military departments to accelerate procurement while ensuring that procurement contracts be distributed as widely as possible to help broaden the nation's industrial base. Administration officials, including Marshall, were also acutely aware of the position of small business in the defense effort; they advocated the maximum possible use of small business concerns and actively encouraged the use of subcontracting by prime contractors. The administration obviously wished to avoid the pitfalls of the last war, which had resulted in the exclusion of many small businesses from prime procurement contracts. It also specifically sought to avoid the creation or strengthening of monopolies, the promotion of industry-specific economic concentration, and the suppression of market competition. In order to enlarge small business's piece of the procurement pie, however, the Munitions Board was not adverse to recommending that "smaller plants . . . get together and form a type of cooperative organization with a good strong leader as its managing director. That cooperative would then attempt to secure contracts for the group."[42] This suggestion was quite startling; what the Munitions Board seemed to be advocating was the de facto cartelization of small manufacturers. Thus, the administration appeared willing to tolerate a concentration of power among small manufacturers as a way to prevent such a concentration among large ones.[43]

Meanwhile, mobilization planners were also attempting to bolster Allied defense production. In late December, the North Atlantic defense ministers unanimously agreed to establish a North Atlantic Defense Production Board to maximize the production of military hardware to meet the needs of the NATO pact. The board would be led by an American who would serve as the overall coordinator of production in the NATO member nations. Defense Secretary Marshall pushed

41. Ibid., 15.
42. Letter to Speaker of the House Sam Rayburn from J. D. Small, January 3, 1951, RG 304, NSRB Office of the Chairman, box 13, file: "Congressional Correspondence M-Z," NA.
43. Memorandum for the Secretary of the Army, the Secretary of the Navy, and the Secretary of the Air Force from G. C. Marshall, December 18, 1950, RG 304, NSRB Office of the Chairman, box 14, file: "Defense Department," NA; Memorandum from the President, December 20, 1950, OF, box 27, file: "277 (May 1951)," HSTL.

hard for this initiative, arguing that coordination of military production among NATO members was critical not only for the immediate Korean effort, for which the United States was providing the lion's share of manpower and resources, but also to ensure the success of the nation's recent troop commitments to Europe. General Eisenhower enthusiastically endorsed the board's creation as did Charles Wilson, General Lucius Clay, and Sidney Weinberg of the ODM. The Munitions Board also backed the creation of the board, asserting that the board's director "will bear an important responsibility second only to that of the Supreme Commander [Eisenhower]."[44] The creation of a NATO defense production board sent a strong signal to the Europeans. First, the United States made it clear that it would not go it alone in the rearmament effort; NATO members would be expected to add their share to the defense program. Second, by engaging its allies in multilateral mechanisms like the defense production board and the International Materials Conference, America was proving to Europe the seriousness of its commitment to continued economic cooperation as a way to contain the Soviets and to continue Europe's economic recovery from World War II.[45]

However preoccupied some planners may have been with industrial expansion and defense production, most officials in the administration continued to focus on the most vexing problem of the new defense program: economic stabilization. Stabilization efforts were made somewhat easier, however, by the president's January 8, 1951, state of the union address and his January 15 annual budget message, both of which laid out the precise extent of the mobilization program and which also prepared the nation for the sacrifices that lay ahead. But they did not solve many of the dilemmas facing stabilization planners. Without a coherent stabilization program, the mobilization effort would be greatly

44. Memorandum for the President from G. C. Marshall, January 3, 1951, President's Secretary's Files, box 176, file: "Defense, Secretary of," HSTL.

45. Ibid.; Memorandum for the President from F. J. Lawton (Bureau of the Budget), January 6, 1951, PSF-Bureau of the Budget, box 150, file: "Bureau of the Budget—Military, 1945–53," HSTL. These initiatives are illustrative of the United States' general shift toward the militarization of containment conceived in NSC-68 and born in the June outbreak of war in Korea. Although the United States would continue to promote economic cooperation and integration as important links in its containment policy, it would become increasingly dependent upon Allied military defense spending. I raise this point as an example of the interconnection of foreign and domestic policy, which became even more pronounced as the Cold War deepened. See Melvyn P. Leffler, *A Preponderance of Power: National Security, the Truman Administration, and the Cold War;* Walter LaFeber, *America, Russia, and the Cold War, 1945–1950,* 5th ed., 62–63; and Pollard, *Economic Security,* 3, 7, 131 for discussion of this shift in strategy.

compromised. Officials knew that unchecked inflation resulted in exorbitant rearmament costs and bigger budget shortfalls. Unmonitored wage increases had a multiplier effect; furthermore, constant wage hikes interfered with productive output by luring labor away from essential defense industries and toward more lucrative positions in nonessential work. And of course, labor strikes were far more prevalent without controls. Stabilization officials spent the first two weeks of January plotting price-and-wage-control strategies. Not surprisingly, there was little consensus on how and when controls should be applied. Only in the third week of January was anything close to a consensus reached, and by then, the turmoil over controls had ESA director Valentine on the ropes. Thus despite the formalization of the mobilization effort, stabilization officials continued to contradict each other both in public and in private.

While OPS director Michael DiSalle publicly maintained that voluntary controls should be continued, he knew those restraints were unworkable. This conviction became even stronger as prices continued to rise throughout the month of January. And DiSalle made little effort to control rumors of imminent comprehensive controls, much to Valentine's irritation. Although the president supported Valentine's position for a time, other administration officials, including Stuart Symington, were on record as supporting DiSalle's approach. They believed controls were needed immediately.[46]

On January 4, Valentine and DiSalle met separately with ODM chief Wilson to apprise him of their respective positions on controls. Both men stuck to their guns: Valentine proposed a gradual approach to controls, and DiSalle lobbied for an immediate across-the-board freeze on wages and prices. On that same day, Truman announced at a press conference that he believed price and wage controls would be invoked as soon as possible. Valentine now felt squeezed by his own team. DiSalle was pushing for immediate controls, and although Ching continued to favor an incremental approach, it appeared that DiSalle had the president's ear.[47]

46. Bernstein, "Administrative History of the ESA," 34, 36; Memorandum to Mr. Symington, December 19, 1950, RG 304 NSRB Office of the Chairman, box 13, file: "Congressional Correspondence, M-Z," NA; Letter to Alan Valentine from Symington, December 7, 1950, RG 304 NSRB Office of the Chair, box 14, file: "Economic Management Office," NA; *Newsweek* 37 (January 15, 1951): 67.

47. Bernstein, "Administrative History of the ESA," 36; "The Coming Wage-Price Controls," *U.S. News and World Report* (January 12, 1951); "Price-Wage Split Undermines Valentine in Stabilization Job," *Washington Post*, January 12, 1951.

When Valentine discovered that DiSalle had presented Wilson, in their meeting on January 4, with a detailed plan to invoke a thirty-day price freeze, he announced that the ESA would *not* invoke a thirty-day freeze but would continue to move toward selective controls as quickly as administrative staffing would permit. Wilson said nothing in public about Valentine's rejection of DiSalle's proposal but privately assured the ESA director that he would support his decision. Valentine's rejection of the freeze actually moved the ESA and OPS a bit closer to agreement. Now Valentine finally seemed to agree that blanket controls would be needed, a position that DiSalle had held since he became OPS administrator. The remaining difference seemed to be over the timing of those controls. Valentine argued that a general freeze should be imposed only when the stabilization agencies were properly staffed to administer it. DiSalle disagreed, arguing that the ESA should announce a freeze regulation whether it was staffed sufficiently or not. DiSalle was acting partially out of his own philosophy on controls but also *reacting* to growing popular sentiment that favored the immediate imposition of a freeze. The reclusive Valentine, who shied away from the spotlight, did not appear to be cognizant of the strong public demand for wage and price controls.[48]

Valentine's cautious approach to controls in part reflected the advice he sought from former (World War II) OPA executives, who had counseled him as early as November to approach the imposition of controls with great caution. Their advice did not waver even after the Korean crisis deepened in December. The OPA advisors were obviously influenced by their World War II experiences and did not wish for Valentine to rush into controls without adequate administrative capacity and staffing. Without a doubt, the ex-OPA group exerted a conservative influence over an administrator who was already inclined toward a cautious approach to economic stabilization. And while the OPA advisors were very helpful in advising Valentine about the techniques of control, they were far less helpful in guiding him through the political minefield of stabilization. Ex-OPA official G. Griffith Johnson admitted

---

48. Bernstein, "Administrative History of the ESA," 36, 46–49; Release from the office of Representative Jacob K. Javits (Rep-Lib, NY), U.S. House of Representatives, January 3, 1951, OF, box 460, file: "Official File 101-B, Defense Production Act (1951)," HSTL; *Newsweek* 37 (January 8, 1951): 60–61; *Newsweek* 37 (January 15, 1951): 67–68. By mid-January, even the conservative magazine *Business Week*, published by the United States Chamber of Commerce, began to acknowledge grudgingly that controls might be needed; see *Business Week* (January 20, 1951): 128.

as much when he wrote "we learned a great deal [from World War II] about techniques but relatively little about strategy except in relation to the special circumstances of the time."[49] Valentine was on his own in this regard, and he seemed unable to maneuver around the politics of his own agency, much less those of Washington.[50]

In his budget message and state of the union address, Truman charted the course he expected the new mobilization program to take. He also detailed the costs of the program and the likely tax increases that would result. Broadly speaking, the president proposed a $140 billion defense commitment for fiscal year 1952 and 1953 and an increase in the annual rate of defense spending from $20 to $50 billion by the end of 1951. This acceleration would effectively bring the defense effort to 18 percent of the nation's total output—unprecedented during a time of technical peace but far below the 45 percent peak of World War II. To achieve this goal, the president pressed for aggregate economic growth—more specifically, an economy 25 percent larger by 1956— through which the huge defense expenditures could be absorbed. He continued to insist that the program be implemented on a pay-as-you-go basis, although many businessmen and policymakers doubted that this could be achieved. And without the $72 billion in federal taxes the president requested, the nay-sayers would be right: the result would be a $16 billion budget deficit. The most stunning single feature of the proposed budget revealed that nearly 69 perent of the $72 billion in federal expenditures was earmarked for national security, that is, defense at home as well as military and economic aid abroad.[51]

Keeping in mind that the fighting in Korea was costing approximately $13 billion per year, how did the president's figures translate into mobilization policy for the larger Cold War rearmament effort? First, according to *Business Week,* what Truman had asked for amounted to a 40 percent mobilization effort; that is, 40 percent of 1944 war expenditures, which marked the peak of the nation's military spending during World War II. The president's goal was a "peacetime" military establishment of 3.5 million combat-ready personnel. To support the

49. G. Griffith Johnston, "Reflections on a Year of Price Controls," *American Economic Review,* 42 (May 1952) 289.
50. Ibid.; Bernstein, "Administrative History of the ESA," 40–41.
51. *The Economic Report of the President,* January 12, 1951, 1–19; 66–83; *The Federal Budget in Brief* (1952), President's Secretary's File—Bureau of the Budget, box 150, file: "BOB, Budget-DPA," HSTL; *Business Week* (January 20, 1951): 128; *Life* 30 (January 22, 1951): 44.

military, he requested the building and maintenance of defense plants that could produce upwards of 50,000 military aircraft and 35,000 tanks per year. Of course, these amounts were not needed at that precise moment; rather, the administration's move toward the development of a permanent mobilization base dictated that an industrial reserve be in place to produce *up to* 50,000 planes and 35,000 tanks. Out of the $54 billion that the Truman administration ultimately committed to the armed forces in 1951, most of it—$41 billion—was earmarked for strategic defense procurement and for long-term defense plant and general industrial expansion. Truman also promised that the Air Force would be expanded from 48 to 84 wings and that the Marine Corps would have two divisions plus additional nondivisional units.[52]

To produce all of this, the administration recommended that steel production capacity be increased from the current 103,000,000 ingot tons per year to no less than 120,000,000 tons by 1955. A big boost in the production of raw materials was called for as was an increase in electrical power generation. Meanwhile, the National Production Authority began issuing more regulations to curb the use of critical materials. It also increased the percentage of Defense Orders (DO's) that manufacturers of specified steel items were required to accept. Thus, for the first time since the outbreak of hostilities in Korea, the Truman administration had laid out a detailed mobilization blueprint that included strategies, expectations, and costs. The price of implementing NSC-68 was finally tabulated.[53]

After the president's state of the union address and his budget message, the ESA began moving forward toward a general wage-and-price freeze. Its job was somewhat easier now that the administration had formally laid out its plans for the next several years. On January 17, Valentine again met with ex-OPA advisors to discuss the timing of the freeze. After much discussion, the group's best guess was that wages and prices could not be frozen any sooner than February 15. DiSalle believed he could move faster, claiming that he would be ready for a full price freeze by the first of the month. As usual, Valentine disagreed, stating that "it would be foolhardy to try it before February 15 or

52. *Business Week* (January 20, 1951): 24–25; *Newsweek* 37 (January 15, 1951): 19–22; *Newsweek* 37 (January 22, 1951): 17–18; Leffler, *A Preponderance of Power*, 374; *The Economic Report of the President*, 4–6, 13–20, 84–96; *Public Papers of the Presidents* (1950), 743; ibid. (1951), 11.

53. *The Economic Report of the President*, 84–96; *Newsweek* (January 22, 1951): 59–60; *Newsweek* (January 29, 1951): 69.

March 1."[54] Charles Wilson wanted to move even more quickly than DiSalle; he favored a complete freeze within a week.[55]

Under increased pressure from both the ODM and the White House, Valentine presented to Wilson a detailed plan for a wage-and-price freeze to take effect on February 1. The next day, January 19, Valentine resigned as the ESA administrator. Although Valentine had narrowed the gap between his position and DiSalle's, it had become obvious that Wilson wanted him out. As the *Washington Post* reported on January 19, "Wilson's office is said to be impatient with what is described as a too-cautious, perfectionist attitude on Valentine's part. More to its liking is the rough-and-tumble technique of DiSalle, politics-wise from his career as former mayor of Toledo."[56] With Valentine pushed aside, the scene was now set for a quick, decisive move toward economic controls.

Valentine's resignation can be attributed to a number of things, including his rather inflexible, introverted management style. In all fairness, however, at the root of Valentine's troubles at the ESA were two structural weaknesses within the stabilization program. They emerged during Valentine's tenure, much to his dismay, and continued to vex the ESA throughout its existence. First, neither the administration nor Valentine was ever able to define specifically the goals of the stabilization program. For example, should the ESA have attempted to stop any increase in prices, or should it rather have tried to keep prices within a predetermined range limit? At what level should the agency have frozen prices and wages? Should wage-and-price action have been implemented simultaneously? Top ESA officials never adequately answered these questions amidst the turmoil of staffing the agency, disagreements over the implementation of controls, and the growing animosity between Valentine and DiSalle. The White House and the ODM offered little help in defining the agency's function in light of their other duties, and the Defense Production Act itself offered no guidance in such matters.[57]

The second flaw in the stabilization setup was organizational in nature. Obviously, neither Valentine's personality nor his management

---

54. "General Ban on Increases Likely Early in February," *Washington Post*, January 19, 1951.

55. Bernstein, "Administrative History of the ESA," 41–42; Cabinet Meeting, January 22, 1951, Papers of Matthew J. Connelly, box 2, file: "Notes on Cabinet Meetings, 1951, 2 January–31 December," HSTL.

56. *Washington Post*, January 19, 1951, 3A.

57. Bernstein, "Administrative History of the ESA," 54–55.

philosophy meshed with Wilson's. By refusing to delegate authority to the WSB and the OPS on operational procedures, Valentine was implicitly rejecting Wilson's centralized/decentralized management approach. Wilson's "holding company" management philosophy was as much functional as it was rhetorical. He clearly recognized the advantages of decentralization—it had helped to propel corporations like General Electric into the forefront of industry. Valentine, a neophyte in the world of business and economics, never seemed to have grasped this concept. Wilson also must have known that a decentralized approach to mobilization could help blunt fears that the nation was moving toward a centralized, regimented garrison state. Again, Valentine did not seem sensitive to these concerns. Valentine's inability to organize the stabilization program along the lines envisioned by Wilson may have had more to do with his failure than any other single issue.

Finally, while Valentine seemed genuinely distrustful of his subordinates, especially DiSalle, it would have been difficult for him to delegate authority even had he wanted to because he had not defined the agency's overall function nor had he established a workable wage/price policy until his position with Wilson had become untenable. Decentralized operations can succeed only if the centralized policymaking is clear and concise; in this case, it was neither. Although the organizational issue was settled by Valentine's successor, Eric Johnston, who granted DiSalle and Ching virtual autonomy in the implementation of controls, the problem of policy coordination and implementation continued to plague the ESA throughout its existence.[58]

Finding a replacement for Valentine was not difficult. On January 24, 1951, Eric Johnston was sworn into office as the new administrator of the Economic Stabilization Agency. Johnston came to the agency from the Motion Picture Association of America, which he had served as president. Prior to that, he had been president of the United States Chamber of Commerce, guiding that organization through the tumultuous World War II years and the equally turbulent postwar reconversion period. The tall and striking Johnston was gregarious, well liked, and a political animal in his own right. In the past, his name had been mentioned more than once as a candidate for political office, including, in some circles, the presidency itself. His position with the Chamber of Commerce naturally allied him with businessmen, many of whom were delighted

58. Ibid., 55.

with his appointment. And his tenure as president of the Motion Picture Association also stood him in good stead. It propelled him into the national spotlight at a time in which television was still in its infancy and Hollywood films and film stars continued to hold the nation's attention and imagination.[59]

Johnston, a self-made man, had led what he called a "penniless, work-filled boyhood." He was also a self-described small business-man, at least in his economic and philosophical outlook. His business experience, however, belied his professed small-business mentality; he was not exactly a typical corner merchant, having assembled the biggest electrical contracting and retail appliance business in the Pacific Northwest. In 1931 he was elected president of the Spokane Chamber of Commerce, marking the beginning of his ascendancy to the pres-idency of the national association in 1942. Regardless of his business acumen and success, however, Johnston remained wedded to the idea of small business as the backbone of America. Not surprisingly, his economic philosophy did not make him an avid proponent of economic controls; he would have preferred a more gradual approach, using less-interventionist methods. However, his pragmatic—and political—side recognized the need for quick, aggressive action against inflation. Fur-thermore, the administration had chosen him to replace Valentine pre-cisely because it knew Johnston would move toward controls quickly and would do so with a significant amount of support from business.[60]

During his first two days in office, Johnston moved decisively toward a wage-and-price freeze. To expedite the implementation of controls and to put the organizational problems of the agency behind him, he formally delegated a broad range of powers to DiSalle and Ching, giv-ing them the authority to operate their parts of the stabilization program

59. Eric Johnston, *America Unlimited,* 1–3; *Newsweek* 37 (January 29, 1951): 17, 25; Herman Kaufman, April 13, 1953, "The Economic Stabilization Agency in the Johnston Period," RG 293, Records of the Wage Stabilization Board and the Salary Stabilization Board of the Economic Stabilization Agency, box 1, file: "ESA," 1, NA.

60. Johnston, *America Unlimited,* 3, 6–11; Kaufman, "The ESA in the Johnston Period," 14–16. Johnston had been lobbying for a national political appointment for quite some time. His blatant posturing, however, apparently did not sit well with many of those in the administration and the Democratic party. Ex-Democratic Senator Clarence Dill, noting Johnston's attempt to preempt Truman by announcing his own grandiose plans for foreign aid in a 1949 speech, wrote that "This man Johnston is a foreflusher and tries to play both ends against the middle." Truman acknowledged that he was "in complete agreement." Letter to Warren G. Magnuson from Clarence Dill, January 31, 1949, PSF, box 144, file: "Economic Stabilization Agency, Eric Johnston, Adm.," HSTL; and Letter to Warren G. Magnuson from Harry S. Truman, February 8, 1949, PSF, box 144, file: "Economic Stabilization Agency, Eric Johnston, Adm.," HSTL.

with a great deal of autonomy. Then, building upon Valentine's plan of price and wage controls, he invoked a general wage-and-price freeze, effective on January 26. The freeze would be followed by carefully tailored adjustments in both wages and prices; however, the implementation of the freeze was a bold and necessary first step. It proved that the Truman administration was finally and firmly committed to an effective stabilization program to mitigate the effects of the new mobilization program. It also established a benchmark upon which further economic and national security policy could be based.[61]

The long-awaited freeze order was announced by DiSalle and Ching at a late Friday afternoon press conference that *Newsweek* described as "wild and wooly . . . the type usually seen only in Hollywood."[62] The ESA's order was a sweeping one, placing strict ceilings on wages and prices. But the freeze was meant as a stopgap measure only, according to DiSalle and Ching. In fact, the OPS was already preparing a series of tailored adjustments for individual commodities and services to eliminate the inequities of a sudden freeze. These adjustments would mean both price rollbacks and price advancements on a case-by-case basis. Thus, as DiSalle pointed out, the price freeze would gradually give way to a thaw at both ends—a sort of selective freeze in reverse. Ching was prepared to take comparable action on the wage front, having just put the finishing touches on a supplemental wage policy that would be quite flexible. It would avoid setting wage ceilings and would leave intact long-term cost-of-living agreements negotiated prior to the freeze date.[63]

As of January 26, prices of applicable commodities were frozen at their highest level attained between December 19, 1950, and January 25, 1951, which marked the period in which prices had risen the fastest. Notable exceptions to the freeze were commodity trade market margins and professional services, which were specifically exempted from price action by the Defense Production Act. Farm and food prices that were

61. Kaufman, "The ESA in the Johnston Period," 15–16; Defense Mobilization Board, Meeting no. 3, January 25, 1951, RG 296, Records Maintained by the Administrator, Classified General Files, box 2, file: "Defense Mobilization Meetings—Foreign Allocations Policy," NA.

62. *Newsweek* 37 (February 5, 1951): 61.

63. Ibid., 61–62; Kaufman, "The ESA in the Johnston Period," 16–18; Rockoff, *Drastic Measures*, 179–81; Industrial College of the Armed Forces, *Emergency Management of the National Economy: Reconversion and Partial Mobilization*, 64–66; George A. Lincoln, *Economics of National Security: Managing America's Resources for Defense*, 492–94.

below government parity levels were also excluded from the freeze—another stipulation of the Defense Production Act. Food prices, in fact, proved to be a major sticking point of the freeze because, with the exception of most meats, nearly all food products were under parity levels and were thereby exempted from controls. Thus, the fight against inflation through price ceilings was hampered by rising food prices until they reached parity level.[64]

To fulfill its mission, the Office of Price Stabilization, perhaps more so than any other mobilization program during the Korean War, underwent constant revision and experimentation during its two-year life span. Modeled loosely after the much more expansive OPA program of World War II, the OPS during the Korean War concerned itself mainly with price control and enforcement of pricing regulations, including dollar and cents ceilings that were applied gradually during the spring and summer of 1951. Because product rationing and recycling measures were not used during Korea, the OPS never approached the size and intrusiveness of World War II's OPA. There were, however, startling similarities between the two programs, which became more pronounced as the mobilization period progressed. In the months immediately following the general freeze of January 1951, which was patterned after the General Maximum Price Regulation of April 1942, the OPS under DiSalle moved quickly to establish thirteen regional offices to assist in consumer education programs, the handling of merchant inquiries, the establishment of industry and consumer advisory committees, the implementation of price stabilization programs, and the policing and enforcement of price regulations. To be sure, like the OPA that preceded it, the OPS worked closely with communities and households and as one historian of the OPA recently noted, it ultimately "enlisted thousands of shoppers as its main shock troops in the fight against inflation."[65]

Reporting to the OPS director's main office in Washington was the Office of Price Operations, which eventually comprised seven

64. *Newsweek* 37 (February 5, 1951): 61–62, 65; Lincoln, *Economics of National Security,* 493–94; Rockoff, *Drastic Measures,* 180–81.
65. David E. Ramsett and Tom R. Heck, "Wage and Price Controls: A Historical Survey," 10–11; Administrative History of the Economic Stabilization Agency under Alan Valentine, 6, RG 293 Records of the WSB and SSB of the ESA, box 1, file: "Administrative History of the ESA," NA; Meg Jacobs, " 'How About Some Meat?' The Office of Price Administration, Consumption Politics, and State Building from the Bottom Up, 1941–1946," 911.

consumer commodity divisions, akin to the NPA's industry divisions. The OPS commodity divisions were divided along product or service lines such as the Food and Restaurant Division and the Industrial Materials and Manufactured Goods Division. Working through these divisions and their various branches, the Office of Price Operations wrote orders and regulations that established price ceilings and processed requests for changes in the ceilings coming from both industries and individuals. In formulating price orders and regulations, the office naturally worked closely with industry and consumer advisory committees at the national and local levels. By 1952, the OPS would peak at a paid workforce of approximately 12,300 working in Washington and in the thirteen regional and eighty-four district offices around the country. The number of unpaid volunteers enlisted at the local level is impossible to determine, though it was significantly higher than the number of paid personnel and would continue to grow as the defense program progressed and as Congress began to cut operating funds of the stabilization program.[66]

Accordingly, the wage freeze applied to wages, salaries, and other types of compensation. The wage regulation froze all of these at the prevailing rates as of January 25. Further, the wage regulation provided that the Wage Stabilization Board was empowered to "modify, amend, or supersede" the regulation by subsequent rules or regulations. Still unresolved was the dilemma of how to treat emergency labor contracts or other disputes that might not have been related to wages alone. Undoubtedly, Ching faced an uphill battle in his role as wage stabilizer. The WSB was irritated by the promulgation of the wage freeze; labor representatives were especially angry that the order came from Johnston and not from the president himself. In fact, the board put Ching in a compromising position by refusing to sign the freeze order; instead, Ching had Johnston sign it. Although the board was not angry at Ching, nor did it oppose the wage regulation per se, its refusal to sign the order was further evidence that board members, especially labor representatives, were increasingly unhappy with their role—or lack thereof—in the mobilization program. They simply felt that they were not being accorded the attention that

66. Administrative History of the Economic Stabilization Agency under Alan Valentine, 16, RG 293 Records of the WSB and SSB of the ESA, box 1, file: "Administrative History of the ESA," NA; Correa, "Organization for Defense Mobilization," 11; Ramsett and Heck, "Wage and Price Controls," 11; ESA Weekly Roundup, June 24, 1952, 8, RG 296 Records of Reports and Secretariat, box 3, file: "ESA Weekly Roundup," NA.

they deserved, especially compared with the attention lavished upon business.[67]

The Wage Stabilization Board was somewhat more prepared than its OPS counterpart for an across-the-board freeze. In preparation for a possible wage freeze, the WSB had held a series of meetings in mid-December and another in mid-January 1951 with a cross-section of members of labor and industry organizations. The purpose of the meetings was to hear the views of as many organized segments of the nation's economy as possible in order to implement wage-stabilization regulations. These meetings included representatives of the Associated General Contractors, the Chamber of Commerce, the National Association of Manufacturers, and the Committee for Economic Development; labor representatives came from the AFL, the CIO, the United Mine Workers, and the United Labor Policy Committee. Although those who took part in the meetings quite expectedly gave a wide variety of conflicting counsel, the conferences allowed the opinions of labor and industry to crystallize and made the WSB's task of implementing the freeze less burdensome. As well, these meetings and consultations followed the decentralized setup of the mobilization process already under way and, at least in the short-term, kept the American public and private sectors as well as management and labor working cooperatively toward microeconomic stabilization during the first critical weeks of the accelerated rearmament program.[68]

Business and industry reaction to the implementation of controls was mixed. Some of the more progressive business associations, like the Business Advisory Council (BAC) and the Committee for Economic Development (CED), which counted Charles Wilson among its most prominent members, lent their general support to the administration's new mobilization policies, including wage and price controls, increased taxes (as part of a pay-as-you-go plan), and controls over credit and industrial materials allocations. More conservative business groups, like

67. *Newsweek* 37 (February 5, 1951): 61–62, 65; *New York Times,* January 27, 1951, 1–2A; Kaufman, "The ESA in the Johnston Period," 16–17. See also Memorandum to Charles Wilson, from the United Labor Policy Committee, January 11, 1951, in which the powerful new committee made it clear to Wilson that it was dissatisfied with the extent to which labor had been included in the mobilization program and the overall decision-making process, Papers of Harold L. Enarson, box 6, file: "Wage and Stabilization Board Policies, 1950–52," HSTL.
68. Wage Stabilization Program, 1950–1953, vol. 1, 5–6, RG 293, Records of the Wage Stabilization Board and Salary Stabilization Board of the Economic Stabilization Agency, box 1, file: "Wage Stabilization Program, WSB-ESA, June 30, 1953," NA.

the National Association of Manufacturers (NAM) and the Chamber of Commerce, joined the ranks of conservatives in both political parties to disparage the administration's increasing reliance upon higher taxes and government controls. Although the Chamber of Commerce as a group was opposed to controls, many individual members grudgingly accepted the need for such measures, and Johnston's presence at the stabilization helm apparently helped in this regard. Even the group's official mouthpiece, *Business Week*, acknowledged that controls were needed—not because members liked the idea of controls, but because "leaders . . . have not had the guts to deal with the root causes of this inflation."[69] Thus the implication was that controls had become necessary because not enough had been done to stop inflation when it began to climb in June. Business support, however fickle, eroded as the year progressed, and the effectiveness of the stabilization program was increasingly called into question.[70]

So it was that the Truman administration finally moved toward an organized, rationalized defense program in the span of six short weeks. The job had been anything but easy. The unexpected Chinese incursion into Korea created a crisis equaled only by the Japanese bombardment of Pearl Harbor in 1941. Administration officials were caught off guard and were forced into a massive acceleration of the heretofore meandering rearmament effort. Thus, they found themselves having to do in a few week's time what should have taken several months. Staffing the myriad new agencies that sprung up to administer the program proved difficult at best, and those few administrators who were in place by mid-December had been chosen before the crisis worsened. For administrators like Alan Valentine, this fact spelled disaster because, while he seemed perfectly acceptable to the administration upon his appointment in October, by December he seemed hopelessly out of step and woefully inexperienced to administer a substantial stabilization program. Compounding mobilization planners' problems were internal bickering over the extent and pace of the stabilization effort, pressure by labor and industry representatives for special considerations,

69. *Business Week* (February 3, 1951): 104.

70. U.S. Congress, House, Committee on the Judiciary, *The Mobilization Program*, H. Rept. 1217, 82d Cong., 1st sess., 1951; Kim McQuaid, *Big Business and Presidential Power: From FDR to Reagan*, 161–68; Robert J. Donovan, *Tumultuous Years: The Presidency of Harry S. Truman, 1949–1953*, 326–28, 331, 368–69; Karl Schriftgiesser, *Business and Public Policy: The Role of the Committee for Economic Development, 1942–1967*, 150–57; and Letter from the NAM to Symington, January 22, 1951, RG 304-NSRB Office of the Chairman, box 17, file: "NAM," NA.

oftentimes conflicting with one another, and the onslaught of the Great Debate and the concomitant McCarthy barbs, which diminished the administration's clout in Congress by further splintering bipartisanship and strengthening the body's conservative coalition.

Above all, the administration did its best to assuage the fears of citizens and convince them that the new and unprecedented "peacetime" mobilization would be an inclusive one that would not lead the nation down the road to economic regimentation and totalitarian repression. Mobilization planners' decentralized organizational impulses reflected their fears of authoritarianism as much as their acknowledgment that decentralization would get the job done with the most efficiency and the least cost. Policymakers like Leon Keyserling and Charles Wilson insisted that private-sector advisory committees be consulted at every step of the rearmament and stabilization process. Many of these advisory committees were already being used by the Departments of Commerce, Labor, and Agriculture; in turn, the Office of Defense Mobilization created its own committees, largely comprising private-sector specialists but also making use of at-large public representatives. The Wage Stabilization Board took this cooperative effort to its logical conclusion by wedding the interests of government, business, and labor through its nine-man tripartite setup. Thus the Korean mobilization, like the ones that preceded it, relied upon New Era–style cooperative management, decentralized operations, and "dollar-a-year" business and production experts.[71]

Finally, the appointment of the suave darling of business Eric Johnston to the ESA, coupled with the administration's almost simultaneous imposition of wage and price controls, primed the nation for a long-haul mobilization program while sending an obvious signal to business that its interests were indeed being tended by one of their own. In fact, after Valentine's departure, the only non-businessman among the top echelon of mobilization planners was Michael DiSalle.

71. For other references to these developments see Kim McQuaid, *Uneasy Partners: Big Business in American Politics, 1945–1990,* 59–72; Kim McQuaid, *Big Business and Presidential Power,* 161–67; Hogan, *Marshall Plan,* 380–84.

III

Labor's Cold Shoulder

*The Price and Wage Freeze and a
Crisis-Filled Spring, February–May 1951*

February through May 1951 was one of the most active—and
divisive—periods of the Korean mobilization. It was a time of constant
adjustment, as the Truman administration tried to structure and pace
rearmament in a manner compatible with the nation's long-standing
traditions and values and that would not convert the country into a regimented garrison state. At the same time, the administration was forced
to deal with a series of military and political crises that threatened
the entire mobilization effort. These months also brought considerable
good news, however. The inflation rate eased, and materials that had
been in short supply began to reappear. The new stabilization program
began to have the desired effect: panic-inspired buying ceased, prices
fell, and production rose. In the early summer of 1951, the United States
was poised to enter one of the most productive and prosperous periods
in its history.

The story in Korea was not as rosy as the domestic economic scene,
however. By early spring, the heretofore topsy-turvy military engagement in Korea had stalemated. General Douglas MacArthur's attempts
to widen the war and question its efficacy undermined the Truman
administration and precipitated a full-blown crisis that called into
question the primacy of the civilian government over the military
establishment. MacArthur's insubordination resulted in his dismissal,
which played right into the hands of Truman's opponents and the
conservative bloc in Congress. By now, the Korean War had become
"Truman's War," a war of stalemate, attrition, and bitter partisan political rhetoric. The uproar over MacArthur's dismissal hampered the administration's efforts to formulate coherent, long-term defense strategy

and bolstered the efforts of those who opposed Truman's economic and foreign policies. Relations between the chief executive and Congress grew increasingly strained as Congress tried to limit the president's authority by diluting his emergency and mobilization powers and stalling on much-needed tax increases.

At the same time, and in spite of the overall progress of the rearmament program, the American people and the Congress began to fret openly over the long-term consequences of mobilization. At issue was the public's dread of a garrison state and a centrally regimented economy dominated by government-sponsored monopoly and oligopoly. Especially troublesome were the effects of materials shortages and defense procurement practices on small- and medium-sized manufacturers. As in World War II, large, capital-intensive firms in the monopoly and oligopoly sectors received the lion's share of prime defense contracts. Complicating this disturbing trend was the inefficient Defense Order (DO) system, which was in place to distribute raw materials and commodities, especially those most urgently needed for defense manufacturing. Small- and medium-sized producers, particularly those who were not vertically integrated or well diversified, were at a comparative disadvantage. Unlike their larger counterparts, they were unable to convert easily to defense production. Thus, smaller manufacturers could not efficiently compete with larger ones for the shrinking aggregate resource base, nor could they easily attract defense work.

The dislocations caused by rearmament even affected corporations that were usually considered to be large. During the early 1950s, the automotive industry, for example, comprised six "independent" firms in addition to the "Big Three" (Ford, Chrysler, and General Motors). In this instance, the so-called independent car makers, which collectively produced about 15 percent of the nation's total output, were at a comparative disadvantage to the industry leaders. Although statistics classified the independents as large corporations, compared with the Big Three, they were dwarfs running among giants. Because of the structure of the auto industry, then, they suffered difficulties comparable to those experienced by much smaller corporations. The Kaiser-Frazer Corporation of Willow Run, Michigan, for instance, was caught in a price squeeze because of the ceiling on automobile prices. Unlike its larger counterparts, Kaiser-Frazer produced only two lines of cars. Thus, it was unable to divert production toward higher-priced cars with greater profit margins. Further, Kaiser-Frazer could neither compete with the auto giants for scarce materials nor sustain prolonged operating losses as the Big Three could. As a result, the president of Kaiser-Frazer, Edgar F. Kaiser, wrote to Michael DiSalle in February 1951 formally requesting exemption from the price freeze under the hardship clause enumerated in the General Ceiling Price Regulation of January 26, 1951. Kaiser-Frazer was granted the exemption, with slight modifications, in May 1951.[1]

At the end of January, Dwight Eisenhower, NATO's new supreme allied commander, provided the nation with its first overview of the defense situation in Europe. His reports, the first ones of their kind since the outbreak of the Korean War, set the pace and mood for the next four months of the rearmament program. On January 30, he briefed Congress on his just-completed tour of Europe. The following day, Eisenhower reported to President Truman and his cabinet. During the briefings, Eisenhower outlined his perceptions of the political, economic, and military situations in Western Europe. What Eisenhower had found in Europe was both troubling and inspiring. On the one hand, the general found the Europeans confused and less than united in the fight against communism. He was especially chagrined at the large number of communists and communist sympathizers in France and Italy. Eisenhower also lamented the lack of efficient production coordination among the nations of Europe. On the other hand, Eisenhower reported that "morale is growing stronger in every country . . . there is a growing confidence in all Western Europe."[2]

The general added that the gravest problem facing Europe was the urgent need for more military equipment. He urged the Truman administration to convert the nation's economy to a full wartime status: "We must get this curve, this damned curve, up quick. We have got to get the stuff into the hands of the Europeans." He went on to say that he did not believe the United States could accomplish its defense goals by merely superimposing the rearmament program on the existing economy. What Eisenhower had called for was nothing short of all-out mobilization. Not surprisingly, Truman and Wilson quietly demurred; they promised to discuss the matter further but gave no firm commitments to the general. By the time Eisenhower returned to Europe on February 21, the White House had convinced him that

1. Letter to Michael V. DiSalle, February 21, 1951, RG 296, box 4, file: "Automotive and Equipment," NA.
2. Cabinet Meeting, Wednesday P.M., January 31, 1951, Papers of Matthew J. Connelly, box 2, file: "Notes on Cabinet Meetings, 1951, 2 January–31 December," HSTL.

full-out mobilization was neither economically feasible nor politically wise.[3]

With public support for the Korean conflict plummeting, and dissatisfaction with economic controls increasing, the administration could not increase the scope or pace of the rearmament effort. In addition, Truman did not wish to draw any more attention to Europe while American soldiers were dying in Asia and conservatives in both parties were still questioning his troop commitments to the Continent. Although officials at the time were reluctant to admit it, the mobilization program was aimed not so much at the Korean theater as toward the general strengthening of U.S. military capabilities around the world, an important part of which was the augmentation of Western Europe's economic and military capacity.

Eisenhower's reports gave the administration a perfect opportunity to seize the moment and to gather public support for the mobilization program. Indeed, by February the public—and Congress—had already begun to grow impatient with the rearmament effort. Especially irksome was the economic stabilization program, which seemed to many to be hopelessly misdirected and poorly executed. These feelings reached fever pitch with the labor showdown later in February. But the Truman administration never used Eisenhower's stature as a wildly popular war hero to help sell its mobilization and economic stabilization programs. The opportunity quickly passed, and although administration officials continued to use Eisenhower's reports to set their own internal benchmarks for the rearmament effort, their public relations efforts were not guided by the same goals. Why White House officials did not make use of this public relations windfall is something of a mystery, although they must have been concerned that Eisenhower's Eurocentric focus would anger the thousands of families who had relatives fighting and dying on the Korean peninsula.

Eisenhower was not the only one concerned about interallied defense production and economic integration. Early in February the Chamber of Commerce of the United States urged the Truman administration to form a single independent government agency under which all foreign economic operations would fall. At the same time, the U.S. Chamber denounced the idea of a "Fortress America," and likened ex-President

---

3. Meeting of General Eisenhower with the President and the Cabinet, Wednesday, January 31, 1951, President's Secretary's Files (PSF), box 132, file: "North Atlantic Treaty, folder 1," HSTL; Letter to the President, February 24, 1951, PSF, box 132, file: "North Atlantic Treaty, folder 1," HSTL.

Hoover's ideas to a bona fide "garrison state . . . which would destroy those freedoms inherent in democracy as we know it." Clearly, the Chamber was rejecting the Hoover-Taft approach to foreign policy and national security; it favored internationalist policies but stopped somewhat short of fully endorsing Truman's plans.[4]

It is clear that the problems and fears engendered by the Korean mobilization program had by this time become inseparable from the much larger and more difficult task of preparing the nation for a protracted global struggle against Communism. In fact, by the summer of 1951, the preceding four months of policy controversies, political crises, and bureaucratic infighting had fused the separate stories of the Korean mobilization and Cold War mobilization into one irrevocably intertwined policy movement.

As February 1951 approached, the Truman administration set its sights on the formulation of wage and price policies that were to supersede the blanket freeze of January 26. This was no simple task. From February through May the administration traveled a tortuous road of price rollbacks, price advancements, and wage-policy adjustments that oftentimes threatened to derail the entire stabilization effort. Even worse, the Wage Stabilization Board's first substantive policy adjustment in February opened a chasm so deep amongst its members that organized labor walked out of the WSB and later refused to participate in the mobilization program in any capacity.

The labor walkout, which began on February 15, was the most serious and destabilizing crisis of the period. Labor representatives to the tripartite wage board walked out of deliberations in protest of the new wage catch-up formula, which was designed to address the inequities of the January freeze and to mollify workers whose wages had not kept pace with prices. Two weeks later, on February 28, organized labor withdrew completely from all mobilization posts, including the Economic Stabilization Agency. The United Labor Policy Committee

---

4. See Chamber of Commerce Release, February 4, 1951, and accompanying letter to W. Stuart Symington, February 8, 1951, RG 304, Office of the Chairman, box 19, file: "U.S. Chamber of Commerce to W. Stuart Symington," NA. See also Memorandum for the President, February 23, 1951, Papers of George M. Elsey, box 89, file: "National Defense, Defense Mobilization," HSTL, for the administration's plans to organize the Allied defense production effort along the lines of the Combined Boards of World War II. Despite a brief foray into this area, however, the Truman administration never re-created the mechanisms of the Combined Boards. The closest it came to such inter-allied production planning was through the International Materials Conference and the NATO Defense Production Board, which were mere shadows of the earlier Combined Boards.

(ULPC) cited as its reason for bolting its dissatisfaction with the lack of adequate labor representation in key mobilization agencies, especially the Office of Defense Mobilization. Labor's boycott of the mobilization program angered administration officials and threatened to disrupt defense production and economic stabilization just as mobilization efforts were moving into high gear. The crisis rendered the WSB inoperable until labor agreed to come back into the fold under a newly reconstituted and enlarged wage board in May 1951.

Once more, the experiences of World War II haunted the Korean rearmament. Labor's disgruntlement with the current mobilization process was uncannily similar to labor's difficulties during the previous war. And unfortunately, the Truman administration's attitude toward labor during the Korean buildup was not well informed by the mistakes made during the last war. Contrary to the conclusions of some scholars, the New Deal and the Second World War did *not* result in a triumvirate in which "Big Labor now took its place beside Big Business and Big Government."[5] No such transformation occurred during World War II, nor did it occur during Korea. Labor's difficulties during both conflicts were essentially the same: organized labor was not given meaningful representation in mobilization agencies; manpower management was deliberately kept out of labor's purview; and fuller labor participation in production planning was never realized. In short, labor's advancements in management relations continued to be realized most fully in the areas of collective bargaining, wages, hours, working conditions, and fringe benefits. Labor continued to be a junior partner in economic policymaking, just as it had been during World War II. The only major difference in 1951 was that organized labor had not agreed to a World War II–style no-strike pledge. Thus, Truman had less room to maneuver than did Roosevelt.[6]

5. Quotation from Carl N. Degler, *Out of Our Past: The Forces That Shaped Modern America*, 406. See also Paul A. C. Koistinen, "Mobilizing the World War II Economy: Labor and the Industrial-Military Alliance," 443–78; Irving Bernstein, *Turbulent Years: A History of the American Worker, 1933–1941*; Arthur M. Johnson, "Continuity and Change in Government-Business Relations," 206–9. For a still cogent New Left viewpoint on the role of labor during the Roosevelt era, see Ronald Radosh, "The Myth of the New Deal," 146–87.

6. Koistinen, "Mobilizing the World War II Economy"; Edythe W. First, *Industry and Labor Advisory Committees in the National Defense Advisory Commission and the Office of Production Management*, 55–64, 169–229; Paul A. C. Koistinen, "The Hammer and the Sword: Labor, the Military, and Industrial Mobilization, 1920–1945," 341–77; Bruno Stein, "Labor's Role in Government Agencies during World War II," *Journal of Economic History*, 17 (fall 1949): 389–408.

Labor—especially the ULPC—distrusted the Office of Defense Mobilization (ODM) from its very inception. Charles Wilson's ODM, in turn, had little regard for labor's criticisms of the mobilization setup. Labor's suspicion of the ODM's modus operandi was focused on two key players: Charles Wilson himself and his right-hand man, General Lucius Clay. Both men had held high posts in World War II's mobilization effort, and neither had shown much sympathy toward organized labor. As executive vice chairman of the War Production Board, Wilson had headed the powerful Production Executive Committee (PEC), which became the de facto source of most of the WPB's authority. As head of the PEC, Wilson saw to it that groups other than big industry and the military—including labor—were given minor, subservient roles. Clay had shown similar disregard for labor when, as James Byrnes's chief assistant of the Office of War Mobilization (OWM) in December 1944, he authored an OWM "work-or-fight" order essentially designed to be a compulsory labor law. The order came at a time in which no real manpower problems existed and no serious labor shortages were reported. Labor balked at the heavy-handed decree, and the Roosevelt administration was forced to water down the order. But labor leaders would not forget Wilson's cavalier treatment nor could they forgive General Clay's dictatorial decree. With the bitter memory of World War II still fresh in their minds, labor leaders cast a wary eye toward the ODM, which was now headed by their two biggest nemeses.[7]

Beyond the personal animosities involved in the impending labor crisis lay more concrete problems. Labor was not satisfied with its level of participation in the mobilization agencies; it was especially rankled by Wilson's refusal to appoint a labor representative to the Office of Defense Mobilization. Labor representatives on the WSB were not pleased with the board's inability to administer wage policies; it could only formulate policy. The nation's major labor unions believed that the wage board should be granted authority to settle labor disputes— especially those arising from WSB policies. At the time, the board lacked such authority. Labor officials were also highly displeased with Wilson's decision to place manpower policymaking and implementation in the hands of an independent agency under the ODM's control; labor believed the proper placement of such functions was in the Department

---

7. Koistinen, "Mobilizing the World War II Economy," 449–50, 459–60; Paul A. C. Koistinen, "The Hammer and the Sword," 637–703, 521–41; Stein, "Labor's Role," 399–401; Kendrick Lee, "Labor in Government," 277–79.

of Labor under the supervision of Secretary Maurice Tobin. Despite these serious concerns, however, the three labor officials on the WSB found one particular issue around which to rally unanimously: the wage catch-up formula of February 15. Well before the vote on the formula was taken, organized labor had its mind set on one—and only one—across-the-board pay increase allowance. By refusing to compromise on that formula, labor was poised to air all of its complaints and to force the issue of labor's role in the mobilization program.[8]

Relations between labor and Wilson's office had deteriorated precipitously by the February 15 showdown, and ESA director Eric Johnston tried to warn the ODM that a crisis was approaching. On February 6 Johnston wrote to Wilson recommending that the Wage Stabilization Board be reconstituted by increasing its membership from nine to eighteen, by establishing a separate board to deal exclusively with salaried workers, and by giving the board specific powers to settle labor disputes. On this last point, Johnston was most emphatic: he simply did not believe that the WSB could function properly without the authority to settle labor disputes arising from its own policies, despite the fact that industry representatives on the WSB did not want such authority extended to the board. Clearly, Johnston was aware of labor's unhappiness with the WSB and was trying to avoid a showdown by addressing some of its concerns. He was also aware that the nine-member board was overburdened and understaffed—an expanded board free from the burdens of salary stabilization would distribute the workload more equitably and might ensure a faster solution to the pending wage catch-up formula. Wilson ignored Johnston's proposals at the time, but he would be forced to accept them in May 1951.[9]

Economic Stabilization officials were not the only ones concerned with the growing rift on the wage board. The White House, too, was worried about the increasingly tense relationship between labor and the Office of Defense Mobilization. Charles Wilson had repeatedly rebuffed the United Labor Policy Committee's request to appoint a

8. Cyrus Stuart Ching, *Review and Reflection: A Half-Century of Labor Relations*, 96–97; U.S. Congress, Joint Committee on Defense Production, *Defense Production Act, Progress Report #3*, 82nd Cong., 1st sess., February 13, 1951, 74–77; B. C. Roberts, "Wage Stabilization in the United States," 149–52; Memorandum to Director of Defense Mobilization from Director of Economic Stabilization, February 6, 1951, RG 296, Office of the Director, box 5, NA.

9. Memorandum to the Director of Defense Mobilization from the Director of the Economic Stabilization Agency, February 6, 1951, RG 296, Office of the Director, box 5, NA.

labor leader to a top-level mobilization post, saying that he "would have to think about it."[10] White House advisers were stumped by Wilson's foot-dragging; presidential aide Harold Enarson wrote to fellow adviser Richard Neustadt that "the net impression of the committee (the ULPC) is that Mr. Wilson does not want a top advisor from the labor movement."[11] What is more, Wilson's rhetoric did not match his actions. He continued to claim throughout the winter and early spring that he *had* made a concrete offer to name a labor representative to an ODM post. This was not exactly the case—Wilson never gave labor a straight answer. First he said he would take the matter under advisement. A few days later, when labor pressed the issue again, Wilson agreed to name a labor man to an ODM post with the stipulation that the nominee resign his union post. Labor balked, and the stalemate held. While Truman personally remained above the dispute, White House officials worried aloud that a labor walkout could lead to strikes and production stoppages. And many White House officials placed a majority of the blame for the labor impasse squarely on Wilson's shoulders.[12]

The labor crisis came to a head on February 15, 1951, when the Wage Stabilization Board finally settled on a new pay policy to replace the temporary freeze of January 26. The United Labor Policy Committee instructed the three labor representatives on the WSB to settle for nothing less than a 12 percent wage-increase allowance. Industry representatives on the wage board initially insisted on an increase of no more than 6 percent. The three public representatives, along with WSB chairman Cyrus Ching, brokered a compromise with industry representatives that allowed for a 10 percent increase. This formula would have permitted laborers to bargain for wage increases up to 10 percent above the level frozen as of January 26 but would have denied fringe benefits and escalator clauses above the 10 percent ceiling. Under more normal circumstances, labor would most likely have been mollified by such an offer. But the ULPC saw the new wage policy as the ultimate weapon in its fight with Wilson's ODM. So the ULPC and the WSB labor representatives held firm. Shortly after midnight, following

10. Memorandum to Richard Neustadt, February 6, 1951, Papers of Harold L. Enarson, box 4, file: "Memoranda, September 1950–May 1951," HSTL.

11. Memorandum to Richard Neustadt, February 6, 1951, Papers of Harold L. Enarson, box 4, file: "Memoranda, September 1950–May 1951," HSTL.

12. Memorandum to Richard Neustadt, February 6, 1951, Papers of Harold L. Enarson, box 4, file: "Memoranda, September 1950–May 1951," HSTL; Memorandum for Mr. (Charles) Murphy, February 16, 1951, Papers of George M. Elsey, box 89, file: "National Defense-Defense Mobilization," HSTL; *Newsweek* 37 (February 19, 1951): 65–66.

a stormy meeting in the Wage Stabilization Board's dark and drab headquarters in an old World War I "temporary" building, Emil Rieve, union leader of the CIO's textile workers, angrily denounced the board's six to three vote in favor of the 10 percent wage formula and stalked out of the building. He was followed by the two remaining WSB labor representatives. Labor had officially bolted from the WSB, crippling its operations and threatening to derail the entire stabilization program.[13]

The ULPC accentuated the crisis with aplomb. On February 16, the three WSB labor representatives publicly submitted their resignations to President Truman. That same day, the ULPC, representing fifteen million non-communist workers unions, drafted a seven-page "manifesto" blasting the Truman administration and excoriating Charles Wilson for "a whole series of shocking developments which we find insupportable."[14] The ULPC concluded its litany against the mobilization setup by asserting that "we have offered our full support to the defense program [but] . . . our offers have been rejected."[15] Clearly labor had used the 10 percent formula as an excuse to pressure the administration into giving it more of a voice in the mobilization program. In fact, WSB chairman Ching later remarked that the labor walkout had more to do with labor's exasperation with mobilization policies in general than with the wage control program. Apparently, labor's strategy was paying off. Now the ULPC had the undivided attention of the White House, Wilson's ODM, and the general public. For many, labor's gripes with the defense program confirmed the fears that the entire mobilization process had been overrun by the interests of big business.[16]

13. *Newsweek* 37 (February 19, 1951): 65–66; ibid., (February 26, 1951): 61; Ching, *Review and Reflection*, 95–97; Marvin Bernstein, *Administrative History of the Economic Stabilization Agency*, "The Economic Stabilization Agency in the Johnston Period," pp. 24–25, RG 293, Records of the Wage Stabilization Board and Salary Stabilization Board of the Economic Stabilization Agency, box 1, file: "Administrative History of the ESA, 4/13/53," NA; "Wage Stabilization Program, 1950–1953, Volume 1," RG 293, box 1, file: "WSB-ESA, 6/30/53," NA; Wage Stabilization Board Transcript, February 15, 1951, pp. 45–46, RG 293, box 18, file: "Transcripts," NA.

14. Statement by the United Labor Policy Committee, February 16, 1951, Papers of Harold L. Enarson, box 6, file: "Wage and Stabilization Board Policies 1950–52," HSTL.

15. Statement by the United Labor Policy Committee, February 16, 1951, Papers of Harold L. Enarson, box 6, file: "Wage and Stabilization Board Policies 1950–52," HSTL; Wage Stabilization Program, vol. 1, 1950–1953, WSB-ESA, 6/30/53, RG 293, box 1, file: "Wage Stabilization Program," NA.

16. Statement by the United Labor Policy Committee, February 16, 1951, Papers of Harold L. Enarson, box 6, file: "Wage and Stabilization Board Policies 1950–52," HSTL; Ching, *Review and Reflection*, 96; *Newsweek* 37 (February 26, 1951): 61; Radio Transcript,

The administration's reaction to the labor crisis was one of anger, confusion, and finger-pointing. In a February 16 cabinet meeting, Charles Wilson seethed at labor's intransigence, bellowing that "labor's position is one of seeking their pound of flesh regardless of the effect on inflation and higher prices."[17] Secretary of Labor Maurice Tobin shot back that had the ODM director agreed to appoint a labor man to a top policy spot, the whole crisis might have been averted. Tobin also implied that he sympathized with labor's call for a 12 percent wage-increase allowance, saying that "50% of labor has had wages frozen at a level below fairness in view of price increases. There are a great many injustices."[18]

President Truman, clearly frustrated by the whole incident, blamed both labor and industry for the showdown, yet he was careful to avoid faulting any one member of his administration for the crisis. Truman's pattern was now firmly established—he wished to remain above the political squabbles engendered by the mobilization program. Others in the administration were far more opinionated about the labor impasse. The Council of Economic Advisers urged the president *not* to allow the inclusion of fringe benefits in a wage "catch-up" formula and further stated that if the WSB continued to be deadlocked, a wage policy should be announced and implemented at a higher level, regardless of the political fallout. The CEA viewed the labor crisis and the lack of a wage policy as the most serious defect of the economic stabilization program.[19]

"The American Forum of the Air," vol. 13, No. 7, February 18, 1951, "Where's Our Economy Headed?," pp. 8–9, Papers of Leon Keyserling, box 19, file: "The American Forum of the Air," HSTL.

17. Cabinet Meeting, February 16, 1951, Papers of Matthew J. Connelly, box 2, file: "Notes on Cabinet Meetings, 1951, 2 January–31 December," HSTL.

18. Cabinet Meeting, February 16, 1951, Papers of Matthew J. Connelly, box 2, file: "Notes on Cabinet Meetings, 1951, 2 January–31 December," HSTL.

19. Cabinet Meeting, February 16, 1951, Papers of Matthew J. Connelly, box 2, file: "Notes on Cabinet Meetings, 1951, 2 January–31 December," HSTL; Memorandum to the President from the Council of Economic Advisers, February 15, 1951, OF, Papers of Harry S. Truman, box 1564, file: "985 (1951–53)," HSTL. For other views held by administration officials see: Memorandum to Dr. John Steelman (assistant to the president), February 15, 1951, which outlines the reasons why the administration had not previously sought a no-strike pledge, and which summarizes the president's concerns about granting dispute-settling functions to the WSB, Papers of Harold L. Enarson, box 4, file: "Memoranda, September 1950–May 1951," HSTL; Memorandum for Mr. (Charles) Murphy, February 16, 1951, which raises the administration's private concerns about the labor crisis and Charles Wilson's handling of it, Papers of George M. Elsey, box 89, file: "National Defense-Defense Mobilization," HSTL; and Memorandum to Mr. Charles Murphy from Charles Brannan (Secretary of Agriculture), February 19, 1951,

Over the next several weeks, the administration tried in vain to placate labor. The ESA went out of its way to soothe ruffled feathers. For nearly ten days following the labor walkout, ESA director Johnston and WSB chairman Ching held a series of meetings with labor officials to try to bring them back into the fold. Labor refused to budge. By the end of February, Johnston had little choice but to sign the controversial 10 percent formula into law. On the same day that Johnston signed the new wage policy, he released to the press a letter that he had sent to Cyrus Ching. In that letter, Johnston stated that he viewed the new 10 percent regulation as only one step in a continuing search for a comprehensive wage policy. He also indicated that he favored the inclusion of pre-freeze escalator clauses, productivity clauses, and major fringe benefit packages in future WSB regulations. Johnston's proposals were a virtual acceptance of labor's opposition to the 10 percent regulation. Other sticking points remained, however, including labor dispute settlement functions for the WSB, Wilson's manpower policies, and labor representation in the mobilization hierarchy. From February 28 until the reconstitution of the wage board in May 1951, Johnston established and implemented wage stabilization policy on his own initiative.[20]

On February 28, the day after Johnston signed the 10 percent regulation, labor withdrew in toto from all mobilization posts. Decrying the new wage regulation and ignoring Johnston's proposed concessions, the ULPC issued a blistering denunciation of Johnston and Charles Wilson. In the long, stinging explanation of its action, the ULPC stated that "we fully realize the gravity of this decision . . . but the Office of Defense Mobilization is staffed at its top level exclusively with men from the executive offices of big business. . . . Mr. Wilson does not want labor participation in the mobilization program."[21] The final

---

which indicates that farm groups too were "worried about business 'stewardship' of the mobilization program," Papers of Harold L. Enarson, box 4, file: "Memoranda, September 1950–May 1951," HSTL.

20. Wage Stabilization Program, 1950–1953, vol. 1, 6/30/53, p. 102, RG 293, box 1, file: "Wage Stabilization Program," NA; *Newsweek* 37 (March 5, 1951): 24–25; *Newsweek* 37 (March 12, 1951): 65; Defense Mobilization Board, Meeting No. 5, February 28, 1951, RG 296, Records Maintained by the Administrator, Classified General Files, box 2, file: "Defense Mobilization Board Meetings," NA. For Charles Wilson's views on the delegation of manpower authority, see Letter to the United Labor Policy Committee from Charles E. Wilson, February 20, 1951, RG 304, National Security Resources Board, Office of the Chairman, box 14, file: "Office of Defense Mobilization," NA.

21. Statement by the United Labor Policy Committee, February 28, 1951, Papers of Harold L. Enarson, box 6, file: "Wage and Stabilization Policies 1950–52," HSTL.

exodus followed on March 1: George Harrison, head of the railway clerks union, quit his post as Johnston's ESA adviser; A. J. Hayes of the machinists union vacated his position as adviser to Assistant Secretary of Defense Anna Rosenberg; Joseph Keenan (AFL) and Ted F. Silvey (CIO) left the National Production Administration; and Philip Murray and William Green dropped their memberships in various advisory committees. Publicly Wilson remained silent, and Truman refused to answer any detailed questions about the walkout, stating that he was unworried about the stalemate and remained fully confident in Wilson's and Johnston's ability to remedy the situation. Labor's final walkout greatly limited its participation in mobilization and stabilization policymaking until the boycott was ended in May 1951.[22]

Labor's boycott of the mobilization program deeply troubled the administration. First, the impasse threatened to sour the president's generally good relations with organized labor—relations established in his 1940 reelection campaign to the Senate, in which labor unions played a vital role. Throughout his political career, Truman had repeatedly identified with labor's social and economic agenda. And nothing better exemplified the president's commitment to organized labor than his very public veto of the 1947 Taft-Hartley Act. Now labor had begun to question Truman's loyalties. The United Labor Policy Committee's actions also made stabilization policies much more difficult to administer. Labor refused to accept anything less than full compensation for each cost of living increase, business balked at any effort to control profit margins, and the public began to question the need for economic controls during a period of falling prices and stabilized battlefield operations in Korea.[23]

All of this highlighted a problem unique to the Korean period. That is, how does a nation mobilize its industrial and emotional resources while engaged in a limited war of indefinite duration? Cyrus Ching, reflecting on the Korean rearmament, summed up the dilemma quite succinctly: "No state of unlimited emergency had been declared. There was no awareness of any immediate or great danger. . . . The willingness to make great sacrifices just didn't exist."[24]

22. *Newsweek* 37 (March 12, 1951): 65; *New Leader* 34 (March 5, 1951): 2–5.
23. For an overview of Truman's relations with labor, see Arthur F. McClure, *The Truman Administration and the Problems of Post-War Labor, 1945–1948*; Alonzo L. Hamby, *Beyond the New Deal: Harry S. Truman and American Liberalism*; Maeva Marcus, *Truman and the Steel Seizure Case: The Limits of Presidential Power*, 17–37.
24. Ching, *Review and Reflection*, 92.

Although the labor standoff was the most pressing issue of the period, administration officials faced other hurdles. These included the formulation of an integrated industrial expansion policy; addressing the rift between the Treasury Department and the Federal Reserve over interest rates; the implementation of a price policy to replace the temporary freeze of January; rectifying spot materials shortages; unclogging the bottleneck in machine tool production; and soothing the concerns of small business owners disgruntled by the mobilization process. None of these problems was solved without a good deal of debate among policymakers, some of which became quite heated. Thus, the winter and spring of 1951 were seasons of considerable adjustment for the rearmament program. The first serious economic and political strains caused by the accelerated mobilization effort were being felt, so it was not surprising that problems ensued.

Still, inflation continued to slacken and production output soared. On April 1, the Office of Defense Mobilization issued its first quarterly report on the state of the defense program. Entitled "Building America's Might," the document's message was clearly upbeat. Stating that the nation was quantifiably safer against attack than it had been only a few months earlier, the report assured the public that the economy was up to the challenges of the mobilization effort. The nation was moving forward at a good pace, according to the ODM, and the future looked even more prosperous and secure. The encouraging and unified picture portrayed by the report, however, belied some rather serious chasms that had begun to develop within the administration toward economic and mobilization policy.[25]

March was a month of confusion for the mobilization effort. Clearly the labor crisis had severely strained relations between the ODM and the Oval Office. Then Wilson's office precipitated another bitter political row, this time over industrial expansion policy. Wilson's team had insisted on a tightfisted policy toward expansion; its members

25. "Building America's Might," April 1, 1951, RG 296, Records and Reports of the Secretariat, box 6, file: "ODM: 1st Quarterly Report, 4/1/51," NA; Release from the Office of Defense Mobilization, April 1, 1951, OF, box 1731, file: "2855," HSTL. U.S. Congress, Joint Committee on Defense Production, *Defense Production Act, Progress Report No. 7, Hearing before the Joint Committee on Defense Production to Hear Charles E. Wilson, on his April 1 Report to the President,* 82nd Cong., 1st Sess., April 4, 1951. The National Security Resources Board saw the report as nothing more than a propaganda ploy. E. C. Welsh, Stuart Symington's assistant, wrote of the report: "It is appropriate that the report is issued on *April First* (emphasis in original). I just hope it doesn't fool everybody!" Memo to Mr. Symington, April 2, 1951, RG 304, NSRB Office of the Chairman, box 14, NA.

believed that government assistance should be extended only to businesses directly involved in the production of military items, a position that rankled the already perturbed White House. Expansion-minded policymakers like Leon Keyserling strongly opposed Wilson's formula. Citing the administration's pledge to build up both military and civilian production capacities, Keyserling argued that Wilson's plan relied too heavily upon the defense sector to boost overall production. The result would be an imbalanced and narrowly defined production policy that would prove disastrous to small industries incapable of converting to defense production. Truman requested that Wilson refashion the expansion policy to allow for greater overall production expansion. The White House prevailed in this fight, but tense relations between the ODM and the Oval Office persisted. The National Security Resources Board (NSRB) and the Council of Economic Advisers were particularly irritated at Wilson's heavy-handed tactics. The CEA took special pains to point out to the president that industrial expansion was not keeping pace with the rest of the economy. It also cited the increasing problem of raw materials shortages, which would only have worsened had Wilson's lopsided industrial expansion plans gone through.[26]

Meanwhile, The NSRB made one last desperate attempt to save itself from extinction. Since late December, when Truman transferred most of the NSRB's mobilization authority to the ODM, the NSRB had been searching for a way to maintain its influence within the administration. Wilson's row with the White House gave the proponents of the NSRB a final chance to reassert the agency's influence. Much of this attempt, of course, amounted to nothing more than a last-ditch effort on the part of bureaucrats to rationalize their existence. But on the other hand, the NSRB and its supporters could rightfully point to Wilson's shortsighted policies and argue that the agency was still needed to balance the rearmament effort over the long term. "It should be clear," NSRB staffer E. C. Welsh wrote, "that the U.S. can not afford . . . to treat the present mobilization efforts as an isolated action which when completed, will

---

26. *Business Week* (March 3, 1951): 19–20; "Wilson's One-Man War," *Nation* 172 (March 3, 1951): 197–98; Defense Production Policy, ODM Doc. 4 (Revised), March 14, 1951, RG 296, Reports and Secretariat, box 14, NA; Letter to the President, March 9, 1951, President's Secretary's File, box 143, file: "Council of Economic Advisers, Reports-Folder 1," HSTL. On March 8, 1951, CEA member Roy Blough remarked to Frederick Lawton, chief of the Bureau of the Budget, that "neither Wilson or [*sic*] any of his immediate assistants gets along diplomatically with other people." See Papers of Roy Blough, diary entry for March 8, 1951, box 14, file: "CEA, Reference-Diary, Jan–Dec 31, 1951," HSTL. There certainly was no love lost between Keyserling's office and Wilson's.

enable the U.S. to go back to the luxury of 'ostrichism.' "[27] White House officials agreed with the NSRB, fearing that national defense—which they assumed was being carried out by the ODM—was being confused with national security—which was supposed to be carried out by the NSRB.[28]

At the heart of this issue lay one of the most implacable problems of the Korean mobilization. That is, how should the nation mobilize for the short term while simultaneously preparing to arm itself for a protracted cold war? Compounding this dilemma, of course, was the public's growing disillusionment with the Korean War and the administration's fervent desire to avoid the creation of an American Sparta. The problem, much to the dismay of the NSRB, was never fully reconciled. Truman had never put much faith in the NSRB, and after Symington resigned from the board in April, the president allowed it to languish. The administration's inability to grapple with the institutional and strategic imperatives of short-term versus long-term mobilization planning demonstrated its tendency to be easily swayed by powerful personalities like Wilson, who looked upon the NSRB with disdain, and its propensity to attempt an almost impossible balance between civilian and military goals.

Despite the administration's difficulty in developing long-term production and expansion policies, March 1951 was decisive in one key controversy: the Treasury–Federal Reserve stalemate over interest rates. At issue was far more than just interest rates. The impasse between the Treasury Department and the Federal Reserve Board affected overall monetary policy, which remained the government's cutting-edge weapon against inflation. The singular goal of monetary policy is that of macroeconomic stabilization: to foster full employment while at the same time providing for economic expansion without inflation. Until March 1951, however, the Federal Reserve's power to affect macroeconomic stabilization had been greatly limited by its commitment to stabilize the government bond market, which by nature undermined its control over the nation's money supply. As the threat of inflation became more ominous in early 1951, the Federal Reserve urged the

27. Memo to Mr. Symington, April 11, 1951, RG 304, NSRB Office of the Chairman, box 14, file: "Economic Management Office," NA.
28. Memorandum to Steelman and Stowe, April 18, 1951, Papers of Harold L. Enarson, box 4, file: "Memoranda, September 1950–May 1951," HSTL; Memorandum for Dr. Steelman, April 25, 1951, Papers of Harold L. Enarson, box 2, file: "NSRB Projects," HSTL.

Truman administration to abandon its policy of strict stabilization of the bond market. But the Treasury Department would hear none of it. The Treasury insisted that the abandonment of pegged government bonds would not necessarily stem the tide of consumer inflation; instead, it would only lead to the increased cost of managing the national debt— at a time when budget deficits were pushing the debt higher. The fight between the Federal Reserve and the Treasury became a public spectacle rather quickly: it confused the public, angered the business community, which believed the administration had not done enough to curb inflation through monetary policy, and threatened the autonomy of the Federal Reserve Board.[29]

Truman at first sided with the Treasury Department, and with good reason. The Council of Economic Advisers strongly urged the president (and Congress) *not* to buckle under to the Fed's pressure. Noting that the entire mobilization program was predicated upon economic expansion, the CEA argued that a tightening of credit would choke off business incentives to expand production—especially defense production.[30] Nevertheless, the CEA urged the president to bring the impasse to a resolution quickly, arguing that "there must be an end to the continuing uncertainty and undermining of confidence . . . when there is on display an unresolved conflict between two major organs of public policy."[31] Truman then directed the heads of the Treasury, Federal Reserve, ODM, and the CEA to study and reconcile their differences so as to strike a balance between public debt management and private credit control.[32]

Although the White House did not immediately support the Federal Reserve's position, business groups and economic experts did. In light of the fact that inflation was expected to increase—despite the current

29. *Business Week* (February 10, 1951): 148; Bert G. Hickman, *Growth and Stability of the Postwar Economy*, 335–37; Rockoff, *Drastic Measures*, 186–87.

30. Letter to Eric Johnston, February 7, 1951, RG 296, box 12, file: "ESA Economics," NA; Statement on Monetary Policy by John D. Clarke, Vice Chairman Council of Economic Advisers to the Joint Committee on the Economic Report Hearings upon the 1951 Annual Economic Report of the President, February 2, 1951, RG 296, box 12, file: "ESA Economics," NA.

31. Report to the President: Monthly Economic Report, February 15, 1951, OF, box 1564, file: "985 (1951–53)," HSTL.

32. Memorandum of February 26, 1951, President's Secretary's File, box 144, file: "Federal Reserve Board," HSTL; Memorandum for the Secretary of the Treasury and the Chairman of the Board of Governors of the Federal Reserve System, no date, President's Secretary's File, box 144, file: "Federal Reserve Board," HSTL.

lull—when the full impact of rearmament hit later in the year, business leaders and many economists believed that it was absolutely essential to curb spending through tighter credit. Many in the business community also believed that the need for ongoing price and wage controls might be mitigated by higher interest rates and stricter monetary policy. The supporters of the Fed's position ultimately triumphed. On March 4, the Treasury and the Federal Reserve System reached an accord that abandoned the commitment to continuous support of government bond prices. The Federal Reserve was now free to pursue monetary policy in the fight against inflation.[33] The Treasury–Federal Reserve Accord was expected to relieve inflationary pressures in two ways. First, it would signal to the public that the Federal Reserve was ready to fight inflation through tighter credit, which would, in turn, dampen inflationary expectations. Second, by reducing the cash value of government bonds, the public would be encouraged to increase savings, diminishing the likelihood of unnecessary buying.[34]

As it turned out, however, the threat of further inflation proved to be largely illusionary. As early as late February, the inflation rate had noticeably slowed. Continuing good news from the Korean front, talk of peace initiatives, record business inventories, and delays in defense production schedules all helped break the inflation. This was certainly good news for American consumers; it was less so for administration officials. Pointing out that the defense program would not reach critical mass until sometime in the third or fourth quarter of the year, they warned that the inflationary lull was only temporary. Administration officials clearly believed that inflation was still enemy number one. One of Eric Johnston's associates at the ESA asked the rhetorical question: "(W)hich is our biggest enemy—inflation or Russia?" The answer appeared obvious: inflation. "As Lenin observed," the memo continued, "a debauched currency is the easiest way to destroy a capitalist country." What mobilization officials feared most was that the slowing of inflation would bring with it a false sense of confidence among the public and the Congress alike. They were concerned that the lull would convince the public that controls were no longer needed and would

33. Joint Announcement by the Secretary of the Treasury and the Chairman of the Board of Governors, and of the Open Market Committee, of the Federal Reserve System, March 4, 1951, President's Secretary's Files, box 144, file: "Federal Reserve Board," HSTL; Hickman, *Growth and Stability*, 337; *Business Week* (February 10, 1951): 148.

34. Rockoff, *Drastic Measures*, 187.

prod Congress into diluting the Defense Production Act, which was scheduled for extension in June.[35]

The extent to which price and wage controls and economic stabilization in general affected the inflation rate is difficult to quantify. To a certain degree, the psychological impact alone of the price-and-wage freeze undoubtedly contributed to the easing of inflation. Realizing that the administration was serious in its fight against inflation, and sensing that shortages were not in the immediate future, consumers concluded that there was no need to panic; buying out supplies and hoarding them were no longer necessary. In retrospect, it is clear that the two most active periods of Korean inflation (June–September 1950 and December 1950–February 1951) were not principally caused by increased military spending, for defense orders did not begin to cut into the civilian economy until the third quarter of 1951. Instead, forward buying of consumers and businessmen brought about these two periods of expectationary inflation. The deflationary trend that began in March, then, was precipitated by unusually large inventories that had been accumulating over the previous six months, combined with the break in consumer expectations of more inflation. Yet the economy continued to boom because, as economist Bert Hickman has observed, the decline in civilian spending was almost perfectly offset by the rise in defense spending. "For a time," Hickman notes, "it was as though two economies existed side by side without touching."[36]

These positive developments were better than anyone would have dared to hope for only a few months before. But now the Truman administration found itself in the untenable position of insisting on tighter controls during a period of booming prosperity and lower inflation. As a result, the public's confusion and frustration with the mobilization program mounted.

In an attempt to quell the negative tide of public opinion, several mobilization agencies, including the ESA, commissioned private studies in the early spring of 1951 to measure public opinion. The polls indi-

---

35. "Is Deflation in the Winds?" *Newsweek* 37 (March 26, 1951): 73–74; Monthly Economic Report, March 9, 1951, President's Secretary's File, box 143, file: "Council of Economic Advisers, Reports," HSTL; Cabinet Meeting, March 20, 1951, Papers of Matthew J. Connelly, box 2, file: "Notes on Cabinet Meetings, 1951, 2 January–31 December," HSTL; Radio Transcript, April 6, 1951, Talk by Eric Johnston, RG 296, box 19, NA.

For quotation, see Memorandum to Mr. Eric Johnston, March 12, 1951, RG 296, Letters, Memoranda of Eric Johnston, ESA, box 98, NA.

36. Hickman, *Growth and Stability*, 91–92.

cated a badly confused and divided populace. Most found the public dissatisfied with the progress of the rearmament effort—especially economic stabilization. And people blamed Washington for the perceived failure. Yet those polled appeared unwilling to allow the government to take stronger measures. Administration officials, in an effort to reshape public opinion and to bolster support for the administration's mobilization programs, tried repeatedly to launch public relations campaigns to blunt the criticism. One such attempt was quintessentially corporatist. On March 12 John T. O'Brien, an information officer attached to the White House, suggested that the administration establish an industry advisory board, "consisting of about twenty top news executives . . . representing all media and regional viewpoints" whose job would be to mold public perceptions of Korea and the mobilization program. The ambiguous and ever-changing military and economic goals, however, made such attempts nearly impossible. Once again, the Herculean task of maintaining high public morale and support over an extended period during a limited war seemed to elude both the Truman administration and the many corporate executives who were continually advising the government.[37]

In the midst of the labor crisis, the Treasury–Federal Reserve Accord, and the other high profile controversies of the late winter and early spring, stabilization officials continued the search for a price policy to replace the January freeze. The responsibility fell most heavily upon Michael DiSalle, director of the Office of Price Stabilization (OPS). And as inflation eased, DiSalle's job became ever more difficult. Business leaders, already frustrated with the price-control setup, resisted efforts to tighten controls, and vehemently protested OPS attempts to roll back prices. Citing the waning inflation rate, many Americans questioned the need for such measures. The administration was unable to blunt public criticism of the OPS; when it tried to do so, the result was internal bickering and external confusion.

DiSalle's office had begun work on tailored price regulations as soon as the January 26 freeze was announced. The task was monumental. The

37. See "Public Thinking on Mobilization and Stabilization Issues," March 19, 1951, RG 296, Reports and Secretariat, box 18, NA; "Public Thinking on Mobilization and Stabilization Issues," April 17, 1951, RG 304, NSRB Office of the Chairman, box 13, file: "Congressional Correspondence, M-Z," NA; "Public Response to the Emergency: A Program of Research," February 5, 1951, Institute for Social Research, University of Michigan, RG 296, Letters, Memoranda of Eric Johnston, ESA, box 98, NA.

For quoted material, see Letter to Joseph Short, March 12, 1951, OF, box 1731, file: "2855-misc.," HSTL. To the author's knowledge, no such program was ever instituted.

inequities of the across-the-board freeze had caught prices in a badly distorted relationship. Retailers were the hardest hit because they were forced to hold the line on retail prices while at the same time spending more to replenish their inventories. Many were simply unable to cover their costs. Immediately after the freeze, the OPS instituted a series of "roll-forwards" for those retailers and other businesses caught short by the freeze. DiSalle had hoped to offset these price advances by rollbacks for goods whose prices had been raised to unreasonable levels. At first, before tailored regulations could be written and implemented, the OPS instituted a maximum margin ceiling on wholesalers and retailers alike; margin regulations used in World War II were temporarily reissued. From that stopgap measure, the OPS set its sights on developing price guidelines specifically suited for the Korean period.[38]

The difficulty of formulating price-control guidelines was increased by two problems: DiSalle tended to be more pessimistic about the inflationary outlook than were most other officials; thus, he favored controls that were more stringent than the administration wanted. Also, the stabilization agencies and the Council of Economic Advisers were not sure what functions—other than inflation fighting—price controls should undertake. For example, besides the obvious function of inflation control, some stabilization officials sought to use price controls as an incentive to increase the production of essential defense products while at the same time discouraging the production of nonessential goods. Not surprisingly, nondefense manufacturers howled in protest. The incentive function was quickly dropped. DiSalle's constant talk about the likelihood of further inflation and the need for stronger controls did not sit well with many administration officials, especially before the deflationary trend had set in. The CEA in particular fretted that such inflation talk might become a self-fulfilling prophesy. Furthermore, with DiSalle actually relaxing some price ceilings, especially in the retail sector, the last thing the administration wanted to emphasize was the possibility of further inflation, which would have added to the public's confusion over price control.[39]

38. U.S. Congress, Joint Committee on Defense Production, *Defense Production Act, Progress Report No. 1, Hearing before the Joint Committee on Defense Production to Hear Eric Johnston and Michael V. DiSalle,* 82nd Cong., 1st Sess., 32–34; Rockoff, *Drastic Measures* 180; Memorandum to Mr. Johnston, March 12, 1951, RG 296, Economic Stabilization Agency, Letters and Memoranda of Eric Johnston, box 98, NA.

39. Memorandum to Ralf Hetzel, ESA, February 8, 1951, RG 296, Economic Stabilization Agency, box 23, NA; Memorandum to Mr. Johnston from G. Griffith Johnson,

By mid-April 1951, the OPS was finally poised to implement price controls specifically tailored to the Korean period. The price control program had two main components: an interim short-term plan and a more permanent long-term plan. In the interim stage, price roll-forwards and rollbacks would be permitted. The interim price-adjustment standard provided upward price adjustments for manufacturers that reflected their increases in costs incurred in factory labor costs up to March 15, 1951, and material costs up to December 31, 1950. These increases were added to the highest price of each seller for any of the four quarters prior to Korea. These liberal adjustment standards, stabilization officials hoped, would remedy the inequities of the January freeze. The long-term plan would be implemented once the inequities of the January freeze had been solved. That plan provided for price increases industry-wide only if a majority in a given industry saw its profits fall below 85 percent of the profits for the three best years of 1946 through 1949.[40]

Once the OPS had defined the tailored price regulations, it became far easier to implement overall price stabilization. The OPS was now also poised to codify and streamline the entire process of price actions. What's more, the decentralized setup of the OPS was at once able to consider local and regional price variances and exceptions while at the same time it was able to blunt public and congressional fears that the rearmament effort was leading to a regimented, garrison state economy dictated from the nation's capital. Nearly all price actions, whether they represented a new commodity price ceiling or merely dealt with the adjustment of an already existing one, originated at the branch level within a commodity division of the Office of Price Operations. The branch chief, responsible for the initial development of the proposal based upon information gleaned from industrial and consumer advisory committees at the district and regional levels, forwarded the price proposal action to the head of the appropriate commodity division. Once there, it was evaluated by the division director, the division counsel, and the division economist. If the price measure cleared that hurdle, then it advanced to the Clearance Committee, where the price

February 23, 1951, RG 296, ESA Committees, box 7, NA; Confidential Memo to the President from Leon Keyserling, February 20, 1951, President's Secretary's Files, box 143, file: "Council of Economic Advisers," HSTL.

40. Memorandum to David H. Stowe from Harold E. Enarson, April 11, 1951, Papers of Harold L. Enarson, box 4, file: "Price Stabilization Issues, 4/51," HSTL; Memorandum to Mr. Symington, April 19, 1951, RG 304, NSRB Office of the Chairman, box 14, file: "Defense Mobilization Board," NA; Defense Mobilization Board Meeting No. 8, April 19, 1951, RG 296, box 2, file: "Defense Mobilization Board Meetings," NA.

action was considered once more before it advanced to the director of price stabilization and the chief economist of the OPS. After that, the OPS director would approve the measure, issue the orders, and channel them back through the appropriate commodity division which would then implement the price order through the regional and district offices.[41]

Reaction to the new OPS price guidelines was mixed at best. The Council of Economic Advisers, along with other White House advisers, asserted that the regulations were inherently inflationary and were not tough enough. Leon Keyserling noted that the interim plan should be scrapped in favor of direct implementation of the long-term plan. Industry representatives voiced their displeasure with both policies, claiming that they were too tough. Johnston and DiSalle argued in turn that the policy provided a formula "under which inequities caused by the existing price freeze could be corrected."[42] The NSRB, watching the deliberations from the sidelines, cynically sniped that the "only possible excuse for the (interim) adjustment procedure was the . . . fact that the OPS was not administratively set up as to handle efficiently a price adjustment policy based on hardship of individual companies."[43] In fact, there was a certain amount of validity to all of the varying administrative viewpoints. The policy was the best the ESA and OPS could muster under the circumstances. Industry complaints were less plausible, however. Profits for American manufacturers were running very high—so high in fact that the chairman of the Federal Trade Commission, Jas. M. Mead, wrote to Eric Johnston on April 21 that "in some manufacturing industries (profits) exceed 50 percent. The figures . . . show that criticisms of the price formulas . . . on the grounds that they are too severe can not be well founded."[44]

The final OPS price control policy emerged from an explosive conference that took place on April 11. In attendance were officials from the ESA, OPS, CEA, ODM, and the White House. When presidential aide David Stowe asked why the OPS was not prepared to implement the price policy in one stroke, OPS officials blew up. One OPS staffer

41. Correa, "The Organization for Defense Mobilization," 12.

42. Defense Mobilization Board Meeting No. 8, April 19, 1951, RG 296, box 2, file: "Defense Mobilization Board Meetings," NA.

43. Memorandum to Mr. Symington, April 19, 1951, RG 304, NSRB Office of the Chairman, box 14, file: "Defense Mobilization Board," NA; Charles H. Lipsett, *Price and Wage Controls*, 149–53.

44. Letter to Eric Johnston, April 21, 1951, RG 296, ESA Committees, box 9, NA.

shouted, "We're working 18 hours a day! We can't handle all the hardship cases as it is!" Johnston, barely keeping his composure, interjected that "we expend vast amounts of manpower and we never come to decisions! No business could operate this way!" Johnston's reaction was typical of most business executives-cum-government policymakers. Whereas most were accustomed to setting policy and seeing it carried out efficiently in the private sector, such was not the case in the public sector. Congressional and public pressures, bureaucratic inertia, and government inefficiency all tested the patience of the businessman turned public servant. In any event, by May 1, the OPS had instituted a workable set of price regulations that were administratively feasible—no small miracle given the fact that they were developed during a time of general deflation and confusion over the direction of the stabilization and mobilization program.[45]

Eventually, the long-term price policy was summarized by a set of four tests for the adequacy of an existing price ceiling. First, an industry had to be earning no less than 85 percent of its average for the best three years of the 1946 through 1949 period. If this was not the case, price advances were justified. Second, on any given product line the average producer had to be breaking even; if not, price increases for that line would be in order. Third, price increases were allowed for individual sellers operating at a loss. Fourth, the preceding guidelines could be nullified and prices increased to protect supplies of goods considered essential to the defense program.[46]

Once the tailored price regulation procedures had been established, the OPS faced one final administrative hurdle: enforcement and compliance guidelines. Not surprisingly, this was one of the more delicate—and potentially divisive—issues that faced price stabilization officials. The first arrest for an OPS pricing violation occurred in April 1951, just as the agency was about to unveil its long-term price regulations. The case involved a Los Angeles auto dealer who was charged with selling a 1950 Cadillac above the price ceiling for cars in the luxury category. Although it is unclear how the violation was brought to the attention of OPS officials, the dealer was later sanctioned but not formally prosecuted. Nevertheless, the first recognized violation, occurring when it did, made headlines around the country. If convicted, the dealer could

<hr />

45. For a fairly detailed transcript of this meeting, see Memorandum to David H. Stowe from Harold L. Enarson, April 11, 1951, Papers of Harold L. Enarson, box 4, file: "Price Stabilization Issues, 4/51," HSTL.
46. See Rockoff, *Drastic Measures*, 180.

have received a maximum fine of ten thousand dollars and one year in prison. The visibility of the first case combined with the likelihood of more cases as the new price regulations were put in place convinced the ESA and the OPS to move quickly to establish policies and procedures for enforcement and prosecution of price violators. Like the rest of the stabilization setup, enforcement and compliance authority was rapidly decentralized.[47]

By early June 1951, the ESA and OPS had established a workable system of enforcement procedures. Working mainly in consultation with the Department of Justice and the Department of the Treasury, the OPS delegated enforcement authority to its field officials in regional and district offices around the nation. Each district had enforcement officers whose job it was to police communities for price violators and to serve as investigators of complaints emanating from local consumers, who were encouraged to report price violations to their local district price office. The district enforcement officers worked with the OPS national enforcement office in Washington. Only when the district and regional price inspectors referred cases to the national office was penal action against accused violators considered. Although there was no enforcement at the regional level, regional chief inspectors did monitor their areas for possible violations and direct investigations by district officers. The OPS enforcement system was modeled after enforcement procedures used by the FBI. Throughout the stabilization program, hundreds of cases were investigated, although the exact number of cases actually prosecuted remains unknown.[48]

With the prickly issue of price controls temporarily laid to rest, administration officials turned their sights on the continuing labor boycott. Their job was made somewhat easier now that the OPS had settled on a price formula. With price guidelines established, both labor and industry representatives could negotiate their respective positions knowing, at least to some degree, what the future might hold in the way of price and cost-of-living increases. As it turned out, the Truman administration was more sympathetic toward labor than it was toward management. To a certain extent, however, the OPS price guidelines gave the administration no other option. Business

47. "Actions Outside the ESA," April 17, 1951, RG 296, Records and Reports of Secretariat, box 4, file: "Activity Outside The Economic Stabilization Agency," NA.
48. Ibid.; "Policy and Organization for Stabilization Compliance," June 18, 1951, RG 296, Secretariat Classified, box 26, file: "National Defense, Organizational Management," NA.

complaints notwithstanding, the OPS regulations were not designed to hold the line on inflation. Instead, they were engineered to keep the cost of living within the bounds of a controlled "creep." Thus, stabilization officials had little choice but to placate labor by capitulating to many of its demands. The administration could ill afford to implement price formulas, which were in fact quite generous to most industries, without giving labor some breathing space. Nor could it allow the stalemate to fester much longer; a labor strike in any of the key industries could seriously impede the mobilization effort.

To break the labor stalemate, on March 15 Truman had formed the National Advisory Board on Mobilization Policy, whose first order of business was to recommend to the president a plan to reconstitute the Wage Stabilization Board. The Advisory Board, a mechanism used during World War II, consisted of sixteen at-large public members, four of whom represented business, four labor, and four agriculture. The board was chaired by ODM chief Charles Wilson.[49] While significant progress had been made to bring labor and management closer together, one major point remained unsolved: the labor dispute settlement function of the WSB. The National Association of Manufacturers, the Chamber of Commerce of the United States, and the Business Advisory Council had already agreed that the WSB should be enlarged to an eighteen-person tripartite board and that the board be given the power to formulate *and* administer wage policies. They were staunchly opposed, however, to any settlement that allowed the WSB to adjudicate labor disputes. Such authority, argued business representatives, effectively stifled private collective bargaining and put the government in the business of doing labor's bidding. It was the Advisory Board's job to break this final sticking point.[50]

On April 17, 1951, the labor crisis was finally resolved. The Advisory Board agreed by majority opinion that the suspended Wage Stabilization Board should be reestablished as an eighteen-person tripartite body with authority to set and administer wage policy as well

49. Memorandum for the President, Mobilization Advisory Board, March 15, 1951, OF, box 1737, file: "2855-A," HSTL; Executive Order Establishing the National Advisory Board on Mobilization Policy, March 15, 1951, OF, box 1737, file: "2855-A," HSTL.

50. Letter to Eric Johnston from the National Association of Manufacturers, Chamber of Commerce, and Business Advisory Council, March 14, 1951, Papers of Harold L. Enarson, box 6, file: "Wage and Stabilization Board Policies 1950–52," HSTL; Letter to Eric Johnston, March 27, 1951, RG 296, box 5, NA; Defense Mobilization Board Meeting No. 6, March 14, 1951, RG 296, Records Maintained by the Administrator Classified General Files, box 2, file: "Defense Mobilization Board Meetings," NA.

as to settle labor disputes affecting the mobilization program. The four industry representatives on the Advisory Board voted against the proposal, but the majority opinion prevailed.[51] Truman hailed the breakthrough, much to the business community's irritation, and set about the task of formally reconstituting the new WSB. On April 21, the president issued an executive order that reconstituted the wage board along the lines suggested by the Advisory Board. Not surprisingly, the administration had a hard time convincing industry representatives to sit on the new board, which would now be composed of six industry officials, six labor leaders, and six at-large public members. Nevertheless, industry officials grudgingly accepted their fate and agreed to send six representatives to sit on the new WSB. They would not forget the administration's strong-arm tactics, however, and decided that the best way to fight the labor disputes function was to take the case to Congress, which was about to begin deliberations on the extension of the Defense Production Act.[52]

On May 8, 1951, the new WSB formally resumed operations. On the same day, the Economic Stabilization Agency established the Salary Stabilization Board (SSB), which removed from the jurisdiction of the WSB any control over salaries of executive, administrative, and professional personnel. Essentially, the SSB would monitor and develop pay policies of most nonhourly workers. Recognizing the sharp differences between hourly and salaried workers, and harking back to the World War II stabilization program, which separated wage and salary stabilization, ESA officials hoped that the SSB would relieve the pressure and workload that faced the new WSB.[53] After a three-month hiatus, the WSB had accrued a formidable backlog of wage questions and

51. Memorandum from Ross Shearer, ESA, April 5, 1951, Papers of Harold L. Enarson, box 3, file: "Letters sent re Steel Strike 1951–52," HSTL; National Advisory Board on Mobilization Policy, Meeting Numbers 1–3, April 9, April 12, April 17, 1951, White House Central Files-Confidential Files, box 26, file: "National Advisory Board on Mobilization Policy, 1951–52," HSTL.

52. Executive Order 10233, April 21, 1951, *Federal Register* 16, 3503.

For business reactions to the newly reconstituted WSB, see Release by the Chamber of Commerce of the United States, April 17, 1951, RG 296 Secretariat-Classified, box 10, NA. The National Association of Manufacturers, historically the most antiunion business group, led the charge against the labor dispute function. See Memorandum to Mr. Murphy, April 16, 1951, Papers of Harold L. Enarson, box 4, file: "Memoranda September 1950–May 1951," HSTL; and Memorandum to Messrs. Steelman, Stowe from Harold L. Enarson, Papers of Harold L. Enarson, box 4, file: "Memoranda September 1950–May 1951," HSTL.

53. The Salary Stabilization Board, May 8, 1951, RG 296, Organization Management, box 27, NA.

hardship cases. George W. Taylor, former chairman of the War Labor Board of World War II and professor of Business Economics at the elite Wharton School of Business–University of Pennsylvania, was named to replace Cyrus Ching as chair of the new WSB. Ching resigned his WSB post to return to the Federal Mediation and Conciliation Service. Once more, the Truman administration had turned to the experienced ranks of World War II mobilization staffers to lead the new wage board. With the new eighteen-person board fully operational and headed by an experienced labor expert, the WSB was ready to bring organized labor back into the fold.[54]

At the same time that the administration struggled to keep the teetering mobilization program under control, it grappled with what was perhaps the seminal event of the Korean War: the dismissal of General MacArthur and the firestorm of controversy it ignited. Journalist David Rees described the firing of the general as the "biggest emotional upheaval in American life since Appomattox was at hand."[55] MacArthur's removal simply cannot be overemphasized. The public uproar it precipitated and the political shenanigans it engendered stymied the administration's foreign policy and rearmament plans. The conservative, quasi-isolationist wing of the Republican party, led by Ohio Senator Robert Taft, along with many Southern Democrats, still stinging from their defeat in the Great Debate, seized the initiative to humiliate Truman and to build up the dubious heroism of MacArthur to epic proportions. As they did during the Great Debate, Truman's congressional foes used the crisis to assert that the president's foreign policies were badly flawed, that his presidential prerogatives had become dictatorial, and, most critically, that his initiatives were bankrupting the nation and were tearing down the pillars of American democracy. In the end, Truman and his military staffers managed to convince the majority of Americans that the rogue general had indeed overstepped his authority. Truman was far less effective, however, at convincing Americans that his foreign and domestic policies were sound. Sensing this, the pro-MacArthur contingent used the controversy to build its case against the president's handling of the Korean crisis—and the mobilization program. Nothing could have been worse for the administration, which was in the midst of asking Congress to strengthen its control powers under the Defense Production Act.

54. Ching, *Review and Reflection,* 96–97; *Newsweek* 37 (May 14, 1951): 60–62.
55. Rees, *Korea,* 213.

Public reaction to the April 11 firing of MacArthur was breath-takingly emotional. Everyone, it seemed, had an opinion about it. Most berated Truman. The president was hanged in effigy in California, and one irate citizen telegrammed the Oval Office informing Truman that "(y)our lousy speech over the radio trying to clear yourself of the blundering mistakes you made at the expense of General MacArthur are as stupid and dumb as your daughter's sand paper singing voice," apparently referring to Margaret Truman's singing career.[56] Congressional Republicans clamored to begin impeachment proceedings. The fact was that the president had little choice but to sack MacArthur. The general had repeatedly circumvented orders and had publicly undermined Truman. His belief that the Korean War should be widened not only to complete Korean reunification but to deal a decisive blow to China was incongruous with the administration's foreign-policy goals, however confused they may have appeared. The MacArthur uproar was finally put to rest during the MacArthur Hearings of May–June 1951, at which time Truman and his advisers won the battle against MacArthur and his supporters. But it was a pyrrhic victory—at least as far as Truman's mobilization and stabilization programs were concerned—for although the MacArthur controversy was settled, the conservative Republican/Southern Democratic bloc in Congress continually evoked the image of MacArthur, "just fading away," to stonewall the administration's economic mobilization program.[57]

Besides the obvious constitutional and political conundrum the MacArthur controversy posed, its effect on Truman's foreign policy—and therefore his rearmament program—was potentially monumental. On the foreign-policy front, it is helpful to view the MacArthur crisis as a continuation of the Great Debate. That is, it was a reiteration of the arguments used against the troop deployments to NATO and, by extension, an indictment of the administration's Eurocentric military and foreign policy. The Truman administration managed to blunt this renewed criticism during the MacArthur hearings and in the end subdued the MacArthurites so conclusively that peace talks began in Korea in the summer of 1951 and the rearmament of Europe was stepped up.[58]

56. As quoted in Halford R. Ryan, *Harry S. Truman: Presidential Rhetoric*, 69.

57. Ibid. For good overviews of MacArthur's dismissal and the ensuing uproar, see Rees, *Korea*, 196–229; Max Hastings, *The Korean War*, 165–207; Foot, *The Wrong War*; and Kaufman, *The Korean War*.

58. Walter LaFeber, *America, Russia, and the Cold War, 1945–1984*, 121–24.

The president's opponents were not, however, so easily vanquished on the domestic front. Building upon MacArthur's bold assault on the president's military and foreign policies, they used the crisis to stir to the surface deep doubts, in Congress and across the nation, about the way in which Truman was running the mobilization program and how it was affecting the economic system and the American way of life.[59]

As April 1951 faded into May, and with the labor flap finally settled, mobilization officials had the opportunity to review the rearmament effort to date. Amidst the overall progress of the program, which in some areas was quite impressive, they found ominous signs of economic dislocation and industrial bottlenecks. Spot shortages of raw materials continued to plague the mobilization effort, while a scarcity of railroad freight cars threatened to disrupt the delivery of both civilian and military items. And, of course, the ever-present threat of additional inflationary pressures worried even the most optimistic mobilization planners. Economic dislocations, public and congressional frustration over the mobilization program, and the possibility of Korean peace talks had some administration officials talking about a "stretch-out" of the mobilization program. In fact, in April, several unidentified administration officials began rumors of a slowdown in the rearmament program. Quoted anonymously, they warned that "Soviet Russia had reason to hope it might eventually achieve victory through American bankruptcy."[60] Ironically, this argument was the same one used by those who opposed Truman's policies.

It was clear that the massive rearmament program had begun to have a deleterious effect on specific industries, especially those producing durable goods. Bloated inventories and tight consumer credit hampered efforts to maintain profit margins and to avoid layoffs. "At the present time important segments of our population are sorely worried about the dislocation in our economy that has taken place within recent weeks. Agriculture is genuinely concerned; many businesses are confronted with growing recession, and labor is being laid off in increasing

59. *Business Week* (May 5, 1951): 19–20; *Newsweek* 37 (May 7, 1951): 63. For an excellent study of the pro-MacArthur contingent in Congress, see Ronald J. Caridi, *The Korean War and American Politics: The Republican Party as a Case Study*, 141–75.

60. *Newsweek* 37 (April 9, 1951): 22. At the time, both Secretary of State Dean Acheson and Defense Secretary George C. Marshall rejected the slowdown approach. By the third quarter of 1951, however, the proponents of a stretch-out prevailed—the confusion and dislocations of the mobilization effort throughout much of the winter and spring undoubtedly helped the cause significantly.

numbers."[61] Although something of an overstatement, Truman administration officials were indeed cognizant of growing economic dislocations as a result of the mobilization program. It was a curious fact, however, that many of the economic problems that began to surface in April and May were not a result of defense production per se, but rather they were a result of overspeculation, bloated inventories, and increased credit restrictions. Especially hard hit were the automotive and electronics/home appliance industries, whose inventories were at record levels by the spring of 1951. At the core of the problem lay two interrelated phenomena. First, many industries had been increasing inventories for months in expectation of the future impact of the defense effort. The fact is, however, that the rearmament program never cut into the civilian economy as much as had been predicted in December or January. The administration's decision to stretch the program out in the third quarter of the year made sure of this. So inventories were at record highs, while at the same time consumer spending—and inflation—were slackening. Second, the Federal Reserve Board's decision to tighten consumer credit, mostly through the so-called Regulation W clause, effectively shut out the much of the lower-middle-class consumer from installment buying plans. As a result, a large portion of potential consumers went untapped: sales slowed, inventories continued to mount, and factories in the affected industries were forced to curtail production and lay off workers.[62]

Other problems became more acute in the late spring as well. Considering that defense production schedules were not expected to reach peak levels for another six to twelve months, materials shortages and a scarcity of machine tools began to crop up with ominous consistency. On May 15, chief mobilizer Wilson reported to the president and the National Advisory Board on Mobilization Policy that "the weight of the

61. Memorandum re the Defense Production Act of 1950, May 22, 1951, OF, box 460, file: "OF 101-B, Defense Production Act (1951)," HSTL.
62. *Fortune* 43 (April 1951): 17–19; Letter to Eric Johnston, from the General Finance Corporation, May 16, 1951, RG 296, ESA Committees, box 8, NA; Letter to Eric Johnston from the National Automobile Dealer's Association (NADA), April 17, 1951, RG 296, box 23, NA; Memorandum re the Defense Production Act of 1950, May 22, 1951, OF, box 460, file: "OF 101-B, Defense Production Act (1951)," HSTL.
Regulation W, a mechanism used by the Federal Reserve to restrict consumer credit in order to limit inflationary pressures while simultaneously freeing capital for industrial expansion and defense production, worked in two ways. First, it required larger downpayments for consumer loans and second, it stipulated shorter repayment times. Naturally, lower income groups, and those with accumulated debt, were thus discouraged from installment buying.

take from the civilian economy for defense purposes is now running about $2 billion per month and will be approximately double that by the end of the year; the toughest part of the production program (will) occur during the next twelve-month period."[63] Raw materials shortages, especially of nickel and tungsten, became so severe that Defense Secretary Marshall had to request a withdrawal of these commodities from the nation's strategic stockpile. The shortage of tungsten threatened to curtail the production of high-velocity armor-piercing ammunition, while the nickel shortfall affected everything from tank production to airplane manufacturing.[64]

Making matters worse was the National Production Authority's inefficient Defense Order (DO) rating system for critical materials. It simply was not getting the job done. Its primary deficiency was that it failed to prioritize material needs. Thus, the Defense Department had no means of rating one material over another or of ranking projects. Suppliers would ship materials only in the sequence in which the DO orders arrived, and no follow-up system was in place to ensure that the shipped DO goods were indeed used for defense production. The DO system was slated for replacement by the Controlled Materials Plan (CMP), but administration officials conceded that the CMP would not be ready before July 1951. In the meantime, materials shortages continued to stymie production, while small manufacturers paid the highest price for the DO system's inefficiency.[65]

A shortage of machine tools—the backbone of an industrial economy—also hampered defense production. One of the leading indicators of economic and industrial strength, machine tools represent an essential building block of any production endeavor. Without them, automobiles, tanks, aircraft, and just about any other modern product of the industrial age were impossible to build. The machine tool bottleneck can be attributed to two factors. First, just as war broke out in Korea, machine tool makers were flooded with civilian orders to keep pace with intense consumer buying. So when the administration decided to accelerate the defense effort in December and January, the machine tool industry was operating very near capacity. By the spring,

63. National Advisory Board on Mobilization Policy, Meeting No. 4, May 15, 1951, President's Secretary's File-Subject File Agencies A, box 142, file: "Advisory Board on Mobilization Policy, National," HSTL.

64. Memorandum to John Steelman, May 15, 1951, OF, box 12, file: "1075 (1950–53)," HSTL.

65. "Report on Rearmament," *Fortune* 43 (April 1951): 96–98.

shortages became acute. Second, the enormous capacity of the machine tool industry accumulated during World War II had been allowed to languish. After the war, a glut of surplus tools became available, so production was slowed. Further complicating the problem, the military had disposed of government-owned machine tools at 25 percent of the list price at the end of the war. Many tool factories had been closed or converted to other uses. Thus, when the U.S. decided to mobilize for Korea, machine tool capacity was well below that used to tool up for the Second World War. The Truman administration tried to remedy the problem by exempting most tool makers from price controls, and by issuing so-called pool orders, a tactic used in the previous war to protect producers in the event that the defense program had to be ended abruptly. The administration also tried to help tool makers by giving them special government financing considerations. Even with these incentives, the machine tool dilemma continued for many more months.[66]

By May 1951, the Korean mobilization had become indistinguishable from the larger Cold War rearmament. And although the strategic situation in Korea appeared stable, the larger context of the mobilization program remained uncertain. Material and machine tool shortages, economic dislocations, congressional and public frustration with the rearmament program, and plummeting presidential approval ratings all led administration officials to conclude that the mobilization program should be stretched out and that the year of maximum danger—1954—be readjusted to 1956 and perhaps 1957. By the end of the year, even rearmament hardliners like Dean Acheson and George Marshall conceded to the readjustment. This decision did not alter the administration's goals, only its strategy. The unique "limited war, indefinite duration" scenario kept mobilization officials in a constant state of adjustment. The result, at least in the public's mind, was a confusing on-again, off-again mobilization program.

The interplay of domestic and foreign/military developments, however, made it next to impossible for Truman to avoid such a course. What had developed was a bonafide crisis management mentality

66. Letter and Report to Charles Wilson on Machine Tools, May 17, 1951, RG 277, Records of the National Production Authority, box 14, file: "Correspondence with Government Agencies," NA; *Fortune* 43 (April 1951): 204. For an overview of the problems of the machine tool industry during World War II see Novick, *Wartime Production Controls,* 42, 44, 271; and Industrial College of the Armed Forces, *Emergency Management of the National Economy: Production,* vol. 13.

that transcended the Korean War and became a permanent fixture of the Cold War. The intricacies of balancing military and national security imperatives with the needs of an American-style democratic free-market system were indeed daunting. The greatest fear was the development of a garrison state, a state in which democratic ideals, normal free-market mechanisms, and the supremacy of civilian control would be subjugated by national security imperatives and the military establishment. This the Truman administration tried valiantly to avoid. Confusion and frustration were often the results, but in the minds of policymakers, they were a small price to pay to stave off the creation of an American Sparta.

As the administration agonized over the size and tempo of the mobilization program, Congress fretted over the effects of the program on small business. The problems that the rearmament effort posed for small business had been the repeated subject of congressional inquiries since the outbreak of war the previous June. These inquiries became more frequent—and more divisive—as the mobilization program was accelerated earlier in the year. The subject of small business participation in the defense effort was carefully monitored by the Joint Committee on Defense Production, Congress's official oversight committee for the mobilization program. What the committee discovered during its investigations, while not unexpected, was troubling: small businesses tended to be excluded from the bulk of the defense effort and were often the last ones to receive government assistance. This despite the fact that the Defense Production Act of 1950 specifically stipulated that small businesses be given equal consideration, whenever possible, in defense contract letting and government assistance.

The failure to include more small businesses in defense planning was more a consequence of the structural imperatives of the procurement process, which tended to be dominated by the Department of Defense, the Munitions Board, and big business, than it was by any intentional action by the Truman administration. The president, a one-time Kansas City haberdasher, had always been sympathetic to the needs of small business. Even the powerful former GE president and ODM chief Charles Wilson considered himself a small businessman at heart, claiming that "they [small businessmen] are the backbone of the nation."[67] To blunt earlier congressional criticism of the defense effort vis à vis small

67. U.S. Congress, Joint Committee on Defense Production, *Defense Production Act Report No. 2*, 82nd. Cong., 1st sess., February 8, 1951, 58.

business, the Defense Production Administration (DPA), under the direction of William H. Harrison, had installed a deputy administrator for small business in February.[68] The Office of Small Business failed to stem the tide of complaints from small business, however. In April 1951, accusations that the DPA had been captured by the interests of big business made it all the way to Capitol Hill. The Joint Committee on Defense Production took the complaints very seriously. The committee relentlessly grilled DPA chief Harrison on government lending policies for industrial expansion and criticized the administration's tardiness in processing accelerated tax-amortization certificates for small business concerns. The committee hearings in April drew to a close with a harangue by Burnet R. Maybank (D-SC), who concluded simply that "the defense effort is strangling America's small manufacturers."[69] Statistics prove otherwise, however. Small business in fact did quite well during the Korean era, despite being largely excluded from the defense effort. Actually, there was more to the small business issue than the state of small business.[70]

In May 1951, the Senate and House Select Committees on Small Business held joint hearings to formally investigate the participation of small business in military procurement. The chairman, John D. Sparkman (D-AL), opened the hearings by asserting that "the impact of the Government's procurement policies upon the Nation's small-business economy has been intensified many times during the present mobilization period . . . (small) businessmen's only hope of survival lies in procuring contracts in the defense effort."[71] Again, the rhetoric did not match reality. There was no shortage of work for small manufacturers, and despite congressional assertions to the contrary, very few small businesses were adversely affected by materials shortages. Congressional rhetoric was aimed directly at the Truman administration's mobilization policy, and Congress knew that one of the most effective ways to rally public support against the administration's policies was

---

68. Ibid., 56.

69. U.S. Congress, Joint Committee on Defense Production, *Defense Production Act Report No. 8*, 82nd. Cong., 1st sess., April 12, 1951, 432.

70. Harold G. Vatter, "The Position of Small Business in the Structure of American Manufacturing," in Stuart Bruchey, ed. *Small Business in American Life;* Mansel G. Blackford, *A History of Small Business in America,* 75; *Business Week* (December 29, 1951): 80–81; *Business Week* (March 8, 1952): 64–66.

71. U.S. Congress, *Joint Hearings before the Select Committee on Small Business United States Senate and Select Committee on Small Business House of Representatives on Participation of Small Business in Military Procurement,* 82nd Cong., 1st sess., May 7, 8, 14, 15, and 16, 1951, 3.

to claim the imminent extinction of small business. This tactic, which dated all the way back to the founding of the republic and the ensuing battle between Hamiltonians and Jeffersonians, struck a sympathetic nerve with an already anxious public. Not coincidentally, the small business hearings ended just as Congress was poised to begin hearings on the extension of the Defense Production Act. At issue then was not the state of small business, but rather the administration's mobilization program and the fears that it would lead the nation inexorably toward monopolistic totalitarianism—a mirror image of the enemy the country sought to subdue.

In this atmosphere of uncertainty, confusion, and political bombast Congress began debating the extension of the Defense Production Act. The battle lines were drawn. Sensing public dissatisfaction and impatience with the rearmament effort, Truman asked Congress for tighter controls and fewer loopholes in the Defense Production Act of 1951. Congress, on the other hand, was leaning toward a relaxation of controls. It was now clear that once the immediacy of the Korean crisis had passed, and the American-led UN forces had stabilized the strategic situation on the peninsula, Congress was prepared to dilute the mobilization effort through legislation. What the Truman administration had failed to do in the months since the Chinese intervention was to convey to the public its intentions of embarking upon a long-term rearmament program, in which the Korean War played only a relatively minor role. The administration watched helplessly as the mobilization program—in the minds of the public—was tied directly to the Korean theater and the political vicissitudes it engendered. Thus, General Eisenhower's January admonitions about the rearmament effort went largely unheeded, and the mobilization program became the victim of political crises such as the Great Debate, the labor stalemate, and the MacArthur controversy. Truman's opponents used these episodes to wage a war against his domestic and foreign policies and, as result, the entire mobilization program suffered.

Despite the changes in mobilization policies that took place in the summer of 1951, the United States achieved unparalleled levels of production (military and civilian). By all accounts, the rearmament effort was a success in terms of output and national security imperatives. Furthermore, the Truman administration had organized and structured an effective mobilization program in less than one year. By contrast, the Roosevelt administration had taken more than two years to effectively mobilize for World War II. It was perhaps the novelty of the Cold War—at which the mobilization program was principally aimed—combined with the nation's remembrances of the last war, which was a clear-cut hot war, that led many to conclude at the time that the Korean mobilization was less than successful. Unlike World War II, the fruits of the Korean mobilization were not so easily plucked. No smashing battlefield victories could be used as propaganda. There were no Hitlers, no Mussolinis, no Tojos. The Cold War was one of ideological foes to be fought through "limited" proxy wars along the perimeters of America's strategic field of vision. Nobody knew how long it would last. The nation seemed to realize, deep in its gut, that the Korean mobilization was really the Cold War mobilization—one that could last for decades. The fears of what this constant state of readiness might do to the American system were largely suppressed. But when they did periodically surface, as they did during the Korean War, Americans, like tongue-tied teenagers on their first date, could not directly express their concerns. Instead, they nibbled at the corners of the mobilization program without getting to the heart of the matter: the massive, ongoing rearmament effort was fundamentally reordering American economic, political, military, and social constructs.

Amidst all of this angst and uncertainty, however, one thing remained constant. That is, the Truman administration remained committed to fulfilling the requirements of the mobilization effort through a program of carefully balanced economic growth. By increasing the nation's productive capacity and boosting Americans' incomes, administration officials hoped to create an enlarged economic base that could absorb increased defense expenditures and protect the American standard of living. Clearly, expanding production and rising incomes were to be the inoculation against the dreaded viruses of excessive government control and economic regimentation.

IV

The Politics of Rearmament

Guns or Butter or Guns and Butter?
June–December 1951

We are fighting for freedom which means our free way of life. It will serve us little good if in the fighting for freedom we become regimented. . . . Therefore, we shouldn't go too fast in our rearmament as to cripple our economy. We are like a boa constrictor swallowing a donkey.

Dwight D. Eisenhower, Supreme Allied Commander, NATO, October 2, 1951.[1]

From here on out, arms output should come ahead of absolutely everything, until the minimum goals of military strength are in being. We must have the courage to put guns ahead of butter.

Senator Lyndon B. Johnson, November 24, 1951.[2]

If the first six months of 1951 witnessed the Herculean task of organizing and tooling up the great American production machine, the last six months of the year saw a general slackening of that effort as the military situation in Korea stabilized and the effects of the overall mobilization program began to have deleterious effects on the economy. In

1. General Eisenhower Interview (with Eric Johnston, ESA Administrator), October 2, 1951, 10:00 A.M., RG 296, Records of Reports and Secretariat of the Economic Stabilization Agency, box 2, file: "Johnston's Statements on European Trip," NA.
2. As quoted in *Business Week* (December 1, 1951): 19. At the time, Johnson was speaking in his official capacity as chairman of the Preparedness Subcommittee of the Senate Armed Services Committee.

light of that, mobilization planners began a fundamental reassessment of rearmament goals. And as the quotations above illustrate, varying opinions on the depth and breadth of America's mobilization program came to the fore. What underlay them all—whether they represented European concerns or congressional angst—was that the rearmament effort was not operating as smoothly or as painlessly as first hoped. By December, the vast majority of Americans, including many of those ensconced in the capital's halls of power, had come to realize that the mobilization program faced some serious problems. They also realized that the time had arrived to reassess the pace and prioritization of mobilization. Some administration officials were caught off guard by these sentiments, however, and thus faced the nearly impossible task of pushing ahead with mobilization in the face of Korean armistice talks, economic dislocations, diluted control mechanisms, labor strikes, and allied fears that rearmament was leading to economic catastrophe.

The last six months of 1951 posed many problems for mobilization planners. Economic dislocations began sprouting up with troublesome regularity. Raw materials shortages shut down civilian production lines, creating pockets of acute unemployment despite record national employment figures. Especially hard hit were Detroit auto workers. In July the administration invoked the Controlled Materials Plans (CMP), which was designed to lessen the impact of materials shortages. Instead, the materials crisis worsened. By the fourth quarter, mobilization planners conceded that the CMP was not working. In response, the Plan was extended to cover nearly all consumers of raw materials—civilian and military alike. Industrial strikes increased at an alarming rate toward the end of the year, and rearing its ugly head in December was the impending steel crisis. Greatly complicating these developments was the renewed Defense Production Act, which hampered the administration's ability to affect economic stabilization. And Congress's failure to raise enough taxes to keep rearmament on a pay-as-you-go basis hamstrung mobilization planners and forced the government into more deficit spending.

Economic hardship was no stranger to Europe, either. The economies of Western Europe strained under the rearmament program, as inflation soared and threatened to undo the successes of the Marshall Plan. The European balance of payments, which had shrunk considerably since the outbreak of the Korean War, took a precipitous turn for the worse. And continued raw materials shortages threatened to derail industrial production. European leaders warned the Truman administration of impending economic and political chaos unless the mobilization effort was stretched out.

The strains placed upon the economies of the West weighed heavily upon administration officials, but even more troubling was the actual performance of the rearmament program. While statistics show a quantum leap in total productive output between June 1950 and December 1951, overall military production schedules continued to lag. Although the troops in Korea in general were receiving adequate supplies, the larger Cold War mobilization program lagged considerably behind schedule. Mobilization planners knew that they faced a tough choice: accelerate military procurement to close the gap, thus further straining the economy, or reassess the entire program and prioritize defense production strictly according to need. They chose the latter, but not very enthusiastically.

As it turned out, 1951 was both the apex and denouement of the Korean mobilization. It was the year that witnessed the greatest activity in both building and partially dismantling the rearmament apparatus. The scale-down began in July with the gutting of the Defense Production Act. From that point forward, a whole host of economic and political contingencies combined to slow down the ongoing mobilization effort. Although the program continued, the zeal and pace of it never again reached the heights set in the first half of the year.

The following pages trace the slow, downward trajectory of the Korean mobilization effort while at the same time revealing the upward thrust of long-term, Cold War preparedness. In them can be seen the germination of intractable Cold War—and post–Cold War—problems: chronic budget deficits; defense-dependent industrial sectors; ballooning federal bureaucracies; and intra-allied tensions.

Always lurking behind public and congressional concerns with mobilization was the dread of an American Sparta and the attendant governmental Hydra such a state might spawn. Nothing better exemplified these fears than the debates over the 1951 Defense Production Act and Revenue Acts. The bitter feuding over control legislation and the agonizingly slow deliberations surrounding the tax bill were ideologically intertwined. At stake in the extension of the Defense Production Act was the president's authority to stabilize the economy through continued direct controls. Many congressmen and senators believed that economic controls were no longer warranted, arguing that their continuation would lead to "socialism," excessive economic regimentation, and even dictatorship. Foes of the 1951 tax package used many of the same arguments. They believed that increased taxes would drain individual initiative, stymie entrepreneurial spirit, and open the way for a centralized, regimented state. Despite these ongoing disagreements over controls and taxes, however, there was one point upon which all agreed: inflation had to be controlled. In short, discord ensued not over *whether* inflation should be controlled, but rather *how* it should be controlled.

Congress began hearings on the Defense Production Act (DPA) of 1951 in May, and the Truman administration wasted no time in lobbying Congress for tighter controls. Arguing that "the great scarcities of materials and hence the greatest need for controlling the flow and use of these materials are yet to come," chief mobilizer Charles E. Wilson urged Congress to extend the Defense Production Act without delay and without disabling its control mechanisms. Echoing those sentiments, Edwin T. Gibson, acting administrator of the Defense Production Administration, pointed out that "defense production has barely begun."[3] The administration's economic stabilizers called for an all-out war against inflation and urged Congress to extend and strengthen the Act. Citing inflation as the nation's greatest domestic threat, Economic Stabilization Agency (ESA) director Eric Johnston asked the Senate Banking and Currency Committee, charged with writing the legislation, to adopt his six-point anti-inflation program. It included a pay-as-you-go tax program; restrictive consumer credit policies; increased savings rates; curtailment of waste by the private and public sectors; equitable division of scarce materials between the civilian and defense sectors; and, most importantly, "the strengthening of direct controls on prices, wages, rents, and credit." Michael DiSalle, director of the Office of Price Stabilization (OPS), added that the extension of the bill was absolutely vital to the success of the anti-inflation program.[4]

3. U.S. Congress, Senate, Committee on Banking and Currency, *A Bill to Amend the Defense Production Act of 1950, Defense Production Act Amendments of 1951: Hearings,* 82d. Cong., 1st sess., 1951, part 1, 18–19 (for Wilson's quotation), 179–91 (for Gibson's testimony). Wilson also testified before the House Banking and Currency Committee. His testimony there was the same as that before the Senate committee, *Congressional Quarterly Almanac* 82d. Cong., 1st sess., 1951, vol. 7, 446. For Gibson's House committee testimony, see ibid., 446.

4. U.S. Congress, Senate, Committee on Banking and Currency, *A Bill to Amend the Defense Production Act of 1950,* 82d. Cong., 1st sess., 1951, part 1, 516–18. See also Summary of ESA Executive Staff Meeting No. 2, May 2, 1951, RG 296, Economic Stabilization Agency, box 23, NA. For DiSalle's complete statement, see U.S. Congress, Senate, Committee on Banking and Currency, *A Bill to Amend the Defense Production Act of 1950,* 82d. Cong., 1st sess., 1951, part 1, 627–42.

During the hearings, it became clear that the Truman administration faced an uphill battle in its efforts to strengthen economic and industrial control legislation; indeed, the administration's adversaries in this regard were potent—and legion. The nation's trade and business organizations simply did not agree with administration officials' assessments or prescriptions. Believing that inflation should be checked by *indirect* controls such as tighter credit policies, higher individual taxes, and curtailment of "nonessential" government spending, William H. Ruffin, President of the National Association of Manufacturers (NAM), recommended that wage and price controls be ended. Ruffin went on to assert that the DPA of 1951 would confer to the president "powers comparable to those exercised by foreign dictators . . . lead(ing) to the destruction of our American economic system."[5] NAM officials also used the opportunity to take aim at the Wage Stabilization Board's recently acquired authority to adjudicate labor disputes. The Association had gone on record as opposing this function when it was conferred upon the new and enlarged WSB in April. Arguing that organized labor had been given an unfair advantage over management, Ira Mosher, chairman of the NAM's Industrial Mobilization Committee, asked that the wage board be disbanded and that labor disputes be handled exclusively through the Taft-Hartley Act.[6] The United States Chamber of Commerce (USCC) supported the NAM's position on the abandonment of the dispute settlement function but stopped short of advocating the total dismemberment of the WSB.[7] By attacking the wage board, organized business interests hit the stabilization program at one of its weakest points. Knowing that public and congressional acceptance of the new WSB was shaky at best, business officials used the example of the wage board to undermine the entire stabilization effort.[8]

5. U.S. Congress, Senate, Committee on Banking and Currency, *A Bill to Amend the Defense Production Act of 1950, Defense Production Act Amendments of 1951: Hearings*, 82d. Cong., 1st sess., 1951, part 2, 1190. For complete statement, see ibid., 1157–1200.

6. U.S. Congress, Senate, Committee on Banking and Currency, *A Bill to Amend the Defense Production Act of 1950, Defense Production Act Amendments of 1951: Hearings*, 82d. Cong., 1st sess., 1951, part 2, 1219–1273.

7. Telegram to Eric Johnston, April 17, 1951, RG 296, Economic Stabilization Agency, box 4, file, "Auto. Equipment Boards," NA.

8. Memorandum to Messrs. Steelman, Stowe, May 25, 1951, Papers of Harold L. Enarson, box 4, file: "Memoranda September 1950–May 1951," HSTL. Business interests were doggedly determined to torpedo the WSB's dispute settlement functions. For other anti-WSB sentiment and testimony, see U.S. Congress, House of Representatives, Subcommittee of the Committee on Education and Labor, *Disputes Functions of Wage Stabilization Board: Hearings*, 82d. Cong., 1st sess., 1951; and U.S. Congress, Senate,

As the DPA hearings progressed, opposition to extending control legislation mounted. The United States Chamber of Commerce sharply criticized the administration's wage and price controls and urged instead a program of indirect controls and the curtailment of nonessential government programs. The National Automobile Dealers' Association railed against the continuation of consumer credit restrictions, claiming that they were choking off automobile purchases and were creating dangerously bloated inventories. And the American Retail Federation simply termed price controls "unworkable and ineffective."[9]

Organized labor, which generally supported the administration's position on controls, used the hearings to draw a sharp line between itself and most business interests, particularly those of the NAM and USCC. Testifying before the Senate Banking and Currency Committee, James B. Carey, secretary-treasurer of the Congress of Industrial Organizations (CIO), accused business interests of trying to "wreck our defense program."[10] The United Labor Policy Committee (ULPC) warned that "a combination of Dixiecrats and reactionary Republicans already have forced through a bill that will increase the cost of living a dollar a day for each American family . . . Congress is succumbing to pressure from special interest lobbies with the excuse that the American people 'just don't care.' "[11] United Auto Workers (UAW) president Walter Reuther blasted big business, claiming that it was promoting "business as usual."[12]

Although industry and labor groups alike agreed that inflation had to be controlled, they parted company on how best to achieve that goal. Generally, industry leaders shied away from the continuation of direct

Subcommittee on Labor and Labor-Management Relations of the Committee on Labor and Public Welfare, *Wage Stabilization and Disputes Program: Hearings,* 82d. Cong., 1st sess., 1951, especially 1–10, 40, 88, 118–19, 121–32.

9. U.S. Congress, Senate, Committee on Banking and Currency, *A Bill to Amend the Defense Production Act of 1950, Defense Production Act Amendments of 1951: Hearings,* 82d. Cong., 1st sess., 1951, part 3, 2056–66, 2076–2084, 2103–2109; Letter to John R. Steelman, May 25, 1951, OF, box 460, file: "OF 101-B, DPA (1951)," HSTL; Memorandum to Dr. Steelman, Harold L. Enarson, Papers of Charles S. Murphy, box 13, file: "Steelman, Dr. John R.," HSTL.

10. U.S. Congress, Senate, Committee on Banking and Currency, *A Bill to Amend the Defense Production Act of 1950, Defense Production Act Amendments of 1951: Hearings,* 82d. Cong., 1st sess., 1951, part 2, 1939–1941.

11. Statement by United Labor Policy Committee, July 9, 1951, RG 296, Economic Stabilization Agency Reports and Secretariat, box 14, file: "Defense Committees, ESA," NA.

12. U.S. Congress, Senate, Committee on Banking and Currency, *A Bill to Amend the Defense Production Act of 1950, Defense Production Act Amendments of 1951: Hearings,* 82d. Cong., 1st sess., 1951, part 3, 2177.

controls, asserting that they would lead to a distorted, regimented economy. Instead, they preferred tax policies designed to drain off excess income and consumer spending, fiscal and monetary policies aimed at curbing demand, and the curtailment of government-funded social programs. The arch-conservative NAM, which rarely ever encountered a social welfare program it liked, saw in the Korean mobilization a perfect opportunity to roll back New Deal era programs and to derail new ones under Harry Truman's Fair Deal. Labor officials, while advocating some of the same inflation-fighting approaches, nonetheless argued that the continuation of direct controls was necessary to distribute more equitably the burdens and sacrifices of mobilization. In fact, the unions wanted even tougher price controls than those in force at the time because they believed that aggregate wages had not kept pace with inflation. They also called for the elimination of parity-based food price ceilings. But Labor's pro-control stance was decidedly in the minority. As the hearings came to a conclusion in early June, an impressive array of anti-control groups had captured the attention of the public as well that of Congress.[13]

By the time the Senate began floor action on the Defense Production Act in late June, the die had been cast for a watered down control bill. In April, the president had asked Congress for tighter inflation controls and greater regulatory authority over the economy. Among other things, he called for more stringent credit restrictions, stronger price-control sanctions against violators, control over commercial and residential rents, and a single-season parity adjustment on food products. But with inflation easing, the prospect of a Korean armistice, and a spectacular show of force by various anti-control groups, Congress was reticent to pass a stronger law than existed at the time. Instead, it busied itself with writing a substantially weaker one.[14]

The battle over controls in the summer of 1951 was a complete reversal of the one that took place a year earlier. Now it was Truman who was lobbying for stiffer controls while Congress demurred. Lobbying pressures and an improving economic and military situation explain

13. *Congressional Quarterly Almanac* 82d. Cong., 1st sess., 1951, vol. 7 (Washington, 1951), 455. See also Kim McQuaid, *Uneasy Partners: Big Business in American Politics, 1945–1990*, 60–61, which synopsizes the NAM's and the USCC's attitudes toward the Korean mobilization.

14. President's Special Message to the Congress Recommending Extension and Broadening of the Defense Production Act, April 26, 1951, *Public Papers of the President, Harry S. Truman, 1951*, 247–48. See also Alonzo L. Hamby, "The Vital Center, the Fair Deal, and the Quest for a Liberal Political Economy," 653–78.

only part of this reversal, however. Debates surrounding the DPA of 1951 not only involved the continuation of direct controls but also raised the specter of a permanently mobilized and militarized society. Thus, the congressional floor debates devolved into a highly partisan, ideological melee that pitted the Truman administration and its supporters against the conservative Republican-Southern Democratic bloc—led by Robert A. Taft (R-OH), Homer Capehart (R-IN), Homer Ferguson (R-MI), and Burnet Maybank (D-SC) in the Senate, and Jesse P. Wolcott (R-MI), Clifford P. Hope (R-KS), and Wingate Lucas (D-TX), in the House. Not coincidentally, this was the same basic coalition that had precipitated the Great Debate and had exacerbated the enmity over MacArthur's dismissal earlier that year.[15]

The opponents of a stronger control bill characteristically attacked the administration's prior handling of economic controls. They argued that if Truman had invoked controls from the very beginning, inflation would have been kept at bay, making tighter ongoing controls unnecessary. Senator Maybank, ever the curmudgeon, accused the Truman administration of deliberately holding off on the imposition of controls because it wanted wages and prices to increase in order to produce higher taxes. In general, the conservative Republicans and Southern Democrats vehemently opposed price rollbacks, arguing that they caused undue harm to business and interfered with free-market mechanisms. Raising the specter of a garrison state, Senator Everett Dirksen (R-IL) rhetorically observed, "one can lean out of a window too far just once, and then he is going to hit the ground. A nation can lean out too far . . . and then the question is, do you finally get your freedom back?" Representative William Buffet (R-NE) likened Truman's "inflationary" policies to those of Germany in the 1920s and insisted that the "OPS . . . fits the pattern by which America is being marched toward socialism and totalitarianism."[16] Bombast notwithstanding, it was clear

15. Maeva Marcus, *Truman and the Steel Seizure Case: The Limits of Presidential Power,* 27–29; Mobilization Advisory Board Meeting, May 15, 1951, President's Secretary's Files (PSF), box 96, file: "Presidential Appointments File, Daily Sheets 1951-May," HSTL; Memorandum for the President, July 5, 1951, PSF, box 96, file: "Presidential Appointments File, Daily Sheets 1951-July," HSTL.

For a good overview of the anti-control, conservative Republican-Southern Democratic coalition in Congress, see James T. Patterson, *Mr. Republican: A Biography of Robert A. Taft,* esp. 443–44, 454, 493, 599–600; Ronald J. Caridi, *The Korean War and American Politics,* esp. 67–69, 138; and Samuel P. Huntington, "Conservatism as an Ideology," 454–73.

16. *Congressional Record,* 82d. Cong., 1st sess., 1951, 97, pt. 5: 7033–34 (for Dirksen quotation see p. 7123); *Congressional Record,* pt. 6: 7727–7729 (for Buffet quotations).

that many congressional conservatives feared the continuation of direct controls. They simply no longer saw any need for them with the slackening of inflation and peace talks in Korea.[17]

As Congress debated the controls issue on the floor, the Truman administration launched an aggressive public relations blitz to build public and congressional support for its policies. On June 19, only six days prior to the scheduled floor debates in the Senate, the president's National Advisory Board on Mobilization Policy released a statement stressing the importance of maintaining and strengthening the stabilization program. The board's statements convinced few people, however. So the White House intensified its efforts, calling upon the Association of National Advertisers and the Advertising Council to help sell its programs. Both organizations suggested using high-profile mobilization officials like Charles Wilson, Eric Johnston, and Michael DiSalle as the first line of fire in the public relations salvo. And that is exactly what administration officials did. Wilson, Johnston, and DiSalle took to the airwaves in a well-orchestrated attempt to swing public opinion toward the extension and strengthening of control legislation. Eric Johnston appeared on television's "Meet the Press," theatrically demonstrating the need for price rollbacks by bringing a rifle, a mop, and combat boots to show that his anti-inflation program meant business. He also appeared on television and radio with such celebrities as Arthur Godfrey and Walter Winchell. In a July 6 cabinet meeting, the president himself suggested that ODM chief Wilson take to the TV and radio airwaves to help sell the administration's stabilization policies, which he did three days later. Former Toledo mayor and OPS director DiSalle was the administration's grass roots contact, crisscrossing the Midwest and pressing the flesh in a last-ditch effort to stir up support. But the White House's efforts were largely in vain. Few minds were changed in Congress, and the public never rallied behind the program. As the final vote on controls loomed in the last part of July, administration officials sensed the futility of their position.[18]

17. The congressional floor debates are voluminous, but the ideological imperatives surrounding the extension of the Defense Production Act make themselves readily apparent. For anti-control sentiments and debate, see *Congressional Record,* 82d. Cong., 1st sess., 1951, 97, pt. 5: 6809–13, 7038–9, 7119–22, 7125, 7201; *Congressional Record,* 82d. Cong., 1st sess., 1951, 97, pt. 6: 7237, 7379, 7660–62, 7669, 7678, 7736, 7743–44. See also *Congressional Quarterly Almanac* 82d. Cong., 1st sess., 1951, vol. 7, 444–46, 448–54.

18. National Advisory Board on Mobilization Policy, Meeting No. 5, June 5, 1951, Papers of Harry S. Truman, White House Central Files, Confidential Files, box 26, file: "National Advisory Board on Mobilization Policy 1951–52," HSTL; National Advisory

Although it was ultimately unsuccessful, the Truman administration's public relations campaign was noteworthy for two reasons. It demonstrated the importance mobilization officials attached to the extension of the Defense Production Act. They knew that the failure to secure an effective control bill might jeopardize the entire mobilization set up, not to mention Harry Truman's already sagging popularity. Furthermore, as a result of the armistice talks that began in June, rumors of a let down in the rearmament program had begun to spread—especially among industry leaders. A strengthened mobilization act would put an end to the rumors and would signal to the nation that Truman was serious in his efforts to sustain the long-term mobilization process, regardless of the developments in Korea.[19] Second, the media blitz indicated that the White House understood just how powerful the new medium of television could be in shaping public opinion and how important corporate sponsors and advertising organizations could be to the political process. White House officials were keenly aware of the power and influence wielded by organizations like the Advertising Council and repeatedly sought their advice in shaping public opinion. Thus, the public-private linkages sought by government policymakers extended far beyond industrialists and financiers.[20]

Board on Mobilization Policy, Meeting #6, June 19, 1951, President's Secretary's Files, Subject File, Agencies A, box 142, HSTL; Letter to John Steelman plus attachments, June 21, 1951, OF, box 1731, file: "2855 February 1951–1953," HSTL; Letter to the President plus attachments, July 3, 1951, President's Secretary's Files, box 144, file: "Economic Stabilization Administration, Eric Johnston, Administrator," HSTL; Cabinet Meeting, July 6, 1951, Papers of Matthew J. Connelly, box 2, file: "Notes on Cabinet Meetings, 1951, 2 January–31 December," HSTL; *Congressional Quarterly Almanac* 82d. Cong., 1st sess., 1951, vol. 7, 460.

19. Cabinet Meeting, Monday, June 11, 1951, Papers of Matthew J. Connelly, box 2, file: "Notes on Cabinet Meetings, 1951, 2 January–31 December 1951," HSTL; National Advisory Board on Mobilization Policy, Meeting No. 8, July 24, 1951, Papers of Harry S. Truman, White House Central Files, Confidential Files, box 26, file: "National Advisory Board on Mobilization Policy, 1951–52," HSTL; "Plant Expansion: Nobody's Backing Out," *Business Week* (July 14, 1951): 21–22; "Peace . . . and the Problems of Peace," *Newsweek* 38 (July 16, 1951): 19–21.

20. Recent literature has demonstrated that the Truman administration was surprisingly adept at using the new technology of television. The State Department especially used television to help sell administration policies. State Department and White House officials like presidential assistant John R. Steelman carefully nurtured ties with the news media, particularly with the nascent television news media. For a good overview of this phenomenon, see William S. Soloman and Robert McChesney, *Ruthless Criticism: New Perspectives in U.S. Communications History*, esp. 294–97. See also Louis Galambos and Joseph Pratt, *The Rise of the Corporate Commonwealth: U.S. Business and Public Policy in the Twentieth Century* for a recent analysis of the postwar trend toward business-government cooperation and the intersects of public-private policymaking in the 1950s.

Administration officials were not happy with the renewed Defense Production Act. Lambasting the new law as he signed it on July 31, 1951, Truman asserted that it would "push prices up" and "threaten the stability of our economy." He also put Congress on notice that he intended to seek amendments and improvements to the law as quickly as possible.[21] The president made it clear that it was the anti-inflation portion of the law that rankled him most, because the emergency powers dealing with production and material controls were actually strengthened to some extent. So the omnibus nature of the bill forced Truman to capitulate. Administration officials conceded that had the bill pertained to anti-inflation controls alone, the president would have vetoed it. But a veto of the omnibus defense act would have brought the mobilization program to a virtual halt.[22]

From the mobilization planners' standpoint, the most egregious component of the new DPA was the Capehart Amendment, which seriously impeded the execution of price controls. The Capehart Amendment, named after its sponsor, Senator Homer Capehart (R-IN), was described by the ESA as "a bulldozer crashing aimlessly through present pricing formulas."[23] The Capehart pricing formula authorized price increases to compensate businesses for all additional costs incurred between June 1950 and July 26, 1951. Essentially, the Capehart amendment unraveled the previous six month's efforts to contain price increases. The new mandate resulted not only in across-the-board price increases, but also in a substantial increase in the workload of the already burdened Office of Price Stabilization. Ironically too, the new labyrinthine pricing formulas resulted in a significant increase in the number of OPS employees. Surely, the creation of an even larger bureaucratic behemoth was the last thing the proponents of the Capehart Amendment had envisioned.[24]

---

21. Statement by the President upon Signing the Defense Production Act Amendments, July 31, 1951, *Public Papers of the President, 1951,* 435.

22. *Congressional Quarterly Almanac,* vol. 7–1951, 454–55; Statement on the Defense Production Act Amendments of 1951 from the General Counsel, ESA, July 30, 1951, OF, box 460, file: "OF 101-B, Defense Production Act (1951)," HSTL; Letter to Frederick J. Lawton (BOB), from Michael V. DiSalle (OPS), plus attachments, July 30, 1951, OF, box 460, file: "OF 101-B, Defense Production Act (1951)," HSTL.

23. Statement on the Defense Production Act Amendments of 1951, from the General Counsel, ESA, July 30, 1951, OF, box 460, file: "OF 101-B, Defense Production Act (1951)," HSTL.

24. *Congressional Record,* 97 pt. 7: 9148; Memo to Eric Johnston from DiSalle (OPS), August 1, 1951, RG 295, Records of the Office of Price Stabilization, Central Files, box 696, file: "ESA Administrator—Memos to and From," NA.

The administration was also troubled with two other amendments to the Defense Production Act: the Herlong Amendment, which required that distributors' price ceilings be maintained at a level high enough to preserve "reasonable" percentage margins, and the Butler-Hope Amendment, which repealed the government's authority to set slaughtering quotas.[25] These amendments, combined with the devastating Capehart Amendment, acted like a huge jack, ratcheting the entire price and wage structure to new heights. Despite vehement protests against the new defense act by the powerful United Labor Policy Committee, which labeled it "a disgraceful surrender to those who stand to benefit from inflation," and a strong push by the administration to have the objectionable amendments repealed or altered, the 1951 Defense Production Act stayed on the books as originally passed.[26] Lulled by the slackening inflation rate, buoyed by armistice talks in Korea, swayed by the lobbying interests of business groups, and spooked by the talk of a garrison state, Congress had no interest and no incentive to continue tough economic controls. As Senator Irving Ives (D-NY) observed, "politics and controls do not mix well—this the administration has taken almost one year to discover."[27]

In spite of these setbacks, administration officials nonetheless found innovative ways in which to work within the confines of the new law. Mobilization planners intensified the trend toward decentralization and came to rely more and more upon industrial and consumer advisory committees at the local, regional, and federal levels. In fact, the number of industrial advisory committees increased eight-fold from December 1950 to January 1952. Mobilization planners, especially those in the economic stabilization agencies, modeled their efforts after the highly successful industry committees of the National Production Authority (NPA), which were established within the Department of

25. National Advisory Board on Mobilization Policy, Meeting No. 10, August 21, 1951, President's Secretary's Files-Subject File, Agencies A, box 142, file: "Advisory Board on Mobilization Policy, National," HSTL.

26. Quotation from United Labor Policy Committee, Statement on Defense Production Act Amendments, July 30, 1951, OF, box 460, file: "OF 101-B, DPA, S. 1717, Misc. Con.," HSTL. For the Truman administration's attempts to overturn the Capehart, Herlong, and Butler-Hope amendments, see Message to the Congress of the United States from the President, August 23, 1951, President's Secretary's Files, Subject File, Agencies D-F, box 144, file: "Defense Production Act," HSTL, and the *Congressional Quarterly Almanac*, vol. 7, 1951, 462–64.

27. As quoted in Marcus, *Truman and Steel*, 29.

Commerce soon after the outbreak of war in June 1950. The OPS and WSB saw the associative-corporative approach of the NPA as the answer to their problems under the new and cumbersome DPA pricing regulations. Instead of hiring thousands of more employees to administer and enforce the new regulations, the OPS turned toward organized consumer groups at the community and regional level to help establish and enforce price controls. By October 1951, for example, the OPS had in place a highly developed and interlocking system of advisory committees that included industry groups at every level, volunteer citizens' and consumer committees at the local level, and a national Consumer Committee comprising representatives from the local and regional level.[28]

It is interesting to note that women dominated a sizable number of mobilization advisory committees. As the primary purchaser of most food and household products at the time, women occupied many of the spots on the OPS Consumer Committees—at all levels. The committees mostly drew their membership from the ranks of women's organizations like the Y.W.C.A., the League of Women Voters, and the Junior League. But consumer committees were not the only outlet for women. They served important roles in other advisory committees too, especially those of the departments of Defense, State, Labor, and the Defense Manpower Administration.[29]

In September 1951, the Wage Stabilization Board established fourteen tripartite regional boards "to enable (it) to get on top of the case load." Upon officially establishing the regional boards, WSB Chairman Nathan P. Feinsinger hoped that their creation would "integrate the

28. Harold Leventhal (Chief Counsel, OPS), "The Organization for Defense Mobilization, part 2: Price Controls under the Defense Production Act as Amended," *Federal Bar Journal* 13 (December 1952 #2): 99–116; Memorandum for Messrs. Clark, Johnson, Tapp from Ralph Hetzel (OPS), June 18, 1951, RG 296 Records of the Economic Stabilization Agency, box 26, file: "National Defense, Organizational Management," NA; Letter to Charles E. Wilson, June 29, 1951, RG 277 Records of the National Production Authority, box 14, file: "Correspondence with Government Agencies," NA; Memorandum to Eric Johnston from DiSalle (OPS), October 11, 1951, RG 295 Records of the Office of Price Stabilization (Records of Joseph Freehill), box 696, file: "ESA Administration (Memos to and From)," NA; Kim McQuaid, *Uneasy Partners,* 61.
29. See for example Memorandum to (Robert) Goodwin, Executive Director of the Defense Manpower Administration, from Mary T. Norton, Vice Chairman of the Women's Advisory Committee on Defense Manpower, August 13, 1951, which offers an excellent analysis of the role of women's organizations in the defense effort, Papers of Robert Goodwin, box 1, file: "Defense Manpower Administration, Operations Bulletins, 1951–53," HSTL.

wage stabilization principles with the freedom of our American way of life."[30] Thus, the move toward greater decentralization, organized volunteerism, and corporatism accomplished two important goals: First, it checked the growth of the mobilization and stabilization bureaucracies and their operating budgets. Second, it allayed the fears of governmental centralization, bureaucratization, and regimentation.

Meanwhile, Congress and the Truman administration locked horns over taxes and the budget. The struggle began with the president's February 1951 tax message, in which he exhorted Congress to keep the nation's defense program on a pay-as-you-go basis. To do this, he asked Congress for an immediate $10 billion tax increase, the largest in U.S. history, to be followed by another supplemental increase amounting to $6.5 billion, which the administration later dropped. These requests came on top of two previous tax hikes since Korea: an emergency $6 billion supplemental in September 1950, and the Excess Profits Tax of January 1951, totaling another $3.9 billion. Republicans balked at these new requests, and Congress took nearly eight months to pass a tax bill, finally approving a $6 billion increase in October. The debates over taxes took on the same ideological and partisan flavor as the fight over controls, so it was not surprising that the administration's request was reduced, just as its controls request was diluted. The main difference was that the Democrats—both northern and southern—tended to agree on the need for some type of tax increase, while the Republicans generally stood alone in their opposition. Many Republicans used the tax issue to protest the administration's spending policies and social programs, insisting that the rearmament program could be funded without more taxes if "non-essential" spending were cut—including social welfare spending and foreign economic and military aid.[31]

Truman, who had traditionally viewed a balanced budget as sacrosanct, insisted from the start that the mobilization program be kept on a pay-as-you-go basis. In this regard, he did not waiver from the majority opinion on Capitol Hill. So when he submitted his tax and budget package to Congress in February, he had expected the body to comply—more or less—with his requests. But by the time lawmakers began to seriously consider the president's tax package during the

30. Memo to Eric Johnston (ESA), September 4, 1951, RG 296, box 5, NA; "Current Board Developments," No. 4, October 1951, page 1, RG 296 Secretariat-Classified, box 10, file: "Current Board Developments," NA.
31. *Congressional Record*, 82d. Cong., 1st sess., 1951, 97, pt. 5: 6889; *Congressional Quarterly Almanac* 82d. Cong., 1st sess., 1951, vol. 7, 409.

summer and fall, the political and economic impact of the mobilization effort had changed dramatically. First came the labor impasse, then the MacArthur controversy, and then the diluted Defense Production Act, all of which greatly eroded Truman's political clout and popularity. Superimposed over all of this, of course, were the continuing attacks on the Truman administration by Senator McCarthy and his minions. Those events and circumstances, combined with the armistice talks that began in June and reports of production bottlenecks and mobilization-related unemployment, convinced Congress that the time had come to reassess rearmament. Thus, still focused on Korea rather than the long-term mobilization prescribed in NSC-68, many lawmakers no longer saw the urgency or the wisdom of an accelerated defense effort. Nor did they believe that taxes had to be levied to historic heights. So as the vote on taxes loomed in September, Truman was in such a weakened political state that he had little choice but to watch hopelessly as Congress eviscerated his proposals.[32]

The House Ways and Means Committee conducted hearings on the tax issue from February 5 through March 14, 1951. During the hearings, administration officials made a solid pitch for increased taxes, arguing that the additional revenue would be needed not only to keep mobilization on a pay-as-you-go basis, but also to keep a check on inflation by draining off excess discretionary income.[33] Organized labor generally agreed with the administration's position, although labor leaders stressed the need for increased taxation of corporations and upper-income individuals instead of higher excise taxes which, in their view, were regressive and discriminatory.[34]

The business community as a whole held very different views, however. Noting the difficulties many small businesses were facing because of the mobilization program, George J. Burgher of the National Federation of Independent Business told the committee that the

32. Cabinet Meeting, March 20, 1951, Papers of Matthew J. Connelly, box 2, file: "Notes on Cabinet Meetings, 1951, 2 January–31 December," HSTL.

33. For the testimony of key administration and mobilization officials see U.S. Congress, House of Representatives, Committee on Ways and Means, *Revenue Revision of 1951: Hearings,* 82d Cong., 1st sess., 1951, parts 1 and 2; For Secretary of the Treasury John W. Snyder's comments, see *Hearings,* parts 1 and 2, 4–14; Bureau of the Budget Director Frederick J. Lawton, 169–75; Economic Stabilization Agency Administrator Eric Johnston, 315–18; Office of Price Stabilization Director Michael V. DiSalle, 353–60.

34. *Revenue Revision of 1951: Hearings,* parts 1 and 2, Statement of the American Federation of Labor, 477–86; ibid., Statement of the Congress of Industrial Organizations, 603–17; See also Memorandum for John R. Steelman, September 21, 1951, Papers of Roy Blough, box 10, file: "Council of Economic Advisors September–October 1951," HSTL.

administration's tax proposals "may push them (small businesses) over the brink to complete disaster."[35] The Council of State Chambers of Commerce, along with representatives of the National Association of Manufacturers, agreed that the defense effort must continue to be based upon the ability to pay, but opposed higher income and corporate taxes, emphasizing instead the need for higher consumption taxes along with a drastic curtailment in non-defense appropriations. The Ways and Means Committee concluded its hearings in March, at which time it went into closed session to draw up a tax plan.[36]

The House took up floor action on the tax bill on June 22 and voted to accept the committee's recommendation of a $7.2 billion tax increase the same day. The vote was not without opposition, however. In a minority dissent, Republicans called for an immediate 10 percent reduction in non-defense spending as well as the elimination of all nonessential spending by the military. The minority report declared that "the Truman administration is under the false illusion that pay-as-we-go means only a one-way street of ever-increasing expenditures paved with higher taxes."[37] Reiterating those sentiments on the floor, Republicans used the opportunity to lambast Truman's spending policies, urging him to curtail all nonessential government services and to cut by half the nation's economic and military aid to Europe. Sounding a familiar warning, Daniel A. Reed (R-NY) asserted that the pending bill would "fulfill the dream of the hard-core . . . Socialist planners within the Truman administration."[38]

Clearly, by arguing that the mobilization program would bankrupt the nation without a draconian curtailment of social spending and foreign economic aid, the Republicans played to the public's concerns about mobilization while they attempted to derail Truman's Fair Deal. Yet the GOP never seriously considered the alternative: cutting back the defense budget. It also became clear that the Republicans' positions on taxes and economic controls were irreconcilable with their professed dread of inflation. In essence, Republicans—and to a lesser extent conservative Democrats—wanted to have their cake and eat it too. They

35. *Revenue Revision of 1951: Hearings,* parts 1 and 2, 556. For the complete statement see 553–65.
36. *Revenue Revision of 1951: Hearings,* parts 1 and 2, Council of State Chambers of Commerce, 893–96; National Association of Manufacturers, 696–730.
37. *Congressional Quarterly Almanac* 82d. Cong., 1st sess., 1951, vol. 7, 419.
38. *Congressional Record,* 82d. Cong., 1st sess., 1951, 97, pt. 5: 6888–6934, for Reed's quotation see p. 6894.

deplored inflation, yet they opposed direct controls and tax increases, all the while tacitly approving mounting defense expenditures.

Disappointed in the House version of the tax bill, the White House lobbied the Senate Finance Committee, which began hearings in June, to increase taxes by a full $10 billion. But administration officials knew that they faced a tough fight, for the Senate turned out to be even more reluctant than the House to raise additional revenues. ODM Director Wilson was especially concerned that the failure to secure sufficient funds for rearmament would stymie the long-term mobilization program. Clearly, he was thinking far beyond the Korean War. On July 3, Wilson told the Finance Committee that taxes "must be raised based not upon the Korean fighting, but upon what we know to be the ultimate aims and present tactics of the Soviet Union."[39] Other mobilization and administration officials repeated the urgency of Wilson's warnings. By separating the Korean conflict from the mobilization and tax scenarios, the administration was attempting to keep the long-term Cold War preparedness program on a pay-as-you-go basis. But neither the Congress nor the public desired to do so. Congress was apparently willing to sign on to Truman's long-haul military plans but was unwilling to provide the necessary taxes to pay for them. This myopia forced the Truman administration to compromise on the speed and expanse of the mobilization effort and resulted in budget deficits that haunted the nation in later years. As it was, officials in June still projected budget deficits of $18.6 billion for FY 1951 and $10.1 billion for FY 1952 even *with* projected new taxes of $7 billion.[40]

In September, the Senate took up floor action on the Finance Committee's recommendation of a $5.506 billion tax increase, which it approved by a better than two-to-one margin on September 28. The Senate version of the tax bill, however, was some $1.7 billion lower than the House version and was almost one-half of what Truman had originally

---

39. U.S. Congress, Senate, Committee on Finance, *Revenue Act of 1951: Hearings*, 82d. Cong., 1st sess., 1951, parts 1–2, 262. For complete statement and testimony see 261–85. See also Cabinet Meeting June 29, 1951, Papers of Matthew J. Connelly, box 2, file: "Notes on Cabinet Meetings, 1951, 2 January–31 December," HSTL, in which Wilson expressed his concerns to Truman and the entire cabinet: "If we stop our production drive after Korean peace, we are sunk. We should on the contrary . . . step up production."

40. Confidential Report to G. Griffith Johnson on Established U.S. Government Receipts and Expenditures, Fiscal Years 1951 to 1954, June 12, 1951, RG 296 Records Maintained by the Administrator, Classified General Files, box 1, file: "Stabilization Issues," NA; Budget Outlook and Proposed Agency Ceilings for Fiscal Year 1953, June 19, 1951, President's Secretary's Files-Bureau of the Budget, box 151, file: "Bureau of the Budget, FY 1952–53," HSTL.

requested. Predictably, the floor debates in the Senate were even more acrimonious than were those in the House. The same issues were debated, however, and the same partisan politics were at play. The most bitter feuding came during the last four days of debate, during which time Senate Republicans bashed Truman's "reckless" spending policies and "wasteful" programs, while the Democrats accused Republicans of catering to the whims of corporate America and balancing the nation's rearmament program on the backs of working people.[41]

On October 19, more than eight long months after the president's original request for $10 billion in new taxes, Congress finally passed a tax package with $5.691 billion in additional revenue. Truman signed the bill into law the next day, but only, in his words, "because we badly need these revenues to help pay for strong defenses we are building." He pointed out that the tax bill failed to yield enough to keep the mobilization effort on a pay-as-you-go basis.[42]

The 1951 tax bill was the second major legislative defeat for the administration's rearmament program. Coupled with the dilution of the Defense Production Act in July, the 1951 Revenue Act severely restricted the parameters in which mobilization planners could operate. Having first lost some of their ability to fight inflation though the 1951 DPA, and then losing any hope of financing rearmament on a pay-as-you-go basis, mobilization officials were hemmed in by the dual fears of inflationary pressures and budget deficits. Neither the American people nor Congress was ready to make the long-term sacrifices inherent in the kind of defense buildup Truman had in mind. The momentum of Korea was lost and with it went the political courage and fiscal responsibility Congress had displayed only a year earlier. The murkiness of arming for the long haul, for a war that everyone hoped would never be fought, seemed too abstract a proposition for most politicians to handle.

Although the legislative setbacks of 1951 no doubt forced mobilization planners to scale back and stretch out their mobilization goals, the Truman administration pushed ahead with its long-term plans nonetheless. It often found creative ways around congressional obstacles and political mine fields, but it did not fundamentally alter its ultimate objectives of rearming Western Europe and building a permanent

41. *Congressional Record,* 82d. Cong., 1st sess., 1951, 97, pt. 9:11597–98; *Congressional Quarterly Almanac* 82d. Cong., 1st sess., 1951, vol. 7, 534–35. For the full floor debates see *Congressional Record,* 82d. Cong., 1st sess., 1951, 97, pt. 9:11940–11984, 12023–12035, 12094–12171, 12206–12261, 12300–12384.

42. *Congressional Quarterly Almanac* 82d. Cong., 1st sess., 1951, vol. 7, 430.

U.S. industrial and military mobilization base. Even the revenue limits placed upon the administration by Congress did not deter it from these Cold War guideposts. In fact, the failure to secure adequate resources to finance rearmament resulted in a wholesale acquiescence to budget deficits that would have been unthinkable only a few years earlier. Leon Keyserling, chairman of the Council of Economic Advisers, summed it up best in November 1951: "Whether the national debt increases by 10 or even 20 billion dollars over the next few years is of great economic importance; but it is of relatively minor importance compared with the satisfaction of defense needs."[43] Keyserling had stood largely alone in his view of fiscal policy before the advent of NSC-68 and the Korean War, but by the end of 1951, economic and political exigencies turned many administration officials into reluctant military Keynesians, most notably the president himself. The alternative to Keyserling's prescriptions was the abandonment of long-term mobilization goals which, in the minds of most policymakers, was far more risky than cyclical budget deficits.

While the White House fought for its economic controls and tax proposals, mobilization officials worked behind the scenes to reimpose World War Two's Controlled Materials Plan (CMP). In January 1951, only days after taking the top post at ODM, Charles Wilson had announced his intention to reactivate the CMP. But because of the monumental job involved in gathering the necessary information and statistics necessary to implement the plan, mobilization planners did not formally begin its operations until July 1. The reactivation of the CMP reflected not only the growing need for centralized control over materials allocations and production programming, but it also reflected the past experience and management philosophy of top mobilization officials, most notably those of Charles Wilson. The CMP was originally used during World War II, from 1943 to 1945, after several other allocation and programming plans had failed. Compared to its predecessors, the CMP had operated relatively well and had seen the nation through the most productive period of the Second World War. Mobilization planners deemed the materials plan a success, and it was admired for its comparative effectiveness long after the guns fell silent. As the former vice chairman of the War Production Board, Charles Wilson was keenly aware of the CMP's legacy and was thus determined to see

43. Letter to the President, November 2, 1951, Papers of Leon Keyserling, box 1, file: "Correspondence between Harry S. Truman and Keyserling (1 of 2)," HSTL.

it resurrected as he again grasped the reins of industrial mobilization in 1951.[44]

The Controlled Materials Plan of 1951 shared many common components with the one that preceded it; there were, however, some important differences. Like its predecessor, the CMP was a vertical control system, decentralized and pyramidical in structure, that was designed to assure an adequate supply-demand balance of the three controlled materials: steel, aluminum, and copper. These materials were the fundamental ingredients of nearly all industrial end-items; thus, by controlling them, mobilization planners could not only address materials supply problems, but they could also control production planning, programming, and delivery of defense items in accordance with the nation's production goals. So in the broadest sense, the CMP was a vertical control system that acted as an allocator of materials *and* as a planner of production. The organizational structure of the CMP was in keeping with the centralized policymaking/decentralized operations of the overall mobilization program and also reflected Wilson's management style and the very successful production-control methods of General Electric, the company over which Wilson had presided before taking the ODM post. Unlike its World War II predecessor, however, the 1951 plan did not originally extend to all producers. Only military and defense suppliers were subjected to the CMP—civilian producers had to obtain their own material from what was left over of the aggregate quarterly supply.[45]

Sitting atop the CMP management pyramid was the Requirements Committee of the Defense Production Administration (DPA). Its job was to gather requests for controlled materials from the various Industry Divisions of the National Production Authority (NPA), which all

44. For good overviews of the Controlled Materials Plan (CMP) during World War II see Melvin Anshen, "Problems in Business and Industrial Mobilization: Production Controls," RG 296, Records of the Economic Stabilization Administration, Economics, box 16, NA; Cuff, "Organizational Capabilities"; Novick, *Wartime Production Controls,* esp. chap. 8 and 9.

45. Memorandum to Charles Wilson, April 17, 1951, RG 296 Reports and Secretariat, box 5, file: "Actions Outside the ESA," NA; Manly Fleischmann, Administrator of the National Production Authority and Defense Production Administration, "Policies and Procedures for Limited Mobilization,": 110–18, esp. 114–18; "ABC's of CMP," National Production Authority pamphlet, RG 277 Records of the National Production Authority, Reference Materials 1951–53, box 16, NA.

For the organizational structure of the CMP and its ties to General Electric see Robert Cuff, "Coordinating Material Flows During World War II: The Controlled Materials Plan 1942–1945," in author's possession, 7–8, 13–14, 54, 65, f.n. 44.

laid claim to a specific area of the economy. The DPA would then match the available supply of the controlled materials for any given quarter against the claims of the Industry Divisions and would apportion the materials to the claimants based upon defense needs and, of course, the aggregate supply. During the first eight to twelve months of the CMP's operations, the amounts of materials requested far exceeded the aggregate supply, frustrating the controlled material planners and in some cases causing real hardship among civilian producers forced to compete for materials on the much-reduced open market.[46]

The decision to exempt civilian producers from the CMP was not popular. Extending the plan only to military producers was justified for two reasons. First, had mobilization planners extended the CMP to all producers, the plan would not have been ready much before the fourth quarter of the year, a delay officials were unwilling to tolerate. Second, by limiting the purview of the CMP, administration officials hoped to avoid assertions that the mobilization program was leading the nation toward a centrally planned and regimented economy. But they soon learned that the implementation of the plan was an all or nothing proposition. Civilian producers, especially the smaller ones, were simply unable to compete with military producers for the limited supply of materials. The debate over the implementation of the CMP occurred behind closed doors for the most part, but it aptly illustrated the disagreement among key mobilization officials over the extent and pacing of the rearmament effort. Manly Fleischmann, NPA director, fought against the exclusion of civilian producers from the plan, arguing that to do so would jeopardize the health of civilian industry. But he lost this battle with ODM officials, who were apparently more concerned that an all-encompassing CMP would elicit howls of protest from industry leaders, not to mention congressional Republicans.[47]

As it turned out, Fleischmann was right. Demand for the three controlled materials was so intense that there was very little left over for civilian use. Not more than six weeks into the revived CMP, most mobilization officials, including Charles Wilson at the ODM, concluded

46. Peter H. Kaskell (Counsel to the National Production Authority), "Production under the CMP," 16–18.
47. Letter to Charles Stauffacher (ODM) from Manly Fleischmann, May 22, 1951, RG 277, Records of the National Production Administration, Reference Materials, 1951–53, box 14, file: "Correspondence with government agencies," NA; Memo to Manly Fleischmann, June 1, 1951, RG 277, box 46, NA; *Newsweek* 38 (July 16, 1951): 63.

that the plan would have to be expanded to include practically all industries—civilian and defense alike. In mid-August, ODM officials, under considerable pressure from civilian producers as well as officials in other mobilization agencies, agreed to extend the CMP to consumer goods manufacturers. On October 1, mobilization officials closed the open-ended features of the Controlled Materials Plan, thus subjecting most civilian industries to CMP allotments for the first time. Although the extension of the plan did help civilian producers, especially in the area of production planning and material inventory control, the overall materials crunch remained troublesome and, in certain instances, was still considered critical.[48]

So critical was the shortage of copper, one of the three "controlled" materials, that the president was forced to authorize the release of some fifty million tons of the metal from the nation's strategic stockpile. As a result of this and other acute shortages, administration officials decided to tackle the shortages head-on. To do so meant the creation of yet another mobilization agency: the Defense Materials Procurement Agency (DMPA). The DMPA would work to centralize all of the various functions involved in the exploration, extraction, and government procurement of strategic materials. Until the creation of the DMPA, materials procurement responsibilities had been spread out among the General Services Administration, the Department of the Interior, the Economic Cooperation Administration, and the Defense Production Agency. On August 28, President Truman formally established the DMPA with Jess Larson, director of the General Services Administration, as its first administrator. The new agency would coordinate the issuance of certificates for the purpose of buying metals and minerals, the granting of government loans to stimulate their exploration and extraction, as well as the distribution of accelerated tax amortization certificates. In addition, the agency would serve as the central coordinating body for the procurement of materials through the Economic Cooperation Administration (ECA). The creation of the DMPA not only centralized and simplified strategic material procurement, but it also served to reassure the United States' allies that the nation was indeed serious about the worldwide raw materials crisis, a crisis that

48. Letter to John R. Steelman plus attached "Facts for Industry," June 13, 1951, Papers of Harry S. Truman, OF, box 1731, file 2855, "Feb 1951–1953," HSTL; Letter to Eric Johnston, July 6, 1951, RG 277, box 15, NA; Memo to Raymond G. Fisher (ODM), August 29, 1951, RG 277, box 14, NA; "NPA Fact Book-Confidential and Restricted," October 1951, RG 277, box 19, file: "Miscellaneous Publications, 1950–53," NA.

had reached epic proportions in countries like Britain, France, and Germany.[49]

The reactivation of the Controlled Materials Plan, the creation of the Defense Materials Procurement Agency, and the United States' participation in the International Materials Conference (IMC) demonstrated a maturing of administration officials' approach to both the worldwide materials crisis and the overall rearmament effort. Recognizing the interconnected nature of commodity markets, U.S. officials came to realize that the only effective way to ease the crisis—both domestically and internationally—was to engage in multilateral agreements designed to bring materials producing and consuming nations together in order to determine aggregate supplies and then distribute the commodities according to need. The IMC was undertaken first, followed by its domestic counterpart, the CMP. Centralized policymaking and decentralized implementation assured that the agencies fit with the existing mobilization structure in the United States. During the last half of 1951, raw material shortages eased and commodity prices began to fall.

By 1952, the materials crisis was largely past. The easing of the crisis was no doubt helped by the slowdown in mobilization that occurred in late 1951. But the efficacy of the IMC, the CMP, and the DMPA cannot be dismissed. First, their creation reassured America's allies of its commitment to multilateral rearmament and its belief in shared sacrifice. Second, the mere fact that these mechanisms *did* exist, with full participation by the United States, tended to serve as a sedative for high-strung commodities markets, instilling in them confidence and stability and thereby reducing raw materials prices.

The copper shortage of 1951 was greatly complicated by the labor-management dispute that had closed one of the nation's largest copper smelters in Garfield, Utah. Administration officials estimated that the strike could diminish copper supplies by nearly 23 million pounds per month. The supply of aluminum was also seriously depleted during the summer of 1951, a situation made worse by a strike that had closed

49. Letter to John D. Small (Munitions Board) from Harry S. Truman, August 6, 1951, President's Secretary's Files (PSF) (Subject File, Agencies D-F), box 144, file: "Defense Materials Procurement Agency," HSTL; Release: Statement by the President, August 1, 1951, PSF (Subject File, Agencies D-F), box 144, file: "Defense Materials Procurement Agency," HSTL; Release: Defense Materials Procurement Agency, September 14, 1951, Papers of the President's Materials Policy Commission, 1951–1952, box 59, file: "Correspondence-DMPA," HSTL.

down the Cleveland, Ohio plant of the Aluminum Corporation of America. The aluminum shortage threatened to reduce substantially the production of aircraft. The last half of 1951 was in fact a period marked by rising labor unrest and an alarming increase in the number and duration of labor strikes. The great steel strike of 1952 was born in the closing months of the year. Some strikes, like the ones in Garfield and Cleveland, threatened both the defense effort and the civilian economy. The copper strike in particular promised the likelihood of more cutbacks in auto production, just as unemployment was on the increase among Detroit auto workers. The dilemma mobilization officials faced was thus twofold. First, they had to deal with an organized labor force that had once again become very unhappy with the mobilization program and that resented caps on its earnings while businesses reaped huge profits. Second, they faced mobilization-related unemployment crises like the one that paradoxically threatened hundreds of thousands of auto workers in the midst of one of America's greatest economic booms.[50]

Labor's unrest was certainly not unjustified. The Korean War's raging economic boom provided organized labor with mere table scraps compared with the bacchanalian feast enjoyed by big business. While most workers' incomes continued to increase proportionately with inflation, many corporations enjoyed unprecedented "peacetime" windfalls: By mid-1952, the Federal Reserve reported industrial production at its highest peak since 1945. Total corporate earnings in the same period were increasing at an annual rate of 7.4 percent, or nearly three times the inflation rate. Some industries reaped incredible profits: aircraft manufacturers averaged a 105.7 percent increase; electronics makers averaged a 99.3 percent increase; and radio and television producers enjoyed a 361.1 percent increase. At the same time, most unions' power was gradually diminishing, and membership increases were falling

50. National Advisory Board on Mobilization policy, Meeting No. 8, July 24, 1951, Papers of Harry S. Truman, White House Central Files: Confidential File, box 26, file: "National Advisory Board on Mobilization Policy, 1951–1952," HSTL; Letter to the President from Charles Wilson, July 25, 1951, President's Secretary's Files (ODM Reports-T), box 148, file: "Stockpiling," HSTL.

At the urging of his top mobilization officials, President Truman ordered the Garfield, Utah, strike referred to the Wage Stabilization Board (WSB) for arbitration on July 26. The copper case was the first one referred to the WSB for strike arbitration. See Memo for the Files, July 25, 1951, PSF (ODM Reports-T), box 148, file: "Stockpiling," HSTL; Letter to Dr. George Taylor (WSB Chairman), July 26, 1951, PSF (ODM Reports-T), box 148, file: "Stockpiling," HSTL.

off. The dilution of the Defense Production Act—especially through the Capehart Pricing Amendment—particularly angered organized labor leaders. The Capehart Amendment essentially demonstrated that price controls had been "captured" by business interests and virtually guaranteed that price increases would be a regular feature of economic "stabilization," while wage increases would not. Furthermore, it was a fact that cheating on price regulations was far easier than cheating on wage regulations, especially given the fact that industry generally applied wage standards *and* determined fringe benefit packages. To make matters worse, management greatly resented the Wage Stabilization Board and routinely attempted to derail its arbitration efforts. The unions were in a no-win situation, and the Truman administration could do little to turn the tide of events toward labor's way. As a result, labor struck with increasing regularity during the last half of 1951. By 1952, a total of 3.5 million workers walked picket lines. It was clear that the administration had now lost much of organized labor's support in addition to that of most business leaders.[51]

"Despite an abundance of war orders and a 'full employment' economy, there are serious and even tragic instances of unemployment. At the same time some (other) areas are suffering from labor shortages," wrote presidential advisor Harold Enarson in December.[52] New England textile towns, industrial cities in the South, as well as Appalachian mining communities, all suffered acute unemployment during the period. But nowhere was the unemployment problem more devastating and potentially embarrassing to the administration than the situation in Detroit. In July the mayor of Detroit, Albert E. Cobo, telegrammed the president warning him that the employment picture in his city would worsen considerably if the administration did not divert more raw materials to civilian production, especially for automotive purposes. In September, Labor Secretary Maurice Tobin warned Truman and his Cabinet that by 1952 unemployment threatened to reach 150,000 in Detroit. Meanwhile cities on the West Coast, like San Diego for example,

51. McQuaid, *Uneasy Partners*, 61–62; McQuaid, *Big Business and Presidential Power;* Gary Mucciaroni, *The Political Failure of Employment Policy, 1945–1982;* Memo for Steelman, October 1, 1951, Papers of Harold L. Enarson, box 3, file: "Labor Disputes Machinery, 1950–1952," HSTL. For corporate earnings and productivity increases see OPS Daily News Digest, October 31, 1952, RG 295, Central Files 1952–1953, box 632, file: "Daily News Digest," NA; Memorandum for the President, November 3, 1952, President's Secretary's Files, box 264, file: "General File-Steelman, John," HSTL.

52. Memo for Mr. Steelman, December 12, 1951, Papers of Harry S. Truman, OF, file: "264 (1951)," HSTL.

suffered from labor shortages, especially in the burgeoning fields of aircraft and avionics design and production. Thus by the summer of 1951, the mobilization program had begun to bite deeply into the nation's civilian labor base. Labor, already disgruntled over its lack of authority in mobilization and stabilization issues, now faced the prospect of spotty yet potentially catastrophic unemployment. In light of these developments, mobilization officials could not help but question the wisdom of continuing the current pacing and prioritization of the rearmament program.[53]

While administration officials grappled with economic dislocations at home, they also had to concern themselves with a growing economic crisis in Europe. The inflationary storm that had lashed the United States in late 1950 and early 1951 roared across the Atlantic, crashing like a hurricane into NATO countries during the second half of the year. To be sure, Western Europe suffered the ravages of inflation as soon as the United States entered Korea and began to rearm—the wholesale price index shot up as much as 30 percent between July 1950 and March 1951. But there was a good side to this, at least temporarily. Because the Korean inflation appeared first in the United States, the early months of the Korean War resulted in a substantial improvement in the European balance of payments, as American buyers turned toward cheaper European products. The infusion of American troops into the Continent further reduced the European dollar drain. Unemployment in Europe dropped and production rose. But these effects were short-lived. After the United States stepped up the mobilization program in December 1950, inflation in Western Europe worsened, production slowed because of raw materials shortages, and high unemployment once again threatened. As production faltered and inflation rose, the improvement in Europe's balance of payments quickly reversed itself. The Truman administration now faced the twin dangers of economic dislocations at home and abroad.[54]

53. Telegram to the President, June 29, 1951, Papers of Harry S. Truman, OF, file: "264 (1951)," HSTL; Cabinet Meeting, September 21, 1951, Papers of Matthew J. Connelly, box 2, file: "Notes on Cabinet Meetings, 1951, 2 January–31 December," HSTL; Letter to the President, October 16, 1951, Papers of Harry S. Truman, OF, file: "264 (1951)," HSTL.

54. Richard M. Bissell Jr., "The Impact of Rearmament on the Free World Economy," 385–405; see Michael J. Hogan, who offers a cogent and concise treatment of European economic difficulties in his definitive *Marshall Plan,* 336–38, 380–81, 393; see also Richard P. Stebbins, *The United States in World Affairs,* 1950, 279–80; and Stebbins, *The United States in World Affairs,* 1951, 217–22; Clarence Y. H. Lo, "Military Spending as Crisis Management: The U.S. Response to the Berlin Blockade and the Korean War," 165–67.

As early as May, European criticism of America's rearmament program made the headlines. And as the economic situation worsened, the criticism grew more intense. Especially critical of the administration's rearmament policies were the British. Leading the charge was Socialist Cabinet Minister Aneurin Bevan, who complained that his country could not afford to devote the amount of resources to rearmament envisioned by the United States. To follow American prescriptions, he claimed, would be to further exacerbate glaring differences in the standard of living among Britons, not to mention the gross disparity of standards between the United States and Great Britain. At the crux of the impasse between American and European policymakers was the means by which rearmament should be accomplished. On balance, the Europeans believed that arms production should fit into a nation's existing industrial capacity and ability to pay. Thus, unlike U.S. policymakers, they did not envision large expenditures to expand production capacity simply to satisfy military needs. Nor did they share in U.S. mobilization officials' acquiescence to defense-related budget deficits and dislocations to the civilian economy. The split between America and its European Allies over these issues was not unlike the growing rift between liberal-internationalist business and government leaders and the ascendant conservative coalition in the United States.[55] At issue in both cases, as Michael J. Hogan points out, were the by-now familiar dichotomies of "government economy versus deficit spending, voluntary restraints versus government controls, guns versus butter." And just as the crises over rearmament weakened the liberal-internationalist coalition at home, so too did they undermine existing political coalitions in Western Europe, most notably Britain's Labour government.[56]

In August 1951, the Truman administration became so concerned over the economic and political situation in Europe that it decided to send chief economic stabilizer Eric Johnston on a European junket to iron out differences between the United States and its European Allies. Johnston planned an extensive itinerary and set ambitious goals for the trip. His major objectives included building unanimity for the defense program; implementing cooperative and coordinating anti-inflation

---

55. "Guns vs. Free Teeth in Britain," *U.S. News and World Report* 30 (May 4, 1951): 24–25; Fritz Steinberg, "Why Our Allies Complain," 443–44; Hogan, *Marshall Plan*, 395–97, 409–10; "Summary of Current Experience of the International Materials Conference: Implications for the Report of the PMPC," June 20, 1951, President's Materials Policy Commission, 1951–52, box 1, file: "Summary of Current Experience of IMC," HSTL.

56. Hogan, *Marshall Plan*, 421–25 (for quotation see pp. 421–22).

policies; achieving stability in the commodities market; and emphasizing the United States' commitment to economic, political, and military integration. When Johnston arrived in Paris on September 29, his
plans included talks with officials in France, Britain, Germany, Italy,
and the Benelux countries as well as a private meeting with General
Eisenhower. In meeting after meeting with European officials, Johnston
heard the same refrain: Western Europe is near the breaking point; the
current rearmament is too much too fast; American dollars—and non-
military aid—must continue to flow into Europe; and the West must
be ever wary of ceding too much control to the military and national
security establishments.[57] Eisenhower admitted to Johnston that the
United States might indeed be rearming too quickly. In an about-face
from his position only ten months before, Eisenhower said that "we
can probably reduce our expenditures at home. . . . Maybe you can cut
down on expenditures in America, but I do feel the amount allocated
to Europe should be given. These people have just about reached the
end of their rope."[58]

Upon his return to the United States, Johnston briefed the president
and mobilization officials on his trip. His reports painted a rather
gloomy portrait of Western Europe's economic landscape. "The inflationary situation in Western Europe," he told the president and
his National Advisory Board on Mobilization Policy, "is most serious
and the prospects are for considerably more inflation in the months
ahead."[59] Among other things, he attributed the inflationary spiral to
higher prices for raw materials; raw materials shortages; weakness
and instability in European governments; and unbalanced budgets.
Johnston strongly urged a three-prong solution to the problems. He
asserted that the United States must provide more economic assistance
to Europe, extend rearmament over a longer time period, and allocate

57. Statement on European Trip, August 20, 1951, RG 296, Records of the Economic
Stabilization Agency, Reports and Secretariat, box 2, file: "European Trip," NA; Paris
Schedule, September 29–October 4, 1951, RG 296, box 2, file: "European Trip," NA; see
also notes from interviews with European leaders by Eric Johnston in RG 296, box 2,
files: "European Trip," and "Reports and Statistics," NA (Interviews include those with
German Chancellor Adenauer, French Minister of Finance and Economic Affairs Rene
Mayer, the venerable European integrationist Jean Monnet, French Foreign Minister
Maurice Schuman, as well as those with British and Italian officials).
58. General Eisenhower Interview, October 2, 1951, RG 296, box 2, file: "Reports and
Statistics," NA.
59. National Advisory Board on Mobilization Policy Meeting No. 12, October 15,
1951, President's Secretary's Files, Subject File Agencies A, box 142, file: "Subject file,
Advisory Board on Mobilization Policy, National," HSTL.

more raw materials to European production.[60] In a written confidential report, Johnston told President Truman that most European officials were convinced that the United States was pushing too far and too fast on rearmament. Johnston ended his report with a blunt caveat: "We obviously face a difficult task of pushing these countries in a direction which they are reluctant to take while at the same time not pushing them so far or so fast that their economies collapse under the strain of rearmament."[61]

Johnston's observances did not go unnoticed. His way of thinking and his prescriptions for easing European travails had already gained grudging acceptance among many American policymakers—even the hawkish ones who had been heretofore insistent upon stepping up rearmament. Thus by the last quarter of the year, the Truman administration could no longer afford to down play Europe's problems. To do so would have meant jeopardizing the whole of European recovery and the international economic system it had helped to build as a bulwark against Communism. All the guns in the world would have been rendered useless had Western Europe descended into economic and political chaos. Under attack at home, and roundly criticized abroad, the administration's mobilization and economic policies were obviously in need of considerable adjustment.[62]

On top of the economic dislocations engendered by mobilization, administration officials had to face the fact that the rearmament effort was not performing as well as first intended. Materials shortages, deficiencies in machine tool production, labor strikes, and disagreements between military brass and civilian planners over the pacing of mobilization all caused a production lag in military items. Confusion abounded within the myriad mobilization agencies, some of which were actually working at odds with each other by the final quarter of 1951. Making matters worse were the watered-down Defense

60. Ibid.
61. Letter to the President plus attached memo, "The Inflationary Situation in Europe," White House Central Files, Confidential Files, box 17, file: "Economic Stabilization Agency (1951)," HSTL.
62. Defense Mobilization Board Meeting No. 19, November 14, 1951, RG 296, Records Maintained by the Administrator, Classified General Files, box 2, file: "Defense Mobilization Board Meetings," NA.
Not only did administration officials now fully realize the deleterious effects of rearmament on the European political economy, but they also came to acknowledge that they could not push European nations in directions that they did not wish to go. Michael Hogan makes this point in regard to the whole of U.S.-European economic relations in *The Marshall Plan,* especially in his conclusion, 427–45.

Production Act, which made economic stabilization far more difficult, as well as Congress's reluctance to raise enough revenue to pay for rearmament. The failure to achieve mobilization goals, coupled with increasing criticism of the Truman administration's economic and mobilization policies, resulted in a wholesale reevaluation of the entire rearmament program. By December, the decision had been made to both slow the pace of rearmament and to stretch out the effort over a longer period of time. Mobilization planners narrowed their goals—at least in the short-term—in order to meet immediate needs while at the same time preserving long-term readiness requirements.

The decisions to slow down and stretch out the mobilization program were the results of an intense debate that occurred in the late summer and fall of the year. Like concentric circles, these debates took place within the administration, Congress, and the business community, and focused upon one common theme: How much mobilization, and over how much time? Those favoring a slower arms buildup spread over a longer period of time finally prevailed, but not before the Truman administration had lost valued respect and support from some important political allies. Corporate liberal business organizations like the Committee for Economic Development (CED) and the Business Council (BC) that had previously backed Truman's policies withdrew their support for economic controls. ESA Administrator Eric Johnston, a member of the CED, resigned his post, reportedly because of disagreements with ODM boss Charles Wilson over mobilization policy. In 1952 Wilson, himself a member of the Business Council, also would resign after a row with Truman over the steel strike. First battered by the conservative coalition in Congress, then bloodied by the likes of the NAM and the USCC, the Truman administration could ill-afford to lose support from the corporate liberal establishment. Once the CED and BC bolted, administration officials had little choice but to yield to the growing pressure and scale back their mobilization goals.[63]

The loss of corporate support during the Korean mobilization demonstrated the true efficacy of business-government cooperation. Once relations between Washington and the corporate world began to deteriorate, policymakers encountered a much more difficult time

---

63. McQuaid, *Uneasy Partners*, 61–62; McQuaid, *Big Business and Presidential Power*, 167–68; Robert J. Donovan, *Tumultuous Years: The Presidency of Harry S. Truman, 1949–1953*, 368–69; Alonzo L. Hamby, *Beyond the New Deal: Harry S. Truman and American Liberalism*, 449–52; Karl Schriftgiesser, *Business and Public Policy: The Role of the Committee for Economic Development: 1942–1967*, 2–3, 35, 50–52.

moving the mobilization process forward. During Korea, unlike the past two wars, the government lacked the requisite authority to prod the corporate world into seeing things its way. No true war emergency existed, so when corporate leaders began turning their backs on the Truman administration, it had neither the popular support nor the legal authority to bring them back into the fold.

Besides the loss of corporate support, indications that defense output was running behind schedule began to surface during the summer of 1951. In mid-July, the administration acknowledged that aggregate production of guns, planes, ammunition, and tanks was some 20 percent behind schedule. As a result, military deliveries were revised downward, and the peak of defense spending—and production—was pushed back six months, meaning that the mobilization program would not hit full stride until the winter of 1952. According to the Office of Defense Mobilization's July 1 Report to the President, the April–June quarter witnessed approximately $10 billion of orders earmarked for the defense program, bringing the total to $42 billion since the Korean invasion a year earlier. Deliveries of end-items during the period reached a level of $1.5 billion per month, and were estimated to increase to $4 billion per month by the middle of 1952. Despite the production lags, however, the nation's output had grown considerably, and the delivery rate of mobilization end-items was still three times higher than it had been a year before. Furthermore, Wilson pointed out that the nation had already reached the first major goal of the buildup: The United States armed forces had reached 3.5 million combat-ready personnel, more than twice the force of June 1950. In addition, Wilson reported that the armed forces now comprised 24 Army divisions, a Navy with 1,100 ships and three Marine divisions and supporting elements, along with an Air Force moving toward a goal of 95 wings.[64]

In spite of the administration's best efforts to solve the lag in defense production, the situation grew worse in the fall. In October, Charles Wilson reported to the president that the backlog of machine tool orders was 22 months off schedule, close to double the size of the backlog during World War II. Aluminum production still lagged badly; new steel

64. "Current Problems and Lines of Action," Monthly ESA Report on the Economy and Rearmament, August 31, 1951, RG 296, Classified General Files, box 1, file: "Stabilization Issues," NA; *Business Week* (July 14, 1951): 27–28; Second Quarterly Report to the President, "Meeting Defense Goals: A *Must* for Everyone," July 1, 1951, RG 277 Records of the National Production Authority, Reference Materials, 1951–53, box 2, file: "ODM-Meeting Defense Goals, 7/1/51," NA, 1, 6–7.

facilities were only one-third completed; and new petroleum plants were only 28 percent completed. Wilson also disclosed that requests for steel, aluminum, and copper—the three materials controlled by the CMP—exceeded supply by 100 percent in some weeks. Even more grim was the delivery rate of war material to NATO. As of November, only five percent of the 1951 appropriation of $4.1 billion had been shipped to NATO countries under the Mutual Security Program. And 30 percent of the previous year's total appropriation remained to be delivered. The shortfalls so disturbed General Eisenhower that he flew back to the United States to meet with mobilization officials in order to survey the delivery difficulties as well as to warn of dire consequences if production were not increased. The only bright spot among the grim figures was the report on prices and wages. Wilson reported that consumer prices in the U.S. continued to decline, keeping the rise in the cost of living to 1 percent in six months. Wage hikes were also kept at bay during the same period.[65]

Many factors explain the disappointing production shortfalls. In large measure, production was held up by the lack of machine tools, a problem that had plagued the rearmament from its inception. And as the mobilization program evolved—especially after the speedup beginning in December—the machine tool dilemma intensified. The problems in the industry were often brought about by the manufacturers themselves: Many machine tool producers had refused to accept government orders because of OPS-imposed price ceilings. Most producers also lacked the requisite working capital to invest in new machinery. The NPA's program of contract "pool orders" helped to alleviate some of the shortages, but the sheer immensity of the problem vexed mobilization planners throughout the entire Korean buildup. Aircraft deliveries especially suffered from the lack of machine tools. Korea was certainly not the first time that industrialists proved reluctant to convert to wartime production. Prior to Pearl Harbor, many U.S. manufacturers, particularly auto makers, resisted attempts by the government to coax them into producing military end-items. It took

65. Third Quarterly Report to the President, "Three Keys to Strength," October 1, 1951, RG 277, Policy Coordination Bureau, box 2, file: "ODM: 3 Keys to Strength, 10/51," NA, 1–3, 6–7, 9, 11–13, 15–17, 31; *Newsweek* 38 (October 8, 1951): 71–72; *Newsweek* 38 (November 19, 1951): 78–81; "Current Problems and Lines of Action," ESA Report on the Economy and Rearmament, November 20, 1951, RG 296, Classified General Files, box 2, file: "Quarterly Report on Economic Situation," NA; Memo for the President plus attachments, "Material Shipments to NATO (Mutual Security Program)," November 15, 1951, PSF, box 132, file: "North Atlantic Treaty (folder 1)," HSTL.

America's entry into World War II and the imposition of mandatory production controls to rally industry around war production. Thus, it is not surprising that machine tool makers during Korea, a limited war, felt disinclined to convert to defense production.[66]

In addition to the machine tools shortage, the rearmament effort continued to suffer from raw materials shortages and labor strikes in strategic industries. And as already noted, industrial strikes were on the increase during the last quarter of the year. In November, strikes and slowdowns at Westinghouse Electric, Allegheny Ludlum Steel Company, St. Joseph Lead Company, General Electric Company, Sharp and Dohm, and Cincinnati-Bickford all threatened to disrupt further the already flagging defense program.[67]

The problems in productive output were also precipitated by civilian and military planners. From the very beginning, civilian mobilization agencies had encountered difficulties in receiving firm—and realistic—estimates of need by the military. Even when military planners decided upon delivery schedules of end-items, they oftentimes changed product specifications and designs in mid-production, causing delays and bottlenecks and resulting in a vast waste of materials and manpower. In September, an NSRB report bluntly stated that "the system for determining requirements broke down to such an extent that as of April 1951 there was no firm statement of requirements based upon an integrated plan for the current defense effort or for full mobilization."[68] Civilian officials did not escape blame for these problems either. Charles Wilson was criticized by members of the president's advisory board on

66. Letter to Charles Wilson, June 28, 1951, RG 277-Correspondence with Government Agencies, box 14, NA; National Advisory Board on Mobilization Policy, Meeting No. 11, September 17 and 18, 1951, Papers of Harry S. Truman, White House Central Files, Confidential Files, box 26, file: "National Advisory Board on Mobilization Policy, 1951–1952," HSTL; "Materials for Inclusion in Annual Report to the Congress," October 18, 1951, RG 277-Reference Materials, 1951–53, box 38, file: "Congress, Report to," NA; *Business Week* (July 14, 1951): 27–28. For the World War II experience vis à vis conversion to wartime production, see Blum, *V Was for Victory*, chapter 4.

67. "An Analysis of Capital Expenditures . . .", RG 304, Records of the Office of Defense Mobilization and the National Security Resources Board, Records of the Office of Program Evaluation, 1951–1953, box 1, NA; Memorandum to Mr. Steelman, November 26, 1951, Papers of Harold L. Enarson, box 4, file: "Memoranda September 51–July 52," HSTL; Memorandum for Members of the Production Executive Committee, November 30, 1951, RG 296-Records Maintained by the Administrator, Classified General Files, box 2, file: "Production Executive Committee Agenda," NA.

68. "Analysis of the Findings of the Military Requirements Survey," September 18, 1951, RG 304-Office of the Chairman, "Safe" File of the Economic Adviser 1951–53, box 2, file: "Requirements Survey (Harvard)(Safe)," NA.

mobilization policy for failing to exercise control over military design changes. The board went on to question whether Wilson or the military was truly in charge of the mobilization program.[69]

Of course, assertions that the nation's mobilization program had fallen prey to the military establishment were nothing new. During the nation's two previous mobilizations, the same accusations had surfaced. As Robert Cuff has shown, the War Industries Board (WIB) of World War I received little cooperation from the military in its attempts to control production and procurement. The military in fact routinely *blocked* the WIB's efforts to establish centralized control. At best, the WIB shared control with the military, it did not rule over it. Thus the sovereignty of civilian control over the military was an ephemeral one at best. The same can be said of the nation's mobilization experience during World War II. Although civilian officials were given specific authority to review and control military procurement, these powers were often ceded to military officials, and the procurement process thus fell victim to unbalanced production and wasteful duplication. So Wilson's seeming inability to assert complete control over the military during Korea came as no great surprise to many.[70]

It was also clear by this time that mobilization planners were loath to cut too deeply into the civilian economy for the sake of rearmament. To do so would have been political suicide with the 1952 elections only a year away. Administration officials could ill-afford to make such a move with the president's reelection decision as yet undecided and the fate of the Democratically controlled Congress in the balance. Neither the public nor congressional conservatives would likely have stood for deep cuts in civilian production either. The DPA and NPA often refused to drastically limit supplies to smaller industries and non-defense producers, even when such a step may have been justified in the name of rearmament. The agencies were fully committed to preserving and strengthening the civilian economy and small business interests to every extent possible. And like other mobilization agencies, they were also determined to carry out the administration's "guns and butter"

69. Letter to Charles Wilson, June 28, 1951, RG 277-Correspondence with Government Agencies, box 14, NA; Memorandum for Members of the Production Executive Committee, November 30, 1951, RG 296-Records Maintained by the Administrator, Classified General Files, box 2, file: "Production Executive Committee Agenda," NA; Memorandum to J. R. S., September 18, 1951, Papers of David H. Stowe, box 3, file: "Formation of National Advisory Board on Mobilization Policy and Relationship to Labor," HSTL.

70. Cuff, *War Industries Board,* 2, 268; Novick, *Wartime Production Controls,* 3, 370, 372, 383–85, 387, 401; Nelson, *Arsenal of Democracy,* xvii, 212–42.

program—a program predicated upon a harmonious balance between civilian and defense production.[71]

All of these problems and differences of opinion formed the battles lines of a substantial debate over the extent and pacing of the rearmament program. The debate took place between military and civilian planners in the Truman administration, among members of Congress, and even among industry leaders. Given the problems spawned by mobilization as well as the deficiencies in the effort itself, it is hardly shocking that such a debate occurred when it did. At issue was far more than the temporary dislocations caused by rearmament, however. The debate once again conjured up ghostly specters of an American garrison state—armed to the teeth and under the hypnotic spell of the military and national security establishments.

During the early summer of 1951, amidst the talk of an anticipated Korean armistice, military planners and the Joint Chiefs of Staff (JCS) began lobbying for an increase in military production above the goals set in January and February. Most notably, they pushed for an Air Force of 130 to 150 wings, up from the 95 wings planned during the winter. The new military demands added up to a $15-billion increase above the rearmament program already under way. Citing growing tensions in Iran, and the drain on long-term readiness because of Korea, military and defense officials decided that current rearmament goals would be insufficient to prosecute the Korean War and assure an adequate defense and mobilization base for the long-haul. In essence, they wanted to ensure the complete fulfillment of NSC-68. The military's request put the administration in quite a bind. Given the fact that current goals were not being met, how could mobilization planners fit increased demand into an already overtaxed delivery system? Because of their commitment to retain uninterrupted production of civilian goods, the only available solution was to space out the production of additional military hardware, just as they had done with the current production program. The peak of production was pushed back once more. Now planners assumed that the peak would not be hit until early 1953.[72]

71. National Advisory Board on Mobilization Policy, Meeting No. 11, September 17 and September 18, 1951, Papers of Harry S. Truman, White House Central Files, Confidential Files, box 26, file: "National Advisory Board on Mobilization Policy, 1951–1952," HSTL; *Business Week* (November 3, 1951): 76–78; *Newsweek* 38 (November 19, 1951): 78.

72. National Advisory Board on Mobilization Policy, Meeting No. 7, July 10, 1951, Papers of Harry S. Truman, White House Central Files, Confidential Files, box 26, file: "National Advisory Board on Mobilization Policy, 1951–53," HSTL; Defense Mobilization Board, Meeting No. 13, July 11, 1951, RG 296-Records Maintained by the Administrator, Classified Files, box 2, file: "Defense Mobilization Board Meetings," NA;

The JCS's request did not go unchallenged. In fact, the planned increases in military production sparked a series of divisive debates over the depth and breadth of mobilization. The first debate took place within the White House—amidst the president's own advisory board on mobilization policy. The board, which White House officials termed a "cross-section of the main pressure groups of the nation," directly challenged the military's recommendations for increased military expenditures over and above current goals.[73] In a September 17 meeting of the Advisory Board, one described as "desultory," by a White House staffer, the consensus of opinion was that the administration had to come to grips with the Cold War rearmament process, to decide whether or not the high level of civilian production could be continued in light of shortages and the anticipated long-term defense buildup. And directly raising the scenario of a garrison state in the making, board members expressed deep concerns that "military authorities may now be controlling the economic destiny of this country . . . (threatening) the American democratic system which requires ultimate sovereignty of civilian authority over military authority."[74] It was at this same meeting that board member and labor leader Walter Reuther doubted Charles Wilson's ability to control military procurement. The board's concerns were not new; they were the very same ones that had been brought to the fore since the Korean mobilization was undertaken. But unlike the complaints lodged by political opponents, the issues discussed at the board could not be dismissed as partisan political rhetoric. The administration had to address the board's concerns and in the process of doing so, conducted an internal debate over the same issues.

By early October, the battle lines among administration officials over the pacing of mobilization were clearly defined. Favoring a continuation of the present buildup were the by-now familiar hawks on the subject—Dean Acheson, George Marshall, and Leon Keyserling. In

---

Memo for the President, July 23, 1951, President's Secretary's Files, box 131, file: "General File-1951, National Advisory Board-Mobilization," HSTL; "Appraisal of the Impact That Could Result from Changes in the Military Program," no date (assumed, however, to be September 12, 1951), RG 296-Classified Files, box 2, file: "Defense Mobilization Board Meetings," NA; *Business Week* (August 18, 1951): 21–23.

73. Memo to J. R. S. [John R. Steelman], September 28, 1951, Papers of Harry S. Truman, WHCF, Confidential Files, box 26, file: "National Advisory Board on Mobilization Policy, 1951–52," HSTL.

74. National Advisory Board on Mobilization Policy, Meeting No. 11, September 17, 1951, WHCF, Confidential Files, box 26, file: "National Advisory Board on Mobilization Policy, 1951–52," HSTL; Memo to J. R. S., September 18, 1951, Papers of David H. Stowe, box 3, file: "Formation of National Advisory Board and Its Relationship to Labor," HSTL.

addition to opposing cutbacks in the already planned mobilization program, they also sympathized with the JCS's requests for additional production. Keyserling, whose economic philosophy heavily influenced mobilization and stabilization decisions, told Truman in early November that the pace of rearmament should move faster, that military deliveries to Europe should be stepped up, and that "it is well within our economic resources as a nation . . . to lift considerably even above current plans and program the size and speed of our defense program and our supply of needed items to forces and peoples overseas."[75] Other White House advisers, as well as ESA director Eric Johnston, did not share these views, however. Concerned about the long-term impact of rearmament, not to mention inflationary pressures, White House aides John R. Steelman and Harold L. Enarson openly questioned the wisdom of Keyserling's approach. Johnston, just back from Europe and deeply concerned with its inflationary problems, decided to resign his ESA post over the pacing of rearmament. Downcast over the earlier dilution of domestic inflation controls, and worried that Charles Wilson would cave in to the wishes of the JCS by increasing mobilization, Johnston chose to opt out of the dispute by resigning and returning to the Motion Picture Association of America.[76]

By late October, those favoring a stepped-up mobilization program lost the battle. But this did not mean that those favoring a rollback won. The administration compromised, choosing to walk a tightrope between the two warring factions. Admitting that the mobilization situation warranted continued urgency, but concerned about economic dislocations, mobilization officials took the middle way. First, they decided to rephase the present program by establishing clear-cut priorities, and adjusting production accordingly. The goal was to speed the production of critical items, while holding off on nonessential production, plant expansion, and long-term mobilization goals. Second, they assured military planners at the same time that their increased demands would be met. Meeting these demands, however, would take time—some production schedules were postponed into 1955.

75. Letter to the President, November 2, 1951, Papers of Leon Keyserling, box 1, file: "Correspondence between HST and Keyserling (1 of 2)," HSTL; see also Memo for Mr. Murphy, August 25, 1951, Papers of Harry S. Truman, OF, box 1737, file: "2855-A," HSTL.
76. National Advisory Board on Mobilization Policy, Meeting No. 12, October 15 and 16, 1951, President's Secretary's Files, box 142, file: "Advisory Board on Mobilization Policy, National," HSTL; Oral History Interview with Leon H. Keyserling, Washington, DC, May 3, May 10, May 19, 1971, by Jerry N. Hess, pp. 137–38, HSTL; McQuaid, *Uneasy Partners*, 61–62; *Newsweek* 38 (September 17, 1951): 67.

The policy trajectory set in October thus did not cut back mobilization per se. Appropriations would stay roughly the same, as would production goals and force strength. What did change was the pacing of rearmament. Expenditures and production would be stretched-out and prioritized over a longer period of time. Implicit in this new approach was the complete and final integration of the Korean mobilization with the Cold War rearmament program envisioned in NSC-68. For the first time, policymakers managed to synchronize the means with the ends of the entire arms buildup.[77]

As soon as mobilization planners charted this new course, Congress and the business community resurrected the debate over rearmament, a debate that then spilled over into the public domain and encompassed far more than just mobilization policy. Lambasted by members of Congress and rebuked by the likes of the CED and other business groups, the Truman administration was forced to redouble its efforts to explain its mobilization, economic, and national security policies. Its efforts were too little, too late, however. By December 1951, it was clear that Truman had lost the support not only from corporate liberals and organized labor, but also from within his own party. Truman's last full year in office reflected this fact, as moderate Democrats and liberal-internationalist businessmen turned against him in droves.

In late November, Senator Lyndon B. Johnson (D-TX) let loose a salvo of criticism aimed at Truman's rearmament program. Johnson, acting in his capacity as chairman of the Preparedness Subcommittee of the Armed Services Committee, berated the Pentagon for complacency, criticized civilian planners for failing to curb non-defense production, and scolded the Department of Defense for trying to cover up production weaknesses by revising schedules downward. Johnson's surprise attack in turn fueled Republican criticism over the alleged failure to adequately supply Eisenhower's NATO forces. Republican Senator Henry Cabot Lodge of Massachusetts presciently intimated that if Eisenhower decided to run for president on the Republican ticket in 1952, he could use the administration's flagging defense program

77. Defense Mobilization Board Meeting No. 16, Addendum No. 1, September 12, 1951, RG 296, Records Maintained by the Administrator, Classified General Files, box 2, file: "Defense Mobilization Board Meetings," NA; Defense Mobilization Board Meeting No. 19, November 14, 1951, RG 296, Records Maintained by the Administrator, Classified General Files, box 2, file: "Defense Mobilization Board Meetings," NA; Letter to Charles B. Stauffacher, December 4, 1951, RG 277, Correspondence with Government Agencies, box 14, NA; *Business Week* (November 3, 1951): 76–78.

and its attempted cover-up as central campaign themes. Although little came of these congressional flare-ups in the short-term, they served to bring mobilization issues to the attention of the American public while at the same time solidifying opposition to Truman's policies.[78]

Once Senator Johnson's allegations hit the headlines, the debate over rearmament was played out once more, and this time it included the business community. Deputy Secretary of Defense William C. Foster, addressing the International Conference of Manufacturers, urged industrialists to step up production as much as possible. Addressing the same group, Philip D. Reed, chairman of the board of General Electric and a prominent member of the CED, urged the Truman administration to trim back the mobilization program by phasing in production goals over a longer time period. Reed warned that the rearmament effort could bring about "serious economic and political disturbances."[79] Robert Wilson, president of Standard Oil of Indiana, echoed Reed's sentiments, asserting that "inflation is a more imminent danger than a Communist attack."[80] Despite the dubious veracity of some of these arguments, business attacks on the mobilization program nonetheless stung the administration hard—especially Reed's critique. Charles Wilson, president of G.E., could not have much appreciated such criticism coming from his own board chairman. Just before Christmas, Wilson felt obliged to defend himself.

Appearing before the Joint Committee on Defense Production, Wilson adamantly asserted that the administration's program was the right course and should continue as planned. "I am more than ever convinced that the program we have is the right program. Between the two poles of criticism, we are carrying out something of a middle-of-the-road policy. Unfortunately, a middle-course program is hard to dramatize."[81] The committee, which had been kept apprised of the mobilization program every step of the way, generally agreed that Wilson's policy course was the correct one to pursue. In a private memorandum to Truman, Wilson defended his policies and derided his critics with a particularly cogent analysis: "There is no way of measuring our score against 'par' for the

78. *Newsweek* 38 (November 26, 1951): 24–25; *Business Week* (December 1, 1951): 19–20; Memorandum for the President, November 23, 1951, President's Secretary's Files, Subject File-Agencies, box 147, file: "Office of Defense Mobilization-Misc.," HSTL.

79. *Newsweek* 38 (December 17, 1951): 21–22 (Reed quoted on p. 22).

80. *Business Week* (December 15, 1951): 24–25 (Wilson quoted on p. 25).

81. U.S. Congress, Joint Committee on Defense Production, *Defense Production Act, Progress Report No. 11, Hearings before the Joint Committee on Defense Production,* 82nd. Cong., 1st sess., December 10, 1951, 700.

course, because the course has never been played before and hence par has never been computed."[82] Wilson was right. The mobilization for Korea and the Cold War defied conventional attempts to appraise its efficiency and efficacy because it was a unique situation. Never before had the nation been involved in a "limited war" in another corner of the world. Nor had it ever attempted to prepare itself for a protracted military and political struggle with a foreign foe. The debates that occurred in the late fall arose from this novel set of circumstances, and engendered all of the fears and uncertainties such a gray area of preparedness naturally wrought.

The debates over mobilization, dating all the way back to the extension of the Defense Production Act, were more than just arguments over pacing and prioritization. They were struggles over the entire makeup of the nation's political, economic, military, and national security landscapes. They were pitched battles over how best to fight the Cold War within the nation's traditional political-economic parameters. Those who viewed the rearmament as a threat to the "American system" fought against its immense costs and government controls. Those who viewed the Soviet Union and the Red Menace as the greater threat appeared willing to accept rearmament as a means to preserve the American way. The Truman administration, sympathetic to both points of view, tried valiantly to forge a middle way between the two extremes. Unable to satisfy completely either contingent, policymakers left themselves open to continual criticism.

The rephasing of the mobilization program, then, was undertaken for a variety of reasons. Political problems at home and abroad, economic dislocations, industry backlash to rearmament policy, labor dissatisfaction, dilution of control mechanisms, failure to raise adequate revenue, and fears of a garrison state all forced changes in the administration's mobilization program. But equally important in these changes was the actual performance of the program itself. The momentum—or lack thereof—in defense production had as much to do with the stretch-out as did outside influences. In the broadest sense then, the Truman administration's Korean mobilization effort, rooted as it was in the traditions of the nation's political economy, was a self-limiting effort. And in the absence of a substantial war that directly threatened the United States, mobilization officials could do little more

---

82. Memorandum for the President, November 23, 1951, President's Secretary's Files, Subject Files-Agencies, box 147, file: "Office of Defense Mobilization-Misc.," HSTL.

than adjust rearmament based upon internal performance and external pressure.

Without a doubt, the Truman administration knew that to push the United States and its allies too far too fast with rearmament could be every bit as detrimental as moving too slowly. In Charles Wilson's own words, "we must not lose sight . . . that a strong economy is the backbone of a long range mobilization program."[83] To risk worsening inflation, materials shortages, and a deterioration in the standard of living would have been tantamount to abandoning the very system the United States and its allies were trying to protect.

On the other hand, American policymakers perceived in the Soviet Union a palpable threat to their national interests. However exaggerated these threats may seem today, they seemed menacingly real to the domestic and foreign policymakers of the early 1950s. To have ignored or downplayed these threats would have been to abdicate the United States' preponderance of influence within the international community. The United States thus took up the gauntlet. But in doing so, it risked altering fundamentally its political, economic, and industrial structure. To avoid this, or at the least to lessen the impact, policymakers turned toward the tried and true gospel of decentralization, corporatism, and volunteerism. In fact, the Cold War and the Korean era mobilization introduced these trends into entirely new arenas.

83. Memorandum for the President, December 21, 1951, President's Secretary's Files-Agencies, box 147, file: "Office of Defense Mobilization-Misc.," HSTL.

V

Crises of Confidence

The Steel Crisis, Congressional Intransigence, and the Evolution of National Security, January–June 1952

Nineteen fifty-two dawned under a pall of uncertainty and frustration. The Korean War, stalemated for many months, dragged on with no end in sight. The president's approval rating stood at an all-time low of 23 percent. Mobilization officials still faced a barrage of criticism for their decision to stretch out the rearmament program. The nation continued to hold its breath as the Wage Stabilization Board worked furiously to avoid a strike of some 600,000 unionized steel workers. And, most disturbing to the Truman administration, its number-one military man and war hero General Dwight D. Eisenhower announced in early January that he was willing to accept the Republican party's presidential nomination. Eisenhower's announcement sent an unambiguous signal to his boss and his party: The Republicans were poised to make Korea the central theme in their efforts to dislodge twenty years of Democratic dominance in Washington.[1]

The first half of 1952 was dominated by the steel crisis, the ramifications of which were monumental. Unable to bring the nation's steel companies and their unionized employees together, Truman authorized the seizure of the companies to avert a stoppage in steel production. For nearly two months the government ran the steel mills. In June, the U.S. Supreme Court ruled the seizure unconstitutional, handing Truman a crushing defeat while at the same time establishing an historic

1. For statistics and analyses of Truman's approval ratings and public sentiment toward the Korean War see John E. Mueller, *War, Presidents, and Public Opinion;* Ronald J. Caridi, *The Korean War and American Politics: The Republican Party as a Case Study;* and George H. Gallup, *The Gallup Poll: Public Opinion 1935–1971,* three volumes. The figure used in this paragraph was provided by the Gallup Poll as quoted in *Newsweek* 39 (January 7, 1952): 13.

legal precedent that set distinct parameters on the president's authority to act in emergency situations. The ruling precipitated a fifty-three–day strike that imperiled the nation's economy and threatened to derail defense production. Furthermore, the way in which the administration handled the steel crisis set the tone for the entire mobilization and stabilization effort. First stung by the Supreme Court's reversal of the steel seizure and then left powerless to avert a massive strike, the Truman administration lost what little support it had for continuing an economic stabilization program.

Besides the immediate vicissitudes engendered by the steel crisis, administration officials continued to grapple with the problems of economic stabilization and price-and-wage decontrol. As frustration with the Korean War and the steel crisis mounted, stabilization officials came under increasing pressure to relax or suspend price controls. As a result, the Office of Price Stabilization (OPS) was forced into a rather hasty decontrol program for certain commodities, despite warnings from other mobilization officials that inflation might soon be on the march again. At the same time, Congress took aim at the administration's economic stabilization programs, further diluting the Defense Production Act, slashing operating budgets of stabilization agencies, and limiting the WSB's purview. It was clear by the spring of 1952 that the most the administration could hope for was a rearguard attack on inflation.

Amidst all of this turmoil, policymakers not only continued to fine tune the pacing and prioritization of rearmament, but they also continued to redefine the nation's overall strategic and national security imperatives. In doing so they altered their conceptions of mobilization planning and Cold War readiness. The decisions that they made in this regard were based not so much upon the perceived motives of the main adversary—the Soviet Union—but rather on other forces: technological advances and mounting domestic pressures to hold down defense spending, lower tax burdens, and relax economic controls. Also shaping policy decisions were the fears of a financially bankrupt garrison state on the one hand and the dread of atomic attack on the other. Guided by the nation's political and economic heritage, national security planners and mobilization officials marshaled a variety of corporative impulses to attempt fundamental changes in the scope and structure of the burgeoning industrial-defense sector. In the end, however, the impetus for many of these changes came not from public policy, but from private enterprise itself.

It became clear during the first half of the year that the Truman administration had come to view the steel crisis as the ultimate litmus test for its economic stabilization program. This was a grave misjudgment. By basing the success of its anti-inflation program upon the outcome of the steel case, administration officials unduly accentuated an already prickly situation. Sensing the administration's exaggerated stake in the crisis, congressional and public opinion turned quickly against the White House—and the entire stabilization program—especially after Truman's seizure of the steel mills in April. The administration thus unwittingly hamstrung its own stabilization efforts and, worse yet, handed the Republicans a ready-made issue for the 1952 campaigns.

The steel crisis of 1952 can be traced back to the fourth quarter of 1951. In October, with the labor contract between U.S. steel companies and the United Steel Workers of America set to expire on December 31, the union and steel officials undertook negotiations for a new contract. Although some administration officials—most notably those concerned with defense production—were deeply troubled by the prospects of a steel strike, White House officials downplayed such a possibility. It was evident from the start that the steelworkers would seek some sort of a wage hike, but Truman and his top advisers remained confident that a new contract could be drafted without government involvement and without a pass-through increase in steel prices. As it turned out, however, the White House seriously miscalculated the steel industry's insistence on price increases commensurate with wage hikes.[2]

By November, it had become obvious that there would be no quick solution to the stalled steel talks. The president of U.S. Steel himself, Benjamin Fairless, remarked that "whether our workers are to get a raise, and how much it will be if they do, is a matter which probably cannot be determined by collective bargaining, and will apparently have to be decided finally in Washington."[3] At the same time, White House officials began to plot their position on the steel dispute. The Council of Economic Advisers (CEA) was firmly against any settlement that would have necessitated an increase in the price of steel. Furthermore, the CEA determined that the steel industry's profits were

2. ESA Executive Meeting No. 7, October 17, 1951, RG 296, Economics, box 23, NA; Memorandum for the President, October 19, 1951, Papers of Charles S. Murphy, box 13, file: "Steelman, Dr. John R.," HSTL.

3. Maeva Marcus, *Truman and the Steel Seizure Case*, 58. Marcus' monograph remains the most detailed and accurate account of the steel crisis. The following section of this chapter is based extensively on that work.

sufficiently high to absorb any reasonable increase in wages. The CEA's position essentially became the administration's position on the subject. From then on, the administration came to identify more with labor's position than with industry management's. As the deadline for negotiations neared, the White House became increasingly anxious to avoid a strike, which it believed would seriously hamper the defense program.[4]

Unable to bring the two sides of the dispute together, and unwilling to invoke the Taft-Hartley Act, which was the bane of organized labor, Truman had little choice but to certify the steel case to the Wage Stabilization Board (WSB). Invoking Taft-Hartley, which Truman had conspicuously vetoed in 1947 much to the delight of labor, would have provoked the unions' wrath in an important election year. Instead, on December 22, the president handed the steel case to the WSB and prevailed upon the steel union to delay strike action until the WSB issued its findings. It took the WSB until March to rule on the dispute.[5]

On January 3, CIO head Philip Murray convened a special convention of steelworkers. At that convention he lambasted the steel companies for their intransigence and greed and told his members that "we re-affirm our determination to achieve our goals . . . We seek only that which is our due. We ask for no more; we will take no less."[6] After the convention, the steel dispute faded into the background as the WSB deliberated on a verdict. On January 2, the WSB appointed a special six-member tripartite panel to settle the steel dispute. On January 8, the steel panel commenced formal hearings on the case, receiving testimony from a wide array of witnesses from both the union

4. CEA Memo, November 14, 1951, RG 295, OPS Records, Records of Joseph Freehill, box 706, file: "Steel," NA; Memo for the President, November 15, 1951, Papers of Leon Keyserling, box 3, file: "Prices and Wages in Steel," HSTL; Memo to the President, November 28, 1951, Papers of Leon Keyserling, box 3, file: "Prices and Wages in Steel," HSTL; Defense Mobilization Board Meeting No. 20, November 28, 1951, RG 296, Records Maintained by the Administrator, Classified General Files, box 2, file: "Defense Mobilization Board Mtgs.-Foreign Allocation Policy," NA.

5. Marcus, *Truman and the Steel Seizure Case*, 58–68; Robert J. Donovan, *Tumultuous Years*, 382–83; Letter to Philip Murray, December 31, 1951, RG 296, Letters/Memos of Eric Johnston, 1951, box 103, NA; "Wage Stabilization Program, 1950–1953," vol. 1, (hereafter "Wage Stabilization," with appropriate volume number) p. xi, RG 293, Records of the Wage Stabilization Board and Salary Stabilization Board of the Economic Stabilization Agency, box 1, file: "WSB-ESA, 6/30/53," NA.

6. Statement and Resolution of the Special Convention of the United Steelworkers of America, Atlantic City, New Jersey, January 3, 1952, RG 296, Letters and Memos of Eric Johnston, 1951, box 103, file: "Statement and Resolution (Steel)," NA.

and the steel corporations. The panel released its final hundred-page report on the steel situation to the full WSB on March 14.[7]

In the meantime, the stabilization agencies underwent important changes in top personnel. First, Truman replaced the recently resigned ESA director Eric Johnston with Roger Lowell Putnam, who was confirmed by the Senate on January 31. Putnam, a Harvard graduate and a direct descendant of the prominent Lowell and Putnam families of Massachusetts, was a lifelong liberal Democrat and a well-weathered politician, having served three terms as mayor of Springfield, Massachusetts. He also was a successful businessman and served as the director of the Office of Contract Settlement after World War II. Throughout his life, Putnam demonstrated a strong affinity for the working class, and his view was apparent as he took the reins of the ESA. Putnam was also determined to keep inflation down, showing even more resolve in this area than had his predecessor. Putnam's fears of inflationary pressures coupled with his sympathy for labor thus set him on a collision course with the nation's steel companies.[8]

On January 23, OPS director Michael V. DiSalle resigned his post to run for the U.S. Senate. Truman named Ellis G. Arnall to replace him. President of the Dixie Insurance Company and the Society of Motion Picture Producers at the time of his appointment, Arnall had enjoyed a brilliant political career in his native state of Georgia. First elected to the Georgia House of Representatives at the age of twenty-six, he moved up the political ladder quickly, becoming the youngest governor in the nation when elected in 1942. As governor, Arnall instituted a variety of liberal reform measures, including the repeal of Georgia's long-standing poll tax. Throughout his political career, he demonstrated a visceral dislike of monopolistic companies and a strong admiration for labor unions, which he believed had become the savior of the working class. When appointed to the OPS post, Arnall pledged a strong commitment to keeping prices at bay. And like ESA Director Putnam, he tended to sympathize with labor rather than with business.[9]

7. "Wage Stabilization," vol. 1, p. xi–xii, RG 293, Records of the Wage Stabilization Board, box 1, file: "WSB-ESA, 6/30/51," NA.

8. Marcus, *Truman and the Steel Seizure Case*, 30; *Business Week* (January 5, 1952): 25–26; ESA Weekly Roundup for the Administrator (hereafter ESA Weekly), January 29, 1952, RG 296, Records of Reports and Secretariat, box 3, NA; Memo for Dr. Steelman, January 24, 1952, Papers of Harry S. Truman, OF, box 1737, file: "2855-A," HSTL.

9. ESA Weekly, January 29, 1952, RG 296, Reports and Secretariat, box 3, NA; ESA Weekly, February 12, 1952, RG 296, Reports and Secretariat, box 3, NA; Marcus, *Truman and the Steel Seizure Case*, 30–31; United State Senate, Committee on Banking and

So it was that as the steel case moved toward its first crisis in March, two of the top four mobilization officials were new to their posts. Their political viewpoints were very much different from that of ODM chief Charles Wilson, who in no way looked upon organized labor with much admiration. The new heads of the ESA and OPS were even less likely than their predecessors to grant price increases that might spark inflation. They were indeed inflation hawks, eyeing warily the steel executives' contentions that wage increases must automatically result in price hikes. The stage was now set for a showdown as the WSB issued its recommendations on the steel dispute.

The Wage Stabilization Board issued its final recommendations on the steel dispute on March 20. Over the clamorous objections of its six industry members, the WSB recommended higher pay, increased fringe benefits, and a guaranteed union shop to the steelworkers. The entire package would have raised the pay of each employee about twenty-six cents per hour. Not surprisingly, the steel companies balked at the recommendations, asserting that they would drive up the price of steel by twelve dollars per ton. Even the public was outraged by the seeming generosity of the WSB package. The business community and much of the national press asserted that the entire anti-inflation program would be wrecked by such a settlement. But the Truman administration had little choice but to accept the recommendations as fair.[10] As presidential adviser Harold L. Enarson observed, "if the action of the Board were repudiated by the administration, there can be little doubt that the Board would break up and the stabilization program would be gone."[11]

Neither the White House nor the OPS had any intention of raising the price ceiling for steel above the limit set by the 1951 Capehart Amendment to the Defense Production Act. Under the Capehart provision, the

---

Currency, *Nomination of Ellis G. Arnall, Hearings,* 82d Cong., 2d sess., 1952, 1; see also Ellis G. Arnall, *The Shore Dimly Seen* for Arnall's political philosophy and his views on economic and political reforms in the South.

10. Donovan, *Tumultuous Years,* 383; Marcus, *Truman and the Steel Seizure Case,* 64–65; "Wage Stabilization Program, 1950–1953," vol. 1, xii, RG 293 Records of the WSB/SSB, box 1, NA; Memo to Ellis Arnall, April 7, 1952, RG 295, Records of the OPS, Decentralized Files of the OPS Directors, box 26, NA.

For business reactions to the WSB recommendations see *Newsweek* 39 (April 21, 1952): 33–34, 37; *Business Week* (April 19, 1952): 180; Statement of the WSB Industry Members (release), March 20, 1952, in U.S. House of Representatives, 82d. Cong., 2d sess., March 24, 1952, *Congressional Record,* 98, 2784; ESA Weekly, March 25, 1952, RG 296, Records, Reports and Secretariat, box 3, NA.

11. Memorandum, note for the files, no date, Papers of Harold L. Enarson, box 3, file: "Letters sent re steel strike, 1951–1952," HSTL.

steel companies were entitled to a price increase of two to three dollars per ton, a far cry from the twelve dollars per ton cited as the necessary pass-through by the steel executives. The crisis deepened. The steel companies refused to accept the WSB recommendations without a concomitant price increase, and the steelworkers would accept nothing less than what the WSB had suggested. ODM chief Charles Wilson was the one administration official who refused to support the wage board's proposal. He believed that the terms were far too generous toward the union and that the steel companies were due price increases sufficient enough to offset wage increases.[12]

On March 24, Wilson flew to Key West to meet with the vacationing president. In that meeting, Wilson spelled out his concern with the WSB proposals, apparently convincing Truman that the steel companies deserved a price increase above the Capehart ceiling. Wilson returned to the capital with an understanding that the administration would permit a price increase of four to five dollars per ton. Four days later, at a White House special conference of mobilization officials, Wilson and Truman clashed. Their recollections of the Key West agreement differed, and now the president was unwilling to allow the price increase envisioned by Wilson. Wilson was furious and believed that Truman had hopelessly undermined his integrity as chief mobilizer. The blustering ODM chief promptly resigned, resulting in a barrage of criticism aimed at the White House. Now the president was in an almost impossible bind. With public support for wage and price controls evaporating, and his top mobilizer gone in a huff, Truman—and his new interim ODM director John Steelman—tried one more time to settle the steel crisis.[13]

12. Arnall Steel Statement, April 3, 1952, RG 295, OPS, Records of Joseph Freehill, box 203, file: "Steel-Press Releases," NA; Memo to the President, March 28, 1952, Papers of Leon Keyserling, box 3, file: "Current Issues and Government Policy in Steel," HSTL; Memo to the President, March 28, 1952, Papers of Leon Keyserling (different memo from preceding one), box 3, file: "Current Issues and Government Policy in Steel," HSTL; Donovan, *Tumultuous Years*, 383–84; Marcus, *Truman and the Steel Seizure Case*, 68–69.

13. Marcus, *Truman and the Steel Seizure Case*, 69–73; Donovan, *Tumultuous Years*, 384. The general details on the Truman-Wilson controversy are well known, although no verbatim, third party notes of the Key West meeting are available. Thus, it cannot be determined whose memory of that meeting is more accurate—Truman's or Wilson's. For a variety of viewpoints on the subject see Harry S. Truman, *Memoirs, Years of Trial and Hope*, vol. 2 (paperback ed.), 469; ESA Weekly, April 1, 1952, RG 296, Records, Reports and Secretariat, box 3, NA; Memo for the Files, April 1, 1952, Papers of Harold L. Enarson, box 4, file: "Memoranda Sept. 51–July 52," HSTL; "Charles E. Wilson's Own Story of Break with Truman," *U.S. News* 32 (May 2, 1952): 11–14; "The Last Days of Charlie Wilson," *Fortune* 45 (June 1952):85–86.

In fact, few were surprised that the president turned to John R. Steelman as a temporary replacement for Charles Wilson. Born in Arkansas and trained as a Ph.D. economist, Steelman was a consummate behind-the-scenes Washington insider. Having first arrived in Washington during the waning days of the New Deal to direct the U.S. Conciliation Service, Steelman was the first person to hold the top White House staff post, "assistant to the president," which Truman had created especially for him in 1946. Prior to that post, he briefly headed the Office of War Mobilization and Reconversion. And somewhat ironically, Steelman had preceded Stuart Symington as the acting chairman of the National Security Resources Board from 1948 through 1950 while simultaneously continuing his duties as assistant to the president. Thus, after Wilson's hasty exit, Truman once again turned to Steelman in a pinch because he trusted him implicitly and because he knew that Steelman was at least familiar with the broad issues of industrial mobilization and economic stabilization issues. Furthermore, Truman realized that by April 1952 the mobilization program was already winding down and that Steelman would be in a "caretaker" role—carrying out policies already set by his predecessors. In fact, as Steelman himself later wrote, "when Wilson left . . . the mobilization emphasis had already shifted from a sharp build-up of controls to the development of an orderly way to decontrol."[14]

Thus, Steelman had little to do with the establishment of mobilization policy, but his talents as a compromiser, a hardworking administrator, and sometimes a "glad-hander," would serve the Truman administration well as it embarked down the slippery slope of the developing steel crisis. Truman, who had always depended upon John Steelman to keep many balls in the air while at the same time keeping needless details and bureaucratic skirmishes out of the Oval Office, hoped that his assistant could hold the line during the crisis while he searched for a permanent replacement for the departed Wilson. Still, though, Steelman's brief five-month stint as acting ODM director was anything but easy. Most of his time was occupied with negotiations between steel

---

For reaction to Wilson's resignation see Memo for Mr. Steelman, April 1, 1952, Papers of Harold L. Enarson, box 3, file: "Lucas Committee Amendment," HSTL; ESA Weekly, April 8, 1952, RG 296, Records, Reports and Secretariat, box 3, NA; Marcus, *Truman and the Steel Seizure Case*, 282, n. 76.

14. Steelman and Kreager, "The Executive Office as Administrative Coordinator," 688–709. For Steelman's quote, see 705; Patrick Anderson, *The Presidents' Men: White House Assistants of Franklin D. Roosevelt, Harry S. Truman, Dwight D. Eisenhower, John F. Kennedy, and Lyndon B. Johnson*, 92–93.

executives and the steelworkers' union. Beyond that, he became more and more preoccupied with issues of price and material decontrol. Furthermore, despite Steelman's considerable clout and experience in the White House, he lacked a firm understanding of the details of the Korean mobilization program because neither of his predecessors—Stuart Symington and Charles Wilson—had much enjoyed sharing power, not to mention information, with other members of the administration.[15]

During the first week of April, the steel companies offered the union a new contract. Their terms were substantially below those recommended by the WSB. At the same time, administration officials told the companies that steel prices could be raised by $4.50 per ton. But neither the union nor the steel executives were mollified by the new terms, and the stage was set for a nationwide steel strike. The United Steelworkers voted to strike effective April 9. Truman was convinced that the steel executives were greedy and unreasonable. He was determined to head off a strike and prepared to appear on national television the day before the strike was to begin. Meanwhile, Truman's top mobilization officials and Defense Secretary Robert Lovett managed to convince the president that a steel stoppage would not only hamper long-term rearmament plans, but would also endanger American soldiers in Korea. Unwilling to imperil the nation's defense effort or its troops in the field, and determined to save the economic stabilization program, Truman decided to seize the steel mills to avoid a work stoppage.[16]

On the evening of April 8, 1952, the embattled president appeared on national television, announcing that he was seizing the nation's major steel mills effective as of midnight. Reactions to the seizure were instantaneous and vituperative—equaled perhaps only by the reactions to Truman's firing of Douglas MacArthur a year earlier. The steel executives, business organizations, newspapers, magazines, and many in Congress excoriated Truman's action as that of a dictator. Some of the president's most stalwart supporters remained conspicuously silent. The volley of criticism aimed at Truman was certainly not surprising. For Truman's political adversaries and those who viewed the Korean War as a fatal mistake sure to lead the nation toward one-man

15. Anderson, *The Presidents' Men*, 92–93; "An Analysis of the Central Management Elements of the Defense Mobilization Program," October 23, 1952, Papers of David H. Stowe, box 3, file: "Organizational Study: ODM-NSRB-NPA-ESA (1952)," HSTL.

16. Donovan, *Tumultuous Years*, 384–85; Marcus, *Truman and the Steel Seizure Case*, 75–82; Truman, *Memoirs*, vol. 2, 469–72; David McCullough, *Truman* 894–99; ESA Weekly, April 15, 1952, RG 296, Records, Reports and Secretariat, box 3, NA.

dictatorial rule, the seizure once again brought to the fore the ghastly apparition of a militarized garrison state. What is more, conservative business organizations and right-wing Republicans saw in the move a detestable capitulation to organized labor, if not an outright bow to radical syndicalism.[17]

Truman's main objective in seizing the steel mills undoubtedly was to avoid a catastrophic stoppage in steel production. But it was by no means the only factor involved in his controversial decision. It was a given that steel supplies, the backbone of the military rearmament program, the fighting forces in Korea, not to mention the economy as a whole, had to be maintained. Truman also realized, however, that to buckle under to the steel companies' demands—or worse yet to invoke Taft-Hartley—would have unnecessarily angered labor in a crucial election year. Furthermore, the White House, along with top stabilization officials like Ellis Arnall and Roger Putnam, had so intertwined the continued success of price controls with their ability to hold steel prices down that any further concessions to the steel executives were unthinkable. Although Truman had announced only a few weeks before the seizure that he would not seek reelection in November, he held firm in his contentions that the steel industry was acting unreasonably and that any upward adjustment in steel prices above the $4.50 per ton already offered would wreck the entire stabilization program. OPS Director Arnall predicted that the price increase sought by the steel industry would drive up the cost of living by at least five percent, adding a minimum of $300 per year to the expenses of the average American household.[18]

17. Donovan, *Tumultuous Years*, 387; Marcus, *Truman and the Steel Seizure Case*, 89–92; McCullough, *Truman*, 888–89; Truman, *Memoirs*, vol. 2, 474–75; ESA Weekly, April 8 and April 15, 1952, RG 296, Records, Reports and Secretariat, box 3, NA; National Advisory Board on Mobilization Policy Meeting No. 16, President's Secretary's Files, Subject File, Agencies A, box 142, file: "Advisory Board on Mobilization Policy, National," HSTL; *U.S. News* 32 (April 18, 1952): 96; *U.S. News* 32 (May 9, 1952): 18–20; *Business Week* (April 19, 1952): 180; *Business Week* (May 3, 1952): 98–99; *Newsweek* 39 (April 21, 1952): 33–34, 37–39; *New York Times*, April 9, 1952, 1, 4–5.

18. "Special Message to the Congress Reporting on the Situation in the Steel Industry," April 9, 1952, U.S. President, *Public Papers of the President of the United States, Harry S. Truman, 1951*, 251; "The People's Stake: Stabilization and Steel Prices," Office of Price Stabilization, Office of Public Information, based upon testimony of Ellis Arnall, director of the Office of Price Stabilization before the Senate Committee on Labor and Public Welfare, April 16, 1952, RG 296, Letters/Memos of the Director, box 103, NA; ESA Weekly, April 22, 1952, RG 296, Reports, Reports and Secretariat, box 3, NA; ESA Release, "Putnam Says Steel Case Tests Nation's Determination to Rearm Successfully," April 25, 1952, RG 295 OPS, Records of Joseph Freehill, box 706, file: "Steel-Press releases," NA.

The steel industry wasted no time in attempting to have the president's seizure order nullified. Invoking the Constitution, the steel companies argued from the start that Truman had no inherent power to seize property. On April 29, U.S. District Court Judge David A. Pine handed the steel industry a temporary victory: He ruled the steel seizure "illegal and without authority of law."[19] Undeterred, the Truman administration won a stay of Judge Pine's order and the Supreme Court of the United States agreed to rule on the dispute. In the interim, the steel mills continued to operate under the government seizure order. It took the Supreme Court one month to rule on the now famous *Youngstown Sheet and Tube Company v. Sawyer* (Secretary Charles Sawyer) case.[20]

On June 2, 1952, the Supreme Court dealt Harry Truman a serious blow. The Court affirmed David Pine's decision by a six to three ruling and declared the president's act of seizure unconstitutional. Truman now had no choice but to hand over control of the mills to their owners. And the steelworkers, all 600,000 of them, walked off the job. Even then, Truman refused to invoke Taft-Hartley. Instead, he went before a joint session of Congress to seek legislation empowering him to seize the steel mills once more until a settlement could be reached. Congress demurred and instead urged the president to invoke the Taft-Hartley Act. Again Truman refused. He preferred to place the blame for a strike on congressional shoulders. The nation thus braced itself for what would be a fifty-three–day steel strike.[21]

Although the steel stoppage was not as catastrophic to the military or the economy as first predicted, it did inflict heavy casualties on certain industries, with auto makers taking the hardest hit. And the longer the strike persisted, the ripple effect on the economy pushed more and more people out of work. On June 9, the National Production Authority (NPA) drastically tightened its CMP control of steel in an effort to keep rearmament programs on schedule. The NPA authorized "crash" priority status to steel orders bearing top priority ratings of military, atomic, and machine tool programs. Thus, for the first time

19. Donovan, *Tumultuous Years*, 388.

20. Marcus, *Truman and the Steel Seizure Case*, 108–9; ESA Weekly, May 6, 1952, RG 296, Records, Reports and Secretariat, box 3, NA.

21. Marcus, *Truman and the Steel Seizure Case*, 130–227, 249–51; Donovan, *Tumultuous Years*, 389–91; McCullough, *Truman*, 900–902; Truman, *Memoirs* vol. 2, 475–77; OPS News Digest (hereafter "OPS News"), June 3, 1952, RG 295, OPS, Central Files, 1952–53, box 632, file: "Daily News Digest, May–August 1952," NA; ESA Weekly, RG 296, ESA, Records, Reports and Secretariat, box 3, file: "ESA Weekly Roundup for the Administrator," NA.

since World War II, top-rated military orders could now automatically push lower priority orders off steel mills' schedules. At the same time, coal mine operators, railroads, and other steel-dependent industries began announcing layoffs and cutbacks. Toward the end of June, military planners began to shut down nonessential production lines of tanks, trucks, bazooka rockets, and mortar shells. Existing inventories were to be depleted before new ones were produced. On June 27, General Electric suspended production of its entire Hotpoint line of appliances, idling four thousand workers in Chicago alone. By early July, the steel stoppage had neared crisis stage; industrial layoffs skyrocketed and the steel reserve for defense needs dwindled to a critically low level.[22]

Under increasing public pressure, and with ominous signs of severe economic and military production dislocations appearing, administration officials redoubled their efforts to end the steel strike. On July 16, Defense Production Administrator Henry H. Fowler wrote to Acting Director Steelman of the ODM that "the cumulative effect of the consequent losses in steel production has mounted to a point where any further delay in reaching a settlement will have extremely serious effects upon the mobilization program and the entire civilian economy."[23] By mid-July, in fact, the forty-five–day steel inventory ceiling established by the CMP was nearly depleted. At the same time, automobile output dropped by more than one-half from the previous month, and the Big Three announced even bigger cuts for the last half of July. In the third week of July, automobile output dropped to a near postwar low.[24]

Finally, on July 24, upon the direct intervention of Truman himself, the steel strike was settled. The United Steelworkers won a union shop clause in their contracts and received a 21.5 cent-per-hour increase in wages and fringe benefits. The steel companies received a total price increase of $5.20 per ton. The agreement was against the judgment of top mobilization and stabilization officials. Roger Putnam, Ellis Arnall, and John Steelman all went on record as opposing the final settlement. Their concern, as it had been since the beginning of the crisis, was

22. OPS News, June 9, 1952, and July 3, 1952, RG 295, OPS, Central Files, 1952–1953, box 632, file: "Daily New Digest, May–August 1952," NA; Wall Street Journal, June 9, 1952, 1–2; ESA Weekly, June 10, 1952, June 18, 1952, and July 27, 1952, RG 296 Records, Reports and Secretariat, box 3, file: "ESA Weekly Roundup," NA; New York Times, July 3, 1952, 5A.

23. Letter to Dr. Steelman, July 16, 1952, RG 277, Records of the National Production Authority, Reference Materials, 1951–53, box 15, file: "Steel Crisis," NA.

24. ESA Weekly, July 22, 1952, and July 29, 1952, RG 296, Records, Reports and Secretariat, box 3, NA; Donovan, Tumultuous Years, 390.

the hike in steel prices. It was clear, however, that the administration settled the crisis because of its deleterious effects on the economy and defense production. Under fire from military planners, Steelman bowed to the pressure and issued a directive raising the ceiling prices on steel. The Council of Economic Advisors estimated that the strike cost the nation some 20 million ingot tons of steel; approximately 520,000 cars (or 12 percent of annual production); and between $600 million and $700 million in lost wages.[25]

The steel crisis resulted in far more than lost production and lost income, however. The crisis precipitated yet another round of hand-wringing over the growth of executive power and prerogative in an era of Cold War—an era already fraught with state secrecy and civil rights abuses. Concomitantly, the nation saw in the steel seizure one more sign of the apocalypse—that the country was becoming a garrison state in which there would be no more room for individual property rights. In the final analysis, by placing so much emphasis on the steel case, and by going toe to toe with the steel companies, administration officials exacerbated the nation's growing ire toward government controls, handed the Republicans and conservative Democrats an easy campaign issue, eroded what little public support remained for the Korean War, and most seriously, severed their last linkage with the liberal business establishment by effectively forcing Charles Wilson to resign. After Wilson's departure from the ODM, business demonstrated a growing reluctance to share its people with mobilization agencies in Washington. In fact, Wilson started a trend; the few long-term mobilization officials still in place had all resigned—or planned to resign—by July, including DPA director Manly Fleischmann and NPA Administrator Henry Fowler. Naturally, the administration found it increasingly difficult to fill vacant mobilization spots.[26]

25. Memo for the President, July 25, 1952, President's Secretary's Files, General Files, box 264, file: "Steelman, John," HSTL; ESA Weekly, July 29, 1952, RG 296, Records, Reports and Secretariat, box 3, NA; Memo to Steelman, July 31, 1952, President's Secretary's Files, General Files, box 264, file: "Steelman, John," HSTL.

26. For various scholarly viewpoints on the steel case vis à vis presidential power and the general concept of an "imperial presidency" see Marcus, *Truman and the Steel Seizure Case*, especially 228–48, 258–60; J. Lawton Collins, *War in Peacetime: The History and Lessons of Korea;* Louis Henkin, *Foreign Affairs and the Constitution;* Alton R. Lee, *Truman and Taft-Hartley: A Question of Mandate;* Robert S. Rankin and Winfried R. Dallmayr, *Freedom and Emergency Powers in the Cold War;* Charles Sawyer, *Concerns of a Conservative Democrat.*

For the exodus of businessmen and mobilization personnel in general see *Business Week* (May 3, 1952): 30.

While the steel case captured much of the nation's attention during the first half of the year, the issue of price decontrol occupied the time of economic stabilization officials. The issue of decontrol, like that of the extension of the Defense Production Act, became intertwined with developments in the steel case. As indicated earlier, the Truman administration was partially to blame for that. There was, however, another important component involved in the public and congressional clamor for decontrol: the performance of the economy itself. As economic output soared and unemployment plummeted, a rather incongruous deflation in some prices occurred. A number of "soft markets" (i.e. goods or services selling below OPS price ceilings) appeared in 1952, leading many Americans to believe that the inflationary threat had passed. Part of this deflationary trend can be attributed to the stretching out of the defense program and the attendant increase in raw materials and labor supplies. But a decline in civilian demand also helped to push prices lower. Business inventories shrunk from their bloated peaks of a year earlier, and consumers began to save a larger proportion of their disposable incomes. Those factors, combined with government actions to slow spending via credit restrictions and tax increases all considerably eased inflationary pressures.[27]

In light of easing inflation, President Truman's State of the Union Address, in which he exhorted Congress to strengthen economic controls, must have appeared very contradictory. In his address, Truman reviewed the past year, lauding the nation's progress in the fields of atomic weapons and defense production. He reported that the nation's economy was at a new peak, with over 61 million Americans employed and wages and business profits at record high levels. He added, however, that in order to match the Soviet's military capabilities, taxes and defense budgets would continue to remain high. To offset high armament expenditures, he asked Congress to strengthen price and wage controls as a hedge against inflation. In February, Truman sent his formal message to Congress requesting the extension and strengthening of the Defense Production Act. He specifically requested the repeal of three amendments: the Capehart Amendment; the Herlong Amendment; and the Butler-Hope Amendment. He also asked for authority to

27. Bert G. Hickman, *Growth and Stability of the Postwar Economy*, 91–98; Fourth Quarterly Report to the President by the Director of Defense Mobilization, "The Battle for Production," January 1952, 5–6, 33–40, RG 277, Records of the National Production Authority, Policy Coordinating Bureau, box 2, file: "ODM: The Battle for Production," NA; *Newsweek* 39 (March 10, 1952): 84; *Fortune* 45 (January 1952): 23–26.

more closely regulate consumer credit. As it turned out, Congress was even less inclined to extend or strengthen the Act than it had been the previous year. With signs of deflation, soft markets, and an easing of the materials crunch, Congress saw little reason to clamp down. And with the steel debacle unfolding just as it considered Truman's request, it came to view wage and price controls as hopelessly ineffective.[28]

Besides congressional reluctance to strengthen controls, the Truman administration came under increasing pressure to move toward decontrol as rapidly as possible. Much of the pressure was exerted by familiar anti-control groups like the National Association of Manufacturers and the Chamber of Commerce. But administration officials were also being pressured by some of their own, including the members of the president's National Advisory Board on Mobilization Policy. On January 8, Clarence A. Putnam, an industry representative on the Advisory Board wrote to Truman asserting that price and wage controls were "a discouraging and disturbing" factor to the economy and should be abandoned. In a particularly contentious meeting of the board in late January, more members began to push for decontrol, urging OPS Director DiSalle to formulate a coherent decontrol policy so that the pitfalls of decontrol after World War II would not be repeated. DiSalle, ESA director Putnam, and Leon Keyserling all resisted premature attempts to decontrol prices and wages, arguing that strong inflationary pressures could reappear at any time. Their assertions fell mostly on deaf ears, however. In the end, the Advisory Board did give its lukewarm support to continued controls, but with a caveat that the ESA and OPS suspend price ceilings whenever and wherever appropriate. In addition, it asked that a decontrol policy be adopted as quickly as possible.[29]

As inflation and materials shortages continued to show signs of easing through the first quarter of 1952, pressure for decontrol grew stronger still. Over the reservations of most mobilization and stabilization officials, the new OPS director, Ellis Arnall, reluctantly began

28. *Newsweek* 39 (January 21, 1952): 21; U.S. President, *Public Papers, 1952,* 2–6; *Congressional Quarterly Almanac,* 82d. Cong., 2d sess., 1952, vol. 8, 305; ESA Weekly, January 22 and February 19, 1952, RG 296, Records, Reports and Secretariat, box 3, NA; *The Economic Report of the President,* January 16, 1952, Papers of Leon Keyserling, box 5, file: "Economic Reports of the President, 1952," HSTL.

29. Letter to the President, January 8, 1952, RG 296, Records, Reports and Secretariat, box 3, NA; Memo for Dr. Steelman, January 24, 1952, Papers of Harry S. Truman, OF, box 1737, file: "2855-A," HSTL; National Advisory Board on Mobilization Policy Meeting No. 14, January 21 and 22, 1952, President's Secretary's Files, Subject File, Agencies A, box 142, file: "Advisory Board on Mobilization Policy, National," HSTL.

to formulate decontrol policies, beginning first with those commodities selling under OPS ceilings. In late April, the OPS lifted price ceilings on some 16 different commodities. Sentiments against continued controls turned into a tidal wave of decontrol as the steel crisis deepened. And after the Wage Stabilization Board issued its ruling in March and Charles Wilson resigned, the administration had all it could do to keep the price and wage program from completely unraveling. At the same time, NPA and DPA officials announced their intentions to loosen CMP metal allotments, moving toward an open-ended program similar to the one used during the CMP's first months of operation. It was speculated that the entire CMP could be abandoned entirely as early as late 1953.[30]

Congress too got into the decontrol frenzy. Just as the Senate hearings on the extension of the Defense Production Act had moved into high gear, Truman seized the steel mills, prompting Senate Banking Committee Chairman Maybank to postpone the hearings. Saying that it would be a "dreadful mistake" to make decisions about the future of controls in the midst of the steel crisis, Maybank suspended hearings for nearly a month. On April 29, the Senate Committee began a series of closed hearings on the steel crisis as part of its larger effort to consider extending the Defense Production Act. Predictably, the committee pointed to the steel dispute as a primary example of how wage and price controls had failed. On May 13, the committee voted to abolish the WSB and replace it with a much weaker all-public panel; it also voted to strip the board of its wage dispute settlement functions. On June 5, the full Senate voted on the new Defense Production Act. Although the final Senate version did not abolish the tripartite character of the WSB, it did strip it of much of its dispute settlement powers and made membership of the board subject to Senate confirmation. The final Senate bill also loosened controls by extending the Capehart Amendment, expanding the Herlong Amendment, and removing price ceilings on fresh fruit and vegetables. The Senate's actions undoubtedly dealt a further blow to the administration's already confused stabilization program.[31]

30. Fifth Quarterly Report to the President by the Director of Defense Mobilization, "Strength for the Long-Run," April 1, 1952, 36–40, RG 277 Reference Materials, 1951–1953, box 2, NA; Memo to Jack Gorrie, NSRB, March 19, 1952, RG 304, safe file, box 1, NA; "Policy for Soft Markets," February 27, 1952, RG 296, Letters and Memoranda of the Director, box 99, NA; Memorandum to Edward Phelps, OPS, April 7, 1952, RG 296, Economics, box 12, NA.
31. *Congressional Quarterly Almanac*, 1952, 305–10; *Congressional Record*, 82d. Cong., 2d sess., 1952, 98, pt. 10: 3256–3381; ESA Weekly, March 4, March 25, April 1, May 6, May 13, June 3, June 17, June 24, 1952, RG 296, Records, Reports and Secretariat, box 3, NA; OPS

As it turned out, the House was even more draconian than the Senate in its attempts to weaken the controls bill. Calling the Defense Production Act "a socialist monstrosity," Representative Clarence Brown (R-OH) implored his colleagues to defeat the bill altogether. His exhortations nearly succeeded, for the final House version of the bill was far more limiting than the Senate's. It called for the total repeal of consumer credit controls; the suspension of all price controls on goods selling below ceilings for three months or for those in adequate supply; the relaxation of limits on the import of strategic materials under the International Materials Conference; and the broadening of the Herlong Amendment. The House version of the controls bill would have effectively ended any meaningful control over the economy.[32]

On June 27, congressional conferees began work to narrow the differences between the two versions of the bill. The next day, a compromise agreement was hammered out. And although it fell far short of what the administration had asked for, it did manage to save many controls that the House had abandoned. The final bill, signed by President Truman on June 30, extended allocation, requisitioning, and priority controls to June 30, 1953, and extended wage and price controls (with many exemptions) to April 30, 1953. The bill also retained the WSB but stripped it of its powers over labor disputes.[33] Truman signed the bill with great caution, pointing out that the law provided "only very limited protection against the dangers of inflation."[34]

The same basic arguments used against the Defense Production Act in 1951 were repeated in 1952. This time, however, the steel crisis intervened, significantly strengthening the already formidable anti-control coalition. Congress resented Truman's attempted usurpation of power during the crisis and, in part, further diluted the Defense Production Act as a check on his power. The steel case also conjured up the apparition of a garrison state and thus played right into the hands of

---

News, May 12, June 11, June 27, July 1, 1952, RG 295, OPS Central Files 1952–1953, box 632, file: "Daily News Digest, May–August 1952," NA.

32. *Congressional Quarterly Almanac*, 1952, 312–15; ESA Weekly, June 24, 1952, RG 296, Records, Reports and Secretariat, box 3, NA; OPS News June 27, 1952, RG 295 OPS, Central Files, 1952–53, box 632, file: "Daily News Digest, May–August 1952," NA. For congressional attempts to limit the purview of the International Materials Conference see Paul G. Pierpaoli Jr., "The Road Not Taken: The International Materials Conference and American Raw Materials Policy, 1950–1954," 35–37.

33. *Congressional Quarterly Almanac*, 1952, 315–16; OPS News, July 1, 1952, RG 295, OPS, Central Files, 1952–53, box 632, file: "Daily News Digest, May–August 1952," NA; ESA Weekly, July 1, 1953, RG 296, Records, Reports and Secretariat, box 3, NA.

34. *Congressional Quarterly Almanac*, 1952, 316.

the ascendant Republicans, who vowed to keep such a ghostly specter under wraps.

What became even more clear in 1952 was the fact that the public, as well as Congress, continued to tie the stabilization program to the Korean War itself. And try as they might, administration officials were never able to dispel this thinking. The actual cost of the Korean War was in fact only a small amount of the approximately $50 billion obligated to defense needs during FY 1952. According to Charles Wilson, the total cost of the Korean War was running about $7.5 billion per year, meaning the remaining $42.5 billion defense budget continued to be earmarked for the larger and more protracted military program envisioned in NSC-68. Thus, the impact of Korea alone was not nearly great enough to adversely affect the economy. This fact obviously did not help the administration sell its stabilization effort. The program became politicized—all the more so after the steel crisis—and thus fell victim to conservative attacks. The Truman administration was partly to blame for this. By linking the steel crisis so directly with the success of its stabilization program and by failing to convince the public of the need for continued controls to prevent inflation and economic dislocation over the long haul, the administration doomed its own stabilization efforts and handed the Republicans a new bloody shirt to wave just as the 1952 elections approached.[35]

While mobilization officials continued to struggle with the day-to-day pitfalls of defense production and economic stabilization, the Defense Department, the JCS, the NSC, and the NSRB faced a different set of concerns. Their problems were ones of strategic and conceptual approaches to military planning and mobilization, but they certainly were no less important than the problems occurring on the operational level. In fact, the decisions reached by military and mobilization planners directly influenced the current mobilization program as well as the nation's long-term strategic plans. In part, the military planners' concepts of national security and mobilization policy changed because of technological imperatives: the advent of atomic and hydrogen weapons as well as the development of viable delivery systems, including long-range jet bombers and guided missiles. These advancements called into question the wisdom and effectiveness of large standing armies

---

35. For Charles Wilson's estimates on the cost of the Korean War see Memo to Dr. Steelman, January 24, 1952, Papers of Harry S. Truman, OF, box 1737, file: "2855-A," HSTL.

equipped with conventional arms. They also laid bare the vulnerability of the nation's industrial and metropolitan centers to air attack. On the other hand, these same planners were under increasing pressure to keep defense spending from spiraling ever higher. Thus they came to view strategic air power and nuclear weapons as the keys to holding defense costs down while simultaneously deterring the Soviets from launching a preemptive strike, especially against a vulnerable Western Europe.[36]

The Truman administration did not, however, abandon its conventional military buildup. There were still those planners who favored large-scale conventional forces, especially in Europe. This viewpoint was made most clearly in the force goals set for NATO. In February 1952, the NATO ministerial meeting held in Lisbon, Portugal, called for no less than fifty combat-ready NATO divisions. The bulk of the manpower was to come from Europe, but the United States was expected to continue supplying NATO forces with war material and weaponry.[37] Thus, although the Truman administration began to move toward a doctrine of strategic air and nuclear deterrence, it stopped well short of a wholesale abandonment of an industrial mobilization base and conventional deterrence. In historian Melvyn Leffler's terms, "behind the atomic shield that served as the principal deterrent to a Soviet attack, the Truman administration was concentrating on developing the capabilities that would allow it to supplant the diminishing power of Great Britain and France." The conventional military hardware rolling off U.S. assembly lines in record volume would thus be used to fortify friends and allies abroad while simultaneously sending a signal to the Soviets that the United States was prepared to fight limited and conventional wars like the one in Korea.[38]

Nothing better exemplified the Truman administration's move toward strategic air superiority than the numerical breakdown of military appropriations for FY 1953. Of the approximately $46.6 billion

36. Michael S. Sherry has written the most definitive book on the subject of air power and strategic nuclear weapons in *The Rise of American Air Power: The Creation of Armageddon*. See also Melvyn P. Leffler, *A Preponderance of Power: National Security, the Truman Administration, and the Cold War*, esp. 485–93.

37. Seyom Brown, *The Faces of Power: Constancy and Change in United States Foreign Policy from Truman to Clinton*, 2nd. ed., 39–40.

38. For quotation see Leffler, *Preponderance of Power*, 490. See also John Lewis Gaddis, *Strategies of Containment: A Critical Appraisal of American Postwar National Security Policy*, esp. 110; Memorandum, July 2, 1952, RG 296, Records Maintained by the Administrator, Classified General Files, box 1, file: "ODM Production Policy Committee," NA.

earmarked for defense, which the Congress finally approved in July, the Air Force was allotted nearly one-half of the total. Of the $21.1 billion apportioned to the Air Force, 60 percent went to the design, development, and procurement of new aircraft, including guided missiles. From then on, the Air Force continued to receive the lion's share of defense appropriations, a trend that became even more pronounced under the Eisenhower administration's "New Look" defense strategy. As the above statistics clearly demonstrate, however, there was little truly "new" in Ike's "New Look"; he merely extended defense doctrines already developed by Truman's advisors.[39]

It was actually during the latter half of 1951 that the administration turned its sights on the problems posed by new weapons. As early as September of that year, defense secretary Lovett briefed Truman and his cabinet on the government's guided missile program, admitting that while there was "no 'push button' war in sight, we are experimenting with guided missiles but we have not had them reach a state of perfection. They may reach (that stage) by 1954 but until then the conventional methods of waging war will be continued."[40] At the same time, the NSRB produced a series of reports studying the impact of atomic weapons on defense strategy. Its findings generally supported the advocates of strategic air superiority. Admitting that the nation's ability to conduct a conventional war could be quickly destroyed by an atomic attack, the NSRB suggested that America's defenses should now pivot around atomic weapons, with only secondary importance given to conventional deterrence. Summing up, the NSRB report stated that "the atomic bomb is now the equivalent of armies and navies. It means that the old idea of destroying an enemy by destroying his armies . . . or his fleet no longer has validity." Until the United States

39. The breakdowns of military and defense appropriations for FY 1953 are as follows:

National Security Council, $155,000;
National Security Resources Board, $625,000;
National Security Training Commission, $37,500;
Office of Secretary of Defense, $409,800,000;
Army, $12,239,500,000;
Navy, $12,842,459,642;
Air Force, $21,118,361,770
for a total of $46,610,938,912.

See *Congressional Quarterly*, 1952, 97–101. See also Brown, *The Faces of Power*, 40; Leffler, *Preponderance of Power*, 488.

40. Cabinet Meeting, September 21, 1951, Papers of Matthew J. Connelly, box 2, file: "Notes on Cabinet Meetings, 1951, 2 January–31 December," HSTL.

built adequate strategic nuclear forces to overwhelm the Soviets, however, the NSRB concluded that "more conventional patterns of preparedness still pertain."[41]

Once the United States reached a preponderance of strategic air and atomic power, policymakers expected the Soviets to reach a similar plateau, at which time, the NSRB stated, "an entirely new situation will exist—one which has never before been met in history. Two major nations will face each other, each possessing the power to destroy the other utterly. Neither could even be reasonably sure of surviving a war in recognizable form."[42] Presaging the Eisenhower administration's doctrine of massive retaliation and the subsequent concept of "MAD"— or mutually assured destruction—the board accurately predicted an atomic arms race. What it did not foresee was the concomitant technology race between the Superpowers, which propelled the arms race to ever higher heights as hydrogen bombs replaced atomic bombs and delivery systems became more and more accurate and sophisticated.

But signs of the emphasis on gaining and retaining technological supremacy over the Soviets were already at hand. It was in fact the intention to best the Soviets in technology rather than match them numerically that factored into the administration's decision to stretch out the rearmament program. As discussed in the previous chapter, reasons for the stretch-out were myriad and complicated, involving domestic and international politics as well as economic considerations. But Charles Wilson, writing to persistent mobilization critic Bernard M. Baruch in February, conceded that "at the outset of our program we could have gone for quantity production . . . at the expense of quality, and achieved a much higher rate of total output. The choice at that time was one that the military had to make, and they elected to put into production our newest, most advanced models." It followed from that premise then that military and mobilization officials would pursue the production of cutting-edge weapons and aircraft, including advanced atomic and thermonuclear weapons in lieu of producing mass amounts of obsolescent and conventional weapons. And because the development and deployment of new weapons require long lead times, production schedules had to be extended. That policy trajectory, combined with the changing nature of warfare and mobilization planning wrought by the atomic age, led the nation inexorably

41. NSRB Memorandum to Oscar L. Endler, October 29, 1951, RG 304, ODM-NSRB, safe file of the Economic Adviser 1951–1953, box 1, NA.
42. Ibid.

toward a policy of nuclear deterrence. As examples, policymakers already had in the works tactical atomic bomb programs, including atomic depth charges, mines, and field artillery. The United States also exploded its first hydrogen bomb in 1952 and had already begun deploying its first all-jet, medium-range B-47 bomber, to be followed quickly by the awesome B-52 and B-60 intercontinental heavy bombers.[43]

In the meantime, the NSRB issued another set of reports detailing the physical impact of an atomic bomb attack on key U.S. industrial and military sites. The predictions were startling. The NSRB calculated the effects of an A-bomb attack on Chicago: three square miles totally destroyed; nine more damaged beyond repair and habitation; another fifty to sixty square miles heavily damaged; up to 259,000 casualties, with 130,000 deaths; major damage to the city's industrial infrastructure. A simultaneous attack on eight to ten other sites around the country would raise death and damage estimates by eight to ten times those of the Chicago scenario. The NSRB's estimates were predicated upon careful analysis of Soviet capabilities. By mid-1952, U.S. intelligence officials estimated that the Soviets held 50 atomic bombs. By 1953, they estimated that the Soviets would possess 100 bombs and from there the numbers would grow by at least 100 new bombs per year. They were also expected to attain thermonuclear capability by 1955, the year in which it was estimated that the Soviets could destroy one-third of America's industrial base.[44]

A key part of strategic military and civilian mobilization planners' attempts to avoid such a chilling scenario was the dispersal of American industry, especially defense plants. Industrial dispersion policy was

43. For the quotation see Wilson's letter to Baruch, February 15, 1952, Records of the National Security Council, box 28, file: "Mobilization Program July 1951–June 1952," HSTL. See also *Defense Programs*, Defense Production Administration, July 30, 1951, RG 277, Miscellaneous Publications, 1950–1953, box 1, file: "Defense Programs," NA; Leffler, *A Preponderance of Power*, 488–89.

For excellent, easily accessible overviews of the United States' desire to achieve technological supremacy and the decisions made vis à vis atomic and nuclear deterrence see "Does Production Matter?" *Business Week* (March 29, 1952): 19–22; Special Report: "Air Program 'Rolls'," *U.S. News* 32 (May 2, 1952): 78, 80–81; "Air Force Atoms," *Newsweek* 39 (March 3, 1952): 25–26; "A-Bomb: New Kinds Force Switch in U.S. Strategy," *Newsweek* 39 (May 5, 1952): 28–29.

44. The Implications of New Weapons," Analysis, Requirements Survey, (no date), RG 304, safe file of the Economic Adviser, 1951–1953, box 3, NA; Brief Statement of the Problem of Post-Attack Industrial Rehabilitation, November 14, 1951, RG 296, box 23, NA; Leffler, *A Preponderance of Power*, 487; Walter Millis et al., *Arms and the State: Civil-Military Elements in National Policy*, 353–54.

specifically assigned to the NSRB by the National Security Act of 1947. Before 1951, however, dispersal plans amounted to nothing more than a few pilot studies. The ongoing ineffectiveness of the NSRB as a planning agency no doubt crippled the early dispersion effort. But also standing in the way was the traditional American fear of government intrusion into private enterprise. A government-imposed industrial dispersion effort would, as one contemporary observer opined in 1947, "require the endowment of government with powers of compulsion so enormous that the 'garrison state' would no longer be a figure of speech."[45]

Nevertheless, spurred on by the new dangers inherent during the Korean War, policymakers finally promulgated a coherent national industrial dispersion policy in August 1951. An earlier attempt to disperse industry during World War II, which was pursued for different reasons, had largely failed because in all except a few cases (like California), local and state private and public sector officials resisted federal coercion. Furthermore, they viewed New Dealers' attempts to disperse industry as a government-mandated program of job and income redistribution. Quite unlike the World War II experience, it is an interesting fact that the impetus for such a policy during Korea came not from Washington, but from certain regional chambers of commerce in coordination with local industry. The pattern that emerged from this effort was a hybridization of corporative impulses, a form of civic and regional boosterism that brought urban leaders and politicians together with key government and military men. The result, in the words of Roger W. Lotchin, was not a military-industrial complex, but rather a "metropolitan-military complex."[46]

The August 1951 dispersion policy announced by the White House had its beginnings not in Washington, D.C. but in Washington state. In 1949 the Air Force decided to locate a new Boeing plant—which was to produce the B-47 bomber—in Wichita, Kansas, rather than in Seattle, Washington, the hub of Boeing's operations. That decision set off a crescendo of concern, especially in Washington state. Many at the time

---

45. For the NSRB's role in the formulation of industrial dispersion policy see Harry Yoshpe, *The National Security Resources Board 1947–1953: A Case Study in Peacetime Mobilization*, 9. For the quotation and other background on early dispersion efforts see Hanson Baldwin, *The Price of Power*, 253.

46. National Industrial Dispersion Policy, plus attachments, August 10, 1951, President's Secretary's Files, NSRB Reports-ODM Personnel, box 147, file: "NSRB Reports," HSTL; Ann Markusen et al., *The Rise of the Gunbelt: The Military Remapping of Industrial America*, esp. 5–6, 230–46. For the concept of a "metropolitan-military complex" see Roger W. Lotchin, *Fortress California, 1910–1961: From Warfare to Welfare*.

interpreted the Air Force's decision as a signal that the government no longer considered the Pacific Northwest as a safe industrial site.[47]

To combat this misperception, the Seattle Chamber of Commerce, in concert with local and regional officials, local industries including Boeing, and the national Chamber, established an industrial dispersion task force. That task force in turn produced a model of industrial dispersion policy that directly influenced the NSRB's 1951 national dispersion policy. And by the middle of 1952, fifty-seven major metropolitan areas had established their own task forces modeled directly after the Seattle Plan. Lauding the success of grass-roots style corporatism, NSRB Chairman Jack Gorrie stated to the Seattle Chamber of Commerce that "this (dispersion policy) is a Federal program in which the major responsibility has been handed to the people of the communities themselves."[48] Even after the national policy was put in place, the NSRB continued to promote local and regional activism in industrial policymaking by sponsoring conferences designed to bring together representatives of national industrial, labor, and planning associations. Thus, in the best tradition of Herbert Hoover's associative vision of the 1920s and the aborted National Recovery Administration of the 1930s, the federal government was acting as a facilitator of discussion and a referee for competing economic interests. By the late 1950s, the kinds of local initiatives started by corporate and civic leaders in Seattle would be extended far beyond the confines of industrial dispersion policy; they would be used to influence a huge array of government-sponsored defense projects all around the country.[49]

This new style of industrial dispersion policymaking was important for a variety of reasons. First, the local public-private initiatives pushed the ineffective and poorly run NSRB into establishing a coherent national dispersion policy. Without such input, it is doubtful that the

47. Aaron L. Friedberg, "Why Didn't the United States Become a Garrison State?" 133–34; Remarks of NSRB Chairman Jack Gorrie, May 16, 1952, Papers of Harry S. Truman, OF, file: "1295 (1951–August 1952)," HSTL.

48. Remarks of Jack Gorrie, May 16, 1952, Papers of Harry S. Truman, OF, file: "1295 (1951–August 1952)," HSTL.

49. Chamber of Commerce of the United States, *Business Action*, Washington, D.C., August 18, 1951, President's Secretary's Files, Subject File-Agencies, box 146, file: "National Security Resources Board," HSTL; Remarks of Jack Gorrie, May 16, 1952, Papers of Harry S. Truman, OF, file: "1295 (1951-August 1952)," HSTL; National Security Resources Board Meeting No. G-1, March 31, 1952, President's Secretary's Files, Subject File-Agencies, box 146, file: "NSRB Meetings," HSTL; Letter to H. Christian Sonne, National Planning Association, October 21, 1951, RG 304-NSRB Name Correspondence File, box 1, file: "General to National Planning Association," NA.

board would have ever moved beyond lip service and pilot studies. Second, the very fact that the impetus for such policy came from below rather than above helped to blunt criticism that the federal government was dictating to the private sector or worse yet, was attempting to implement industrial policy under the ruse of national security. Third, although industrial dispersion efforts would fade as the decade progressed, the corporative, grass-roots process used to implement the policy was successfully used again and again throughout the Cold War. It would become, to a large degree, the nation's de facto regional industrial policy.

The August dispersion policy was a relatively limited foray into public-private industrial planning. The administration took great pains to emphasize that the policy was aimed not at existing industry, but rather at new and expanding facilities. In order to implement the policy, the administration's main prod to industrialists was the use of certificates of necessity aimed specifically at facilities that met satisfactory dispersal standards. The government also used accelerated amortization and low-interest loans to influence the placement of new defense facilities. The national dispersion standards were designed in such a way as to avoid a fundamental remapping of industrial America. The program called for the location of new defense plants and industrial areas ten or more miles away from any densely populated or highly industrialized area or major military installation. Clearly, the point of the standards was to lessen the impact of an atomic air attack, not to alter fundamentally the industrial landscape. In the final analysis, new defense and industrial facilities had to be located close enough to established industrial areas so that they could utilize existing transportation networks, manpower, and utility resources.[50]

As the political scientist Aaron L. Friedberg has ably demonstrated, the Truman administration's industrial dispersion policy did not accomplish a great deal nor did it fundamentally alter government-industry relations. Later, the Eisenhower administration played a large

---

50. National Industrial Dispersion Policy, Appendix "A," August 10, 1951, President's Secretary's Files, Subject File-Agencies, box 147, file: "NSRB-Reports," HSTL; Appendix "B," Standards for Industrial Dispersion, box 147, file: "NSRB-Reports," HSTL.

The administration defined "major military installations" as those considered important enough to be a prime target for atomic air attack. A "densely populated area" was one in which a 4-mile diameter circle contained a population of 200,000 people or more. A "highly industrialized area" was one in which a 4-mile diameter circle contained defense-supporting plants with combined employment of 16,000 or more.

role in limiting the efficacy of dispersal through its constriction of government subsidies. Eisenhower's hands-off philosophy toward government planning and business-government relations simply was not suited to the implementation of industrial dispersal. Dispersion efforts failed, according to Friedberg, because the government lacked the requisite power to force industry to relocate. The advent of powerful thermonuclear weapons, combined with the inexorable growth of the metropolis also tended to render dispersion policy moot.[51]

What Friedberg failed to realize was that the major impetus for dispersion came not from Washington but from specific industries and localities. And once the threat of air attack became overwhelming and inescapable, industry itself decided to abandon dispersal efforts. Thus, his argument that the policy failed because of a weak central government cannot be entirely sustained: From the start, the policy worked its way from the bottom up, not the top down. As the decade of the 1950s progressed, industrialists, in conjunction with the government, did manage to decentralize certain industries. This trend in fact began in earnest during the Korean rearmament. But decentralization decisions were based not principally upon dispersion standards. They were based instead on pragmatic business concerns: labor costs and availability; access to transportation networks; tax structures and the business climate of a locality; and, of course, the willingness of local officials to provide special incentives to attract new industry.[52]

Industrial dispersion efforts during Korea provide an ideal example of the evolution of public-private decision making during the early Cold War. They also demonstrate how the fears and rhetoric of America as garrison state influenced how public and private sector policymakers reacted to the ongoing rearmament program and the problems it wrought. In other words, the traditional American values that public and private officials hoped to respect guided not only the decisions they reached, but also the *way* in which those decisions were reached. In attempting to construct the Cold War national security state—as opposed to a garrison state—policymakers in some instances altered their views of traditional American values. But overall, these values

51. Friedberg, "Garrison State," 134–35; Robert Griffith, "Dwight D. Eisenhower and the Corporate Commonwealth," *American Historical Review,* 87–122.

52. "Plant Decentralization," *Business Week* (September 8, 1952): 22–24; Ann R. Markusen, "Defense Spending: A Successful Industrial Policy?" 105–21; Markusen et al., *Rise of Gunbelt,* 5–6, 36–37, 244.

did not change. Instead, they tended to act as a steering mechanism on certain policy, propelling it in directions not originally mapped.

The midpoint of 1952 affords a convenient vantage point from which to view the entire depth and breadth of the nation's largest peacetime military buildup. Two years after North Korea provoked war on the Korean peninsula and eighteen months after the Chinese intervention, it was clear that the massive rearmament effort and the resulting reorientation of the federal budget had begun to change the way in which American government and industry did business. At the same time, it was also clear that the Truman administration's efforts to mitigate some of the worst effects of rearmament—like inflation and shortages—had indeed paid off. And despite partisan accusations to the contrary, the Korean rearmament had not resulted in the ruination of small business or the rigid regimentation of the economy. In fact, the economy continued to reach new heights of productivity and output well into 1953.

Although defense production was not scheduled to hit its peak until early 1953, what the nation had accomplished in the two years since war broke out was nothing short of extraordinary. The total value of military deliveries during the second quarter of 1952 stood at $8 billion, 20 percent higher than the first quarter and more than 6 times the rate of output in June 1950. The $8 billion mark was approximately three-fourths of the way toward the anticipated peak goal of $10.5 billion per quarter scheduled to be reached in 1953 and then maintained through 1954 as the plateau of production. More than 300 M47 medium tanks rolled off assembly lines each month. Over 800 military aircraft per month spewed forth from defense factories—three times as many as in 1950. Aircraft production was of the most sophisticated models of the day: the B-36 heavy bomber, the B-47 "Stratojet" bomber, the F-84 "Thunderjet," the F-86 "Sabre," and the F-89 "Scorpion," just to name a few. In April, the Air Force staged successful test flights of the B-52 and B-60 bombers. Even the nagging machine tool shortage was moving toward resolution. And most spectacularly, electronics and avionics production was running at seven times the pre-Korea rate.[53]

The nation was also well on its way to completing the construction of its mobilization base. Total investment in new plant and equipment

53. "The Shield Against Aggression," July 1, 1952, Sixth Quarterly Report of the Office of Defense Mobilization, RG 277, Reference Materials 1951–1953, box 2, file: "Defense Mobilization, July 1952," NA; Defense Programs, "Military Procurement," Defense Production Administration, May 22, 1952, RG 277, Reference Materials 1951–1953, box 2, file: "Defense Mobilization, July 1952," NA.

was running at an annual rate of $24.1 billion, 35 percent higher than the $17.8 billion of 1950. More than one-half of industrial projects targeted for tax amortization certificates were in place. Completions were running at the rate of about $2.5 billion per month. The Office of Defense Mobilization estimated that when the accelerated tax amortization program was completed, total investment covered by amortization certificates would amount to between $27 to $30 billion. In the meantime, civilian production continued to boom.[54]

Not surprisingly, all of this government-sponsored activity had a profound effect on the makeup of the federal budget. The $85 billion budget set for FY 1953 was the largest amount expended in one year since 1945. Of that $85 billion, more than *three-fourths* was allocated to national security programs, defined by the administration as all military and defense-related goods and services, international security, atomic energy programs, and government loans and subsidies to defense industries. Prior to Korea, national security expenditures made up only about 6 percent of the nation's gross national product (GNP); by 1953 they would take up 18 percent.[55]

More impressive still was the fact that the Truman administration managed to achieve these results without rampant inflation or major economic dislocations. For all the griping and partisan sniping over wage and price controls, their legacy was a solid one. For example, although the January 1952 Consumer Price Index (CPI) was 13 percent higher than it was in June 1950, it still was 1.6 percent lower than in January 1951, the month in which mandatory controls were imposed. Although the break in the inflationary spiral was influenced by a number of different forces converging at once, most of which have already been discussed, there is little doubt that wage and price controls contributed to the stability in prices by providing a powerful psychological disincentive to demand-pull inflation. At the same time, civilian unemployment remained astoundingly low from 1951 through 1952, running at 3 percent, and personal savings remained high, amounting to an estimated 7.5 percent of disposable income. Raw

54. "The Shield Against Aggression," RG 277, Reference Materials 1951–1953, box 2, file: "Defense Mobilization, July 1952," NA.

55. Memorandum for Mr. Joseph Short plus attachments, May 13, 1952 (Address by Frederick J. Lawton, Director of the Bureau of the Budget, May 14, 1952), Papers of Harry S. Truman, OF, box 365, file: "OF 79 January–July 1952," HSTL; Memorandum, "The Economic Picture Today," June 1, 1952, RG 295 Central Files, 1952–1953, box 496, file: "Economics," NA.

materials shortages also eased considerably during the first half of 1952. The civilian sector, with the exception of steel, saw a nearly across-the-board increase in its share of industrial raw materials.[56]

But how did all this affect the makeup of the United States' political economy? Once more, statistics show the way: Prior to Korea, only about 7 to 10 percent of business activity was derived from national security spending; in May 1952, the nation's top government economists estimated that up to *one-third* of American business activity stemmed from defense spending. Given that policymakers sought to create new industrial capacity rather than convert existing facilities to meet the needs of military production, this meant that the United States was building an alternate "defense economy" next to the already existing civilian economy. The cost of building this new economy would top $60 billion by the end of 1953 and would cost billions more to maintain and operate over the long-term.[57]

It is this new "defense economy," or "military-industrial complex," that helped spark the growth of the so-called Sun Belt. The administration's decision to construct excess industrial capacity as part of the nation's mobilization base, combined with its decision to pursue technological supremacy in military hardware, resulted in the beginning of a remapping of America's industrial landscape. A major example of this trend was the eclipsing of the nation's traditional industrial heartland, most notably Detroit and the surrounding east north central states, by newer regions of industrial prowess such as the South and South Atlantic coast, Texas, California, and the Pacific Northwest. Although statistics show that during the Korean buildup the largest aggregate share of defense dollars continued to be funneled into the Northeastern and North Central regions, the West and South received a proportionately larger share of defense spending than its existing industry would have indicated. The South and Southwest especially benefited from large amounts of new plant construction. Alabama received the most, followed by Florida, Louisiana, Virginia, and West Virginia. By

56. ESA Weekly, March 4, 1952, RG 296, Records of Reports and Secretariat, box 3, file: "ESA Weekly Roundup for the Administrator," NA; Memorandum to the President from the Council of Economic Advisers, April 21, 1952, RG 296, Records of Reports and Secretariat, box 2, file: "Reports, Statistics," NA; "The Shield Against Aggression," RG 277, Reference Materials 1951–1953, box 2, file: "Defense Mobilization, July 1952," NA; Hickman, *Growth and Stability*, 79.

57. OPS News, May 26, 1952, RG 295 Central Files 1952–1953, box 632, file: "Daily News Digest May–August 1952," NA; "Our Permanent War Economy," *New Leader* 35 (January 7, 1952): 2–4.

late 1952, Texas ranked fifteenth in the volume of new defense orders and plant construction. And of course, California continued to benefit from the ascendancy of the U.S. Air Force, receiving huge contracts for aircraft production and electronics and avionics.[58]

The statistics on industrial activity and new plant construction are most revealing of the trends under discussion. In 1947, Texas manufacturing accounted for only 4.1 percent of total U.S. output; by 1952, however, it had received 14.8 percent of government-subsidized new plant construction. In 1947, Alabama, Mississippi, Tennessee, and Kentucky's manufacturing made up only 3.9 percent of the U.S. total; by 1952, those states had received 8.7 percent of new plant construction. Looking at the downside, the nation's most active manufacturing region in 1947 (Wisconsin, Illinois, Indiana, and Ohio), whose manufacturing accounted for 31.5 percent of the U.S. total, had received only 27 percent of government-subsidized new plant construction by 1952. Thus , the statistics clearly indicate a trend that would continue throughout much of the Cold War: the percentage of new industry going to the South and West was larger than those regions' share of preexisting manufacturing. Those regions' good fortune came mostly at the expense of the nation's old traditional industrial heartland.[59]

This industrial remapping was in no way the conscious policy of the United States government, however. While the decision to build a mobilization base and to emphasize technological superiority and strategic air power as the bulwarks of defense rested squarely upon the shoulders of civilian and military planners, the new trends in industrial placement and decentralization were the results of a "complex chain of structural causes and choices made by various public-and private-sector parties."[60] In fact, the same kinds of corporative impulses that had brought about the national industrial dispersion policy were at work once more. And although industrial dispersion never gained momentum, the dynamics of its public-private decision making did. As the Cold War progressed, defense spending became an institutionalized part of the federal budget, never again to revert to pre-Korean levels.

58. *Small Business Participation in Military Procurement*, Joint Hearings before the Select Committee on Small Business, United States Senate and House of Representatives, 82d. Cong., 1st sess., May 7, 8, 14, 15, and 16, 1951, pp. 18–19; *New Leader* 35 (January 7, 1952): 2–4; *U.S. News* 31 (August 17, 1951): 24–25; Markusen et al., *Rise of Gunbelt*, 3–5, 8–25.

59. For an excellent analysis of this trend see Joint Congressional Hearings (ibid.) and *Business Week* (September 8, 1952): 22–24.

60. Markusen et al., *Rise of Gunbelt*, 5.

These billions upon billions of dollars became captured by the interests of local, regional, and national political leaders working in tandem with industrial constituents and government officials. The result was the creation of a large, military-dependent economy located along the nation's western and southern perimeters. The firms that constituted this new economy were almost exclusively high-tech, capital-intensive companies that tended to employ highly skilled and educated non-union workers. For the most part, the employees that flocked to these defense-related jobs were predominantly white, male suburbanites—engineers, scientists, and midlevel managers.[61]

Many of the nation's largest companies took it upon themselves to decentralize and relocate, deciding to locate new plants—including those designed for defense production—in the new high growth areas of the South and West. These firms were drawn to the new growth areas for a number of reasons. Local and regional efforts to entice new business certainly helped: Companies were given special tax incentives; zoning laws were made "industry-friendly"; and utility rates were adjusted to favor new manufacturing. Labor and living costs also tended to be lower than they were in the old industrial heartland. As one example, the auto industry, which had garnered more than $2 billion to build new plant capacity, resisted the conversion of its Detroit-based plants to defense work. First, auto makers did not want to interfere with the booming car market—they had to keep production lines open to meet demand. Second, the older industrial concept of integration had given way to decentralization after World War II. Thus, the new defense orders provided car makers with the perfect opportunity to decentralize their manufacturing operations. So they began building plants along the Atlantic coast, in Texas, and in California. Of the major auto makers, General Motors led the way toward decentralization. In late 1951, it announced plans to build what would be its largest assembly plant outside Detroit in Arlington, Texas.[62]

Viewed within the wider historical context of the 20th century, the trends under way at mid-century reflected the continuing evolution of public-private discourse and decision-making that began in the mid-1930s. As the political scientist Thomas Ferguson has argued, Franklin Roosevelt's sweeping electoral victory in 1936 ushered in a new political

61. Ibid., 7, 16–17, 235.
62. Robert Dean, "Our Permanent War Economy," *New Leader,* 35 (January 7, 1952): 2–4; Alfred P. Sloan, *My Years with General Motors,* 50; Robert Lacey, *Ford, the Men and the Machine,* 290–93.

coalition and by consequence a new era of business-government relations, one in which capital-intensive industries, investment banks, internationally minded commercial banks, and growth-oriented business people worked in unison with government ostensibly to affect New Deal socioeconomic reforms. Many of these business people moved in and out of government service, first as staffers in New Deal agencies, then as dollar-a-year men during World War II, and then again during the Korean War, the most obvious one being Charles E. Wilson. This new political coalition, or the "System of '36" swept away the older Republican-controlled "System of '96," which had traditionally been beholden to low-tech, labor-intensive, and protectionist industries.[63]

As World War Two approached, however, the new System of '36 changed its focus from one aimed principally at implementing limited socioeconomic reform to one that eschewed government-imposed social reform and instead sought to use the institutional and associative/corporative mechanisms of the New Deal to build a national security state. In the final analysis, these trends can be viewed as attempts at state building. But in a land governed by a "weak state," as political scientists and sociologists have categorized the U.S. government, state building became an amalgam of public-private interests. According to the historical sociologist Gregory Hooks, the reorientation of the New Deal coalition's objectives was not because of the existence of a weak centralized state, but rather was the result of conscious decisions made by public and private planners to transfer institutional and functional resources from domestic agencies to national security agencies, especially those influenced by the Pentagon. Korea permanently entrenched this trend by providing huge sums of money for defense purposes.[64]

63. For the concepts developed by Thomas Ferguson see "From Normalcy to New Deal: Industrial structure, party competition, and American public policy in the Great Depression," 41–93. See also Walter Dean Burnham, "The System of 1896: An Analysis," in Paul Kleppner et al., *The Evolution of American Electoral Systems*, 147–202.

64. Gregory D. Hooks, *Forging the Military-Industrial Complex: World War II's Battle of the Potomac*, 1–12, 30–37. For the concepts of state-building and "strong" versus "weak" states see Theda Skocpol et al., eds., *Bringing the State Back In*; Stephan Skowronek, *Building a New American State*; Friedberg, "Garrison State?," 109–10; Stephen Krasner, "United States Commercial and Monetary Policy: Unravelling the Paradox of External Strength and Internal Weakness," 57–60; Stephen Krasner, *Defending the National Interest: Raw Materials Investments and U.S. Foreign Policy*, 55–90; Samuel P. Huntington, *The Promise of Disharmony*, 31–60; and Charles Bright and Susan Harding, "Processes of Statemaking and Popular Protest: An Introduction," 1–15.

For a thought-provoking treatment of the linkages between Thomas Ferguson's theories and state-building concepts see Kenneth Finegold and Theda Skocpol, "State,

Other scholars, most notably historian Alan Brinkley, have argued that the 1936 "shift" described by Ferguson occurred later and did not fully coalesce until the advent of World War II. In contrast to Ferguson, Brinkley portrays this shift in the New Dealers' approach to macroeconomic control in ideological terms. To his way of thinking, New Dealers' older attempts to effect economic reform through regulation, or "social Keynesianism" gave way to a more conservative "commercial Keynesianism," which was predicated upon proactive government fiscal policy designed to spur aggregate economic growth. No matter which theory one prefers, the outcomes were much the same: The federal government increased its control over the nation's economy, and burgeoning high-tech, capital-intensive industries (like those that dominated the defense sector) reaped the most benefits from the ascendance of "commercial Keynesianism."[65]

Although it is true that by 1952 most industry leaders had rebelled against Truman's statist implementation of the postwar national security state, all seemed to agree that there could be no turning back. The national security state was there to stay and defense-related industries stood poised to reap huge benefits from its institutionalization. They also stood ready to work closely with military and civilian officials, although they much preferred the less-intrusive approaches to such cooperation advocated by the ascendant moderate Republicans. President Eisenhower would come to personify this differing approach to national security, which deemphasized interventionist federal spending, taxing, and controls in favor of less interventionist business-regulated controls. The linchpin of the Republican approach was to become monetary policy, which would protect business from inflation through the use of the semiautonomous and business-friendly Federal Reserve Board.[66]

The issue of statist intervention in the building of the national security state naturally became one of the focal points of the 1952 elections. And Truman's actions during the first half of the year no doubt added fodder to the Republicans' cannons. The constant skirmishing over wage and price controls offered a glimpse at what was to

Party, and Industry: From Business Recovery to the Wagner Act in America's New Deal," 159–91.

65. See Steve Fraser and Gary Gerstle, eds., *The Rise and Fall of the New Deal Order, 1930–1980*, especially the Introduction, ix–xxv and Alan Brinkley's essay entitled, "The New Deal Order and the Idea of the State," 85–121.

66. McQuaid, *Uneasy Partners*, 64–66.

come; however, the steel seizure case provided the Republicans with irrefutable evidence that although Truman's defense goals were well placed, his implementation of those goals had run seriously askew.

In sum, despite Truman's preference for government-mandated wartime controls, the final results of those controls devolved into a public-private partnership in which decentralization became the guiding principle. Industrial and economic mobilization for Korea and the Cold War thus took the form of a vertically integrated, *decentralized* corporation whose influence rested not so much upon Washington, but rather upon the myriad of local, regional, and national advisory and decision-making committees that proliferated throughout the country. Economic concentration, at least in Washington, was thus hard to prove. Political rhetoric and continued fears of a garrison state however, suggested otherwise.

By mid-1952, the Truman administration and the nation had already endured the toughest part of the massive rearmament program. The economy was booming; production was soaring; inflation had eased; and shortages had diminished. Frustrated though they were with stalled armistice talks, administration officials had also managed to stabilize the military situation on the Korean peninsula, ensuring at least for the short term a stable and pro-American regime in the South. By doing so, the United States sent an unequivocal message to the Soviet Union and the Peoples' Republic: The United States would resist aggression wherever and whenever it presented itself. Indeed, by 1952 American military and civilian leaders were infinitely more confident in their ability to resist hostile Communist moves than they had been only two years before. So why the continued angst? Why did many Americans feel trapped—even betrayed—by the events of 1952? Why had the partisan attacks on the administration become so vitriolic, even after Truman had taken himself out of the 1952 election? These questions are not so easily answered. Disgust with the stalemated war in Korea no doubt grated on the nerves. Two years of gruesome fighting with no clear victory rang hollow to a citizenry accustomed only to unconditional success. Twenty years of Democratic rule had also begun to grow old, and reports of cronyism and corruption in the administration did little to help. Americans also seemed pessimistic about their future: Was a cataclysmic Third World War in the offing? How long would such a pall of gloom prevail? Finally, the cultural and political atmosphere created by McCarthyism created an air of paranoia and mistrust that—

justified or not—took aim at Truman and the Democrats and virtually assured their loss at the polls in November 1952.

Above all, weariness of a growing and ever more intrusive government raised eyebrows and ire from one coast to the other. Continued wage, price, and credit controls undoubtedly fed the fires of resentment toward government intrusion. But no less a catalyst to these feelings was the steel seizure crisis, in which Truman unwisely raised the stakes so high that the reputation of his party was put on the line. When the Supreme Court rebuked his handling of the crisis in June, Republicans pounced on the opportunity to lambaste Truman and the Democrats for their handling of their crisis—and by insinuation—their handling of the entire mobilization program. Even the affable General Eisenhower, to whom Truman had given a great deal of influence over the rearmament program turned against him. In a June speech, the general cum presidential candidate humiliated Truman by suggesting that his administration was overreacting to the Soviets, who were, in his words, like "pollywogs swimming down a muddy creek."[67] To be sure, Eisenhower was engaged in pure political rhetoric. After all, it was he who had asked Truman to launch full mobilization only 18 months earlier. What underlay Eisenhower's tactics, however, had nothing to do with the perception of the Soviet threat. At the heart of the matter was the *way* in which the nation was to counteract the threat. Republicans shunned the kinds of government intrusions upon which Truman had relied. Instead, they favored greater private-sector initiative, to be underwritten by the government only when necessary. Regardless of the approach, however, the results were the same: the inexorable growth of a military-industrial sector fused together by public-private linkages.

67. Quoted in Donovan, *Tumultuous Years,* 394.

VI

Toward a Tenuous Normalcy

Decontrol and the General's Arrival,
July 1952–February 1953

Electoral politics and renewed confusion over controls and stabilization policy dominated the last half of 1952. The effects of the steel strike settlement on the wage structure hampered efforts by stabilization officials to hold the line on wage increases and inflation. Internal bickering over wage and price policy and the likelihood of renewed inflation stymied Truman's advisors. Making matters worse, constant changes in top stabilization personnel did little to reduce flagging morale and institutional continuity within the ESA and OPS. And to add insult to injury, the Wage Stabilization Board (WSB) precipitated another row with organized labor over coal miners' wages. The result was the demise of the WSB and the final repudiation of economic controls. Superimposed over these concerns were the issues brought to the fore by the pivotal 1952 elections, in which the Republicans captured the White House for the first time in twenty years and regained control of both the House and Senate. The elections marked not only a mandate for the Republicans and their standard-bearer Dwight Eisenhower. They also signified voters' final repudiation of the Korean War and the manner in which the Cold War military buildup had been waged.

In the meantime, more than a year after peace talks began, the war still raged in Korea. While most issues had been settled, one major sticking point remained: the repatriation of North Korean and Chinese prisoners of war. Unwilling to allow the forceful repatriation of POW's held by U.N. forces, Truman refused to move the peace talks toward a final cessation of hostilities. Thus the fighting continued and casualties mounted. Throughout 1952, the American Air Force actually increased the number of air attacks on North Korea, despite the ongoing peace talks. They did little good. The Korean War, like the peace talks ostensibly designed to end it, remained stalemated. And as a result, Americans grew increasingly frustrated and disillusioned.

It should come as no surprise that campaigning Republicans concentrated on the issues of Korea, taxes, controls, administration corruption, and government spending. Eisenhower pledged that if elected he would go to Korea and put an end to the war, and Americans believed him. The Republican platform, echoing the sentiments of most business organizations in 1952, called for the reduction of taxes, an end to wage and price controls, and a return to balanced government budgets. Republican goals of national security and foreign policy differed little from Truman's; however, the execution of those policies would now deemphasize government initiative and rely more heavily on private initiative and free-market mechanisms.[1]

Although the Democrats waged a brave campaign in 1952, it was apparent from the start that the Republicans enjoyed significant advantages. Eisenhower artfully dodged a challenge from the right wing of his party and was nominated as its presidential candidate on the first ballot during the Republican convention in July. His running mate, Senator Richard M. Nixon (R-CA), was nominated by unanimous acclamation. Eisenhower's enormous recognition and popularity as a war hero and as NATO's first military chief gave him an air of unquestioned suitability for the presidency. In contrast, the Democratic presidential nominee, Governor Adlai E. Stevenson (D-IL), had repeatedly rebuffed his party's overtures to make him its candidate. In fact, he did not bow to the pressure until the very last minute. Eleven names were put into nomination during the Democratic National Convention, and Stevenson did not capture the top spot until the third ballot. His running mate, Senator John J. Sparkman (D-AL), was nominated by default, after two other names were withdrawn. Thus the Democrats began the 1952 campaign on a rather reluctant note and were never able to overcome the Republican advantage. By the fall of the year, more and more voters came to view General Eisenhower as the man they hoped

---

1. For good overviews of the 1952 elections and the various themes of the elections see Ronald J. Caridi, *The Korean War and American Politics*, esp. 209–45; Harry S. Truman, *Memoirs: Years of Trial and Hope*, 2, 493, 498–505; Donald R. McCoy, *The Presidency of Harry S. Truman*, 281–310; Donovan, *Tumultuous Years*, 392–401; Stephen E. Ambrose, *Eisenhower: Soldier, General of the Army, President-Elect, 1890–1952*, vol. 1, especially chap. 25–27; and *Congressional Quarterly Almanac*, 82d. Cong., 2d sess., 1952, vol. 8, "The Presidential Election—1952," 484–89 and "Congressional Elections—1952," 458.

would lead them out of the quagmire of Korea and into what some historians have called the "age of fragile consensus."[2]

Upon taking office, Eisenhower, in keeping with his campaign promises and reflecting his philosophy toward government controls, promptly liquidated the ESA, OPS, and WSB. In addition, he closed out the Controlled Materials Plan (CMP) and consolidated the NSRB into the Office of Defense Mobilization. Thus, Eisenhower's presidency marked the return of a tenuous normalcy in the nation's political economy. Although inflationary pressures and other dislocations caused by America's large and perpetual readiness program would lie just under the surface during the Eisenhower years, the new administration managed to keep them at bay. It did so partly on its own initiative, but the fact remained that the toughest part of assembling a permanent national security establishment was accomplished by Truman. In an important way, Truman's struggles during his last years in office paved the way for Eisenhower's comparatively trouble-free tenure in office. When Harry S. Truman handed the reins of government to Dwight Eisenhower in January 1953, the nation was in enviably good shape. Its economy was booming, its rearmament program was nearing its peak, and its ability to uphold domestic and global national security imperatives had never been stronger or more sophisticated.

Late summer and early fall of 1952 proved especially frustrating for stabilization officials. Congress continued to stymie the administration's stabilization program by slashing the operating budgets of the ESA and OPS. At the same time, a temporary spike in inflation, caused largely by drought-induced increases in food prices, befuddled administration officials and played right into the hands of the campaigning Republicans. Even worse, the recent increase in steel prices threatened to resonate throughout the economy, pushing prices even higher. And much to the chagrin of the White House, the recently settled steel controversy emboldened other labor unions to seek wage and fringe benefit increases commensurate with those

2. See sources cited above for more details on the 1952 presidential nominations and subsequent campaign. For varying interpretations of the "age of consensus" during the Eisenhower era see Paul A. Carter, *Another Part of the Fifties;* Elaine Tyler May, *Homeward Bound: American Families in the Cold War Era;* William L. O'Neill, *American High: The Years of Confidence, 1945–1960;* Richard H. Pells, *The Liberal Mind in a Conservative Age: American Intellectuals in the 1940s and 1950s;* and William H. Chafe, "Postwar American Society: Dissent and Social Reform," in Michael J. Lacey, ed., *The Truman Presidency,* 156–73.

accorded to the steel workers. Meanwhile, stabilization officials and Cabinet members engaged in an embarrassing public shouting match over the extent of inflationary pressures and the means by which to control them. OPS director Ellis Arnall promptly resigned his post as a result. By September, Truman's economic stabilization program was in complete shambles, and it became obvious that the best he could do was to resist the growing pressure to decontrol in toto the American economy.

In addition to limiting the administration's ability to control wages and prices by further diluting the Defense Production Act in June, Congress also tried to force the issue of decontrol by slashing the operating budgets of stabilization agencies. The House, always the harsher critic of controls, led the charge to cut the ESA budget by nearly 40 percent. The Senate hesitantly followed suit. The result was a reduction from the president's request of $102 million to a mere $60 million. Calling the cut a "kick in the teeth," ESA director Roger Putnam vowed to continue the war against inflation despite the setback. The war, however, would turn out to be more like a skirmish.[3]

Privately, stabilization officials acknowledged that their anti-inflation efforts would be severely limited. The administration was forced to eliminate 1,700 OPS jobs by September 1. And the already besieged WSB was also pressured into sharply reducing its staff. Thus Congress not only limited by decree the administration's ability to stabilize wages and prices, but it also further restricted stabilization policy through the power of the purse. These moves, led mostly by Republicans and conservative Democrats, placed the administration in a very awkward position. With the one hand they gave to it de jure power to continue— albeit on a limited basis—wage and price controls; with the other hand they forced de facto decontrol by withholding operating and enforcement funds. The result was frustration on the part of stabilization officials and confusion on the part of the public. In the end, this congressional sleight of hand worked to the great advantage of the Republicans. For the most part unaware of congressional legerdemain, the public blamed the administration for the failure to control rising prices during the autumn of the year, and the Republicans, including

---

3. ESA Weekly, July 1, 1952, RG 296, Records, Reports, and Secretariat, box 3, file: "ESA Weekly Roundup for the Administrator," NA; OPS News, July 10, 1952, RG 295, Central Files, 1952–53, box 632, file: "Daily News Digest, May–August 1952," NA. For quotation see *New York Times* July 10, 1952, 3A.

Eisenhower, could only point to this failure and denounce wage and price controls as a sham.[4]

At the same time that Congress was destroying some of the administration's anti-inflation weapons, wholesale and retail prices began to surge upward. This spike in prices was a result of three phenomena: a hefty increase in food prices, the increase in steel prices, and increasing demands by labor unions for higher wages. Higher processing costs and severe drought throughout much of the South and Midwest pushed retail food prices up 1.5 percent between June and July, an inflation rate of 18 percent per annum. In August the Consumer Price Index peaked at an all-time high. Meanwhile, as a result of the $5.20 per ton increase in steel prices, the ESA came under increasing pressure to grant price increases for those industries using steel. On August 27, Ellis Arnall reluctantly issued an order permitting manufacturers who processed steel to pass through, at each stage of fabrication, the increases in ceiling prices for steel, aluminum, and copper. Taking the opportunity to blast the steel companies for the "excessive" prices for steel, Arnall predicted that the pass-through would result in a direct increase of $750 million per year in the prices of products made from steel, aluminum, or copper. To add insult to injury, the wage increase in the steel industry resulted in pressure for similar increases in other industries, which in turn generated even more inflation. Although the OPS and WSB tried to "isolate" the steel case, they were in no position to deny similar settlements in other industries. Indeed by late August, it seemed as if the dam on prices had burst.[5]

The renewal of inflationary pressures also resulted in a spate of public bickering among administration officials, adding to the growing sentiment that wage and price controls had become completely unworkable. Inflation hawk Ellis Arnall's persistently pessimistic

4. Report to the President by the Director of Defense Mobilization, August 1, 1952, pp. 22–23, President's Secretary's Files, Subject File Agencies A, box 142, file: "Advisory Board on Mobilization Policy, National," HSTL; Memo to Putnam, July 8, 1952, "Planning in Connection with Budget Cuts," RG 295, Records of Joseph Freehill, box 696, file: "ESA Administrator Memos to and from, December 1951 to January 1952," NA; Mobilization Executives Staff Meeting No. 34, July 2, 1952, RG 296, ESA Records Maintained by the Administrator, Classified General Files, box 3, file: "Mobilization Executive Staff Meetings," NA.

5. ESA Weekly, August 12, 1952, RG 296, Records, Reports and Secretariat, box 3, file: "ESA Weekly Roundup for the Administrator," NA; Report to the President, August 1, 1952, pp. 3, 20, President's Secretary's Files, Subject File Agencies A, box 142, file: "Advisory Board on Mobilization Policy, National," HSTL; Press Release, August 27, 1952, RG 295, Records of Joseph Freehill, box 706, file: "Steel-Press Releases," NA.

inflationary outlook angered other administration officials, most notably Secretary of Agriculture Charles F. Brannan and Secretary of Commerce Charles Sawyer. Brannan categorically denied that the drought would "drastically" force food prices up as Arnall had claimed. And Sawyer, desperately trying to distance the administration from renewed inflation, publicly rebuked the OPS director, claiming that his "baleful predictions" were not based on all of the facts. Undeterred, Arnall stated publicly that "everybody's entitled to their [sic] own opinion. And time will tell who is right. I am sure that it will show that I am right."[6] Amidst this uproar were persistent rumors that Arnall was ready to quit. They turned out to be true. Angered and disillusioned over the steel settlement, which he took as a personal setback, Arnall had made up his mind to resign in early August. And despite attempts by the White House to keep him on the job—including a direct plea from Truman himself—Arnall left the OPS effective on September 1.[7]

Viewed from a wider perspective, Arnall's departure was probably for the best. The more he predicted inflationary pressures, the more ineffectual the administration appeared. And the angrier the victims of the anticipated inflation became. Arnall's statements certainly confused the public and played right into the hands of the Republicans. Presidential candidate Eisenhower wasted no time in jumping into the fray, asserting that the handling of emergency economic controls had been "badly bungled (and that) will be a very definite part of the campaign."[8] Beyond causing embarrassment on the part of the administration and confusion on the part of the public, the squabble over inflationary pressures may have itself brought about additional inflation. Markets and consumers are highly susceptible to speculative statements, making the mere mention of future inflation something of a self-fulfilling prophesy. Farmers, outraged at Arnall's prognostications and fearful that consumers might curb their spending, lobbied the president to issue a gag order for Arnall. Even federal economists not associated with the price office publicly doubted Arnall's crystal ball

6. ESA Weekly, August 14, 1952, RG 295, Central Files, 1952–53, box 632, file: "Daily News Digest May–August 1952," NA; Washington Post, August 13, 1952, 12A; quotation from New York Herald Tribune, August 13, 1952, 3.

7. OPS Daily News, August 7, 1952, RG 295, Central Files 1952–1953, box 632, file: "Daily News Digest, May–August 1952," NA; Letter to Governor Arnall plus attachment, President's Secretary's Files, ODM Reports-T, box 148, file: "Office of Price Administration," HSTL.

8. Washington Post, August 22, 1952.

ruminations. So just as inflation and the presidential campaign began to heat up, the administration suddenly found itself without a price administrator.[9]

Along with Ellis Arnall's departure from the OPS in September came the replacement of John Steelman, who had been acting director of the Office of Defense Mobilization since April. President Truman, who had never intended for Steelman to head the ODM after the settlement of the steel strike, replaced him with Henry Fowler, a Truman friend and supporter who had already served the mobilization program as administrator of the National Production Authority. Steelman, who was overburdened with his duties as acting ODM chief *and* assistant to the president, was now needed in the White House full-time, where his talents and experience could be tapped for the upcoming elections and the transition to a new administration.[10]

President Truman wasted little time in naming Arnall's successor at the OPS. With his days in office dwindling, and amidst growing pressure from both Democrats and Republicans to stem the tide of inflation, Truman quickly tapped Tighe E. Woods, Director of Rent Control, to succeed Arnall. Although many viewed Arnall's departure as the effective end of meaningful price control, Woods was determined to take up the gauntlet and to continue the fight against inflation. Almost unknown to the public and certainly less colorful than his predecessors, Woods announced soon after he took over the OPS that he would test the consumer waters to see how much support remained for the continuation of price controls. Woods' startling hint that price controls might no longer have been necessary certainly muddied the stabilization waters. The day after Woods announced his plans to tour the nation in order to gauge consumer's views toward price controls, the *New York Post* conducted a poll of local consumers. The vast majority of those polled favored the continuation of price controls, a view that apparently held true throughout much of the country. Woods' approach to price controls was certainly a novel departure from that of his immediate predecessor. As it turned out, Woods was never ready to completely scrap price controls—especially prior to the November elections—instead he took the issue directly to the American people,

9. OPS Daily News, August 18, 1952, RG 295 Central Files 1952–1953, box 632, file: "Daily News Digest, May–August 1952," NA.
10. Wage Strabilization Program, 1950–53, vol. 2, 127–29, RG 293 Records of the Wage Stabilization Board and Salary Stabilization Board of the ESA, box 1, file: "Wage Stabilization Program," NA.

announcing on September 4 his plans to travel to at least six cities throughout the nation to meet directly with consumers.[11]

Since June 1951, at which time the OPS established the National Consumer Advisory Committee in Washington, D.C., the agency had begun gradually to implement more and more community-oriented advisory pricing and enforcement committees. The National Committee, made up of representatives from twenty-six national organizations including women's clubs, labor unions, consumer cooperatives, PTA's, YWCA's, and religious and veterans' groups, was very instrumental in establishing community pricing in the various OPS districts. As an example, the community pricing program allowed shoppers and merchants alike to know at a glance the dollars-and-cents ceiling prices of more than four hundred staple market-based items in neighborhood and community grocery stores. The pricing lists were printed and distributed by the OPS and were displayed in prominent locations in and around the stores. In the spring of 1952, the National Consumer Advisory Committee also recommended the establishment of ten local community-based advisory committees to work with OPS district offices. The OPS went forward with the local committees, which as Tighe E. Woods explained as he embarked on his tour, were "invaluable in explaining to consumers how the stabilization program operates and what limitations Congress has imposed."[12]

The ten local committees that were already up and running played a number of important roles in the price stabilization effort. Besides helping in the establishment of price ceilings and code enforcement, the local committees participated in radio and television programs that tried to increase public awareness of the price program; distributed pamphlets and fact sheets; arranged talks and displays to inform the public on price control policies and operations; published a weekly newsletter for consumers on current problems; and served as a panel to explain official OPS programs at public meetings. To be sure, this kind of corporative volunteerism had by now become the linchpin of the Korean mobilization and stabilization program, at once keeping the fears of a centralized, garrison state at bay while also empowering

11. OPS Daily News, August 27, 1952, RG 295 Central Files 1952–1953, box 632, file: "Daily News Digest, May–August 1952," NA; *New York Post* August 29, 1952, 2–3; OPS Daily News, September 5, 1952, RG 295 Central Files, 1942–1953, box 632, file: "Daily News Digest," NA.

12. OPS Release, September 16, 1952, RG 295 Records of Joseph Freehill, box 699, file: "Consumer Advisory Committees," NA.

and enlisting average citizens at the grass-roots level, most critically women.[13]

Woods' peripatetic survey of consumer attitudes was both a novel and instructive approach toward price controls. It also fit the general trend of the administration's control programs during the Korean War. That is, as resistance to certain controls grew and as public and partisan support for government-mandated programs eroded, administration officials turned to more decentralized approaches that empowered and more clearly informed constituents at the local and regional levels. Woods' nationwide tour eventually took him to ten cities and towns across the nation. Halfway through his tour, Woods called for the creation of more local consumer advisory committees, which were to work in tandem with district OPS offices. Although such committees had already been put into place in ten of the nation's cities—not to mention at the national level—Woods wanted such committees established in all of the eighty-four cities that housed OPS district offices. It was much too late in Truman's term to accomplish such a feat, but Woods' attempts to gauge public support through his town meetings with consumers was quite helpful in two important ways. First, the meetings were a splendid public relations success for an agency that sorely needed a boost. Second, it confirmed top administration officials' convictions that to end altogether price and wage controls before the November elections would be folly.[14]

Woods' meetings with "housewives," to use the language of the day, brought to the fore several issues. First, Woods reported to President Truman on November 3 several attitudes he discerned from his meetings: Consumers were indeed greatly concerned over inflation; consumers thought that the price control system was not very effective yet at the same time believed it should be continued; they blamed the weakness of the law itself (i.e. the Defense Production Act) for most of the system's failures; and finally, Americans seemed largely unaware that the need for price controls was the result of defense mobilization. Of course, the Republicans came to rather different conclusions over the same issues and tried to convince the public that the only

13. Ibid; Memorandum to Michael V. DiSalle, October 11, 1951, RG 295 Records of Joseph Freehill, box 696, file: "ESA Administration, Memos to and From," NA.

14. OPS Release of Woods' Report to the President, November 3, 1952, RG 295 Records of Joseph Freehill, box 699, file: "T.E. Woods-Consumer Mass Meetings," NA; OPS Release, "Local Consumer Advisory Committees," September 16, 1952, RG 295 Records of Joseph Freehill, box 699, file: "Consumer Advisory Committees," NA.

reason price controls were needed was not because of mobilization per se, but rather because the Truman administration was mishandling mobilization. Still, administration officials believed that price controls should continue through the November elections, not wanting voters to get the idea that Democrats did not care about the rising cost of living. The implication of Woods' findings was by then recognized as one of the central dilemmas of the Cold War. That is, how does a nation assemble—and maintain at high readiness over an indefinite period—a huge military complex without resorting to economic and political regimentation on the one hand or bankruptcy on the other? And concomitantly, how do leaders in a democratic system keep the populace informed and willing to sacrifice during such a period?[15]

Part of the answer to these prickly questions may be found in policymakers' organizational and institutional approaches to national security. The Office of Price Stabilization's attempts to decentralize and localize price control policy and enforcement is an ideal example of this. First, OPS officials' moves toward decentralization served highly utilitarian purposes: As Congress diluted their attempts to stabilize prices first by weakening the Defense Production Act and then by cutting their budgets, local consumer advisory committees became indispensable to making and enforcing pricing policies. Volunteers at the local, regional, and national levels thus did the work that paid government bureaucrats had done in the past. Second, by informing and empowering consumers at the local level, policymakers helped to mitigate growing concerns that the workings of government had slipped from the control of the people. Thus, by localizing OPS policymaking, stabilization planners literally took the fight against inflation into Americans' living rooms. Stated simply, the corporative volunteerism at work in the OPS helped to blunt criticism that the nation was moving toward a centralized, regimented garrison state.

There were more subtle—but certainly no less important—motives in the administration's moves toward decentralization and corporative

15. OPS Release of Woods' Report to the President, November 3, 1952, RG 295 Records of Joseph Freehill, box 699, file: "T.E. Woods-Consumer Mass Meetings," NA; OPS Daily News, September 9, September 22, and October 3, 1952, RG 295 Central Files, 1951–52, box 632, file: "Daily News Digest, September," NA; Mobilization Executives Staff Meeting No. 37, September 17, 1952, RG 296 Records Maintained by the Administrator, Classified General Files, box 3, file: "Mobilization Executive Staff Meetings," NA; National Advisory Board on Mobilization Policy, Meeting No. 19, September 22–23, 1952, Papers of Harry S. Truman, White House Central Files, Confidential Files, box 26, file: "National Advisory Board on Mobilization Policy, 1951–52," HSTL.

volunteerism. By forming local consumer advisory committees, which were composed almost exclusively of women, government officials were in the same breath acknowledging women's growing participation in the nation's institutions while at the same time emphasizing women's traditional societal roles as consumers, wives, and mothers. Rarely, in fact, did OPS officials refer to the women with whom they met and worked as "consumers" or "citizens." They were almost always referred to as "housewives" and were very often addressed as "Mrs. John Doe," or were in some other fashion linked with their husbands or other male relations. As Elaine Tyler May has ably demonstrated, the Cold war ethos in America stressed women's traditional roles as wives and mothers. Thus, the "cult of domesticity" served as a bulwark against Communism; women were expected to maintain and strengthen traditional American and family values thereby providing a crucial moral edge in the waging of the Cold War. But as Susan Hartmann has shown, despite the dominance and discourse of traditional gender roles in the early Cold War, American leaders and experts repeatedly tried to include women in the shaping of public policy and public relations, in recognition of women's growing power and participation in the workplace and in politics. This inclusion of women, however, was almost always couched in the discourse of traditional gender roles and family life and was either implicitly or explicitly linked to the waging of the Cold War.[16]

The gendered discourse described here is fully apparent in a splendidly revealing memorandum to OPS director Tighe E. Woods. In that memo, OPS staffer and liaison to the OPS Consumer Advisory Committee Merle W. Huntington explained to Woods the operations and makeup of a consumer group called "Housewives United." Housewives United was formed in July 1951 as an informal, grass-roots organization whose primary aim was to curb inflation by informing consumers, establishing boycotts when necessary, and protesting government policies when they were deemed antithetical to inflation fighting. In the memo, Huntington hinted at the Red-baiting atmosphere of

16. May, *Homeward Bound*; Susan M. Hartmann, "Women's Employment and the Domestic Ideal in the Early Cold War," 84–100. For other good overviews of women's roles in mid-century American society and the evolution of those roles see Susan M. Hartmann, *The Home Front and Beyond, American Women in the 1940s*; Eugenia Kaledin, *Mothers and More: American Women in the 1950s*; William H. Chafe, *The American Woman: Her Changing Social, Economic, and Political Roles, 1920–1970*; Joanne Meyerowitz, "Beyond the Feminine Mystique: A Reassessment of Postwar Mass Culture, 1946–1958," 1455–82.

the times, assuring Woods that "the women who spearheaded Housewives United are above reproach . . . the organization has been spared
the fate of some shoppers groups during World War II which attracted
some vociferous spokesmen (sic) of the extreme left." Huntington went
on to identify the founding women as "Mrs. Louis B. Wright" and
"Mrs. Donald J. Detwiler." "Mrs. Wright," wrote Huntington, "is the
wife of the Folger Shakespearean Library Director and Mrs. Detwiler
is the wife of a Navy Commander," as if these women's spouses and
their social standing somehow affirmed the womens' right to form the
group. At the same time, Huntington's description suggested that the
women were solid wives, mothers, and "housewives," and were thus
by definition anti-communist.[17]

Despite administration officials' concerns over resurgent inflation,
as the autumn of 1952 progressed, inflationary pressures began to ease.
By mid-October prices had stabilized and the supply-demand situation
of critical industrial materials was nearing equilibrium. This was both
good news and bad news for the Democrats, however. Adlai Stevenson
could point to the inflation front and declare that his party—through
the use of economic controls—had kept prices at bay. But at the same
time, Republicans used the improving news on inflation to assert that
controls were no longer needed. Stabilization officials were caught in
the middle. Although they continued to move toward decontrol, even
going so far as to exempt small retailers from price controls in October,
they were still wary of total decontrol. Such a move prior to the election
would have left the Democrats wide open to criticism had inflation
rebounded. Instead, the administration continued to move cautiously
on the wage and price front, especially in light of Eisenhower's sizable
lead in the polls.[18]

While stabilization officials walked a tightrope between immediate
decontrol and gradual decontrol, they pondered the immediate and
distant future of wage and price controls. Not surprisingly, stabilization
officials were not of one mind on the future of controls. Within the

17. Memo to Tighe E. Woods plus attachments, September 23, 1952, RG 295 Records
of Joseph Freehill, box 699, file: "Consumer Advisory Committees," NA.
18. ESA Weekly, August 19, 1952, RG 296 Records, Reports and Secretariat, box 3,
file: "ESA Weekly Roundup for the Administrator," NA; Report to the President by the
Director of Defense Mobilization, November 1, 1952, pp. 17–19, President's Secretary's
Files Agencies A, box 142, file: "Advisory Board on Mobilization Policy, National,"
HSTL; OPS Daily News, October 15 and November 19, 1952, RG 295 Central Files 1952–
53, box 632, file: "Daily News Digest," NA; Memo "Exemption of Small Business,"
October 23, 1952, RG 295 Records of Joseph Freehill, box 692, file: "Small Business," NA.

ESA, the majority consensus asserted that economic controls should be continued until April 30, 1953 at the latest, with attempts to end them earlier if at all possible. The majority position was predicated upon the continuance of the present pace of mobilization. But some stabilization officials challenged this view. Benjamin Ginzburg, an ESA staffer, argued that the Agency should say or do nothing that would imply that controls would be ended in a given period of time. Noting that the economy was then capable of supporting a stepped-up mobilization process, Ginzburg suggested that a new administration might wish to increase defense production; thus, controls should not be ended prematurely. He added that the Agency should do nothing to "interfere with the freedom of decision of the next administration."[19]

With the issue of controls at the heart of the 1952 presidential campaign, White House and stabilization officials had to tread gingerly when the subject arose. And as it became increasingly clear that the Democrats might not capture the White House—and indeed might lose their majority in Congress—stabilization officials were reticent to discuss controls at all. When asked to provide a statement in support of continued controls for campaigning Democratic senators and congressmen, the OPS demurred. In fact, OPS staffer W. W. McClanahan told the Democratic National Committee in September that "what [we are] trying to avoid is laying ourselves open to the charge that we are promoting the control program purely as a political measure rather than because we feel that it is essential to the economic welfare of the nation." However politically insightful that strategy may have been, it bode no good for the future of wage and price controls. The Truman administration continued to enforce controls as they currently stood, but it sensed that an extension or strengthening of control legislation would not be forthcoming from Congress.[20]

Upon the realization that Congress was in no mood to extend or strengthen economic controls, the best the administration could do was to draw up plans for legislative action aimed at provisional, standby control powers once the current powers lapsed in April 1953. What the OPS hoped for was a stronger, standby law that could be invoked by executive order in the face of some future emergency. As part of

19. Memo to Mr. Putnam, September 10, 1952, RG 296 Letters, Memos of Roger L. Putnam, box 100, file: "Position Papers," NA.

20. Memo to Woods, September 9, 1952, RG 295 Central Files 1952–53, box 351, file: "OPS Office of the Director, 7–8-9/52," NA.

this standby legislation, stabilization officials called for the continuation of a skeletal control staff that could quickly swing into action as soon as the president invoked his control powers. What stabilization officials envisioned was akin to what mobilization planners had put into place soon after the Korean War rearmament was begun: a stand-ready mobilization base that could swing into full-scale mobilization relatively quickly, thus avoiding the long lead times necessary to mobilize from scratch. Unlike the military and industrial mobilization base concept, however, the standby economic controls smacked of ongoing economic regimentation and gave to the president more power than the Congress was willing to grant him over the long-term.[21] Reacting to the suggestion of standby controls, Laurence F. Lee, president of the U.S. Chamber of Commerce, once again conjured the ghostly specter of a garrison state: "we are holding up to the world our way of life, our conceptions of freedom and free enterprise and for this reason we should resolve every doubt in favor of the prompt termination of all controls and should view with considerable skepticism even the idea of stand-by controls."[22]

Amidst the bureaucratic wrangling over controls, Republicans and Democrats conducted their own boisterous debate over the efficacy of economic controls and the manner in which the Cold War was to be waged. The 1952 presidential election had become a muddy slugfest even before the parties declared their nominees. After the July nominating conventions, the campaign became even more unseemly. In fact, historian and Eisenhower biographer Stephen Ambrose pronounced the campaign as "one of the bitterest" of the century and one that arguably "featured the most mudslinging."[23] President Truman was deeply troubled and hurt by the antics and words of Eisenhower himself, who Truman had heretofore greatly respected. Truman almost certainly cringed at Eisenhower's repeated assertions that his administration had "lost" China and had brought about the Korean War by its capitulation to Communism abroad. Nothing, however, rankled Truman more than Republican accusations of Communist duplicity within the administration. Richard Nixon's infamously scornful barbs

21. Memo to Joseph Freehill, September 15, 1952, RG 295 Central Files 1952–53, box 688, file: "Programs," NA; ESA Executive Staff Meeting, September 24, October 8, 1952, RG 296 Secretariat-Classified, box 11, file: "Executive Staff Meetings," NA.

22. Letter to Henry H. Fowler, October 16, 1952, RG 296, Letters and Memoranda of Roger Putnam, box 101, file: "National Advisory Board on Mobilization Policy," NA.

23. Ambrose, *Eisenhower,* vol. 1, 567.

aimed at Adlai Stevenson were also meant to strike at the Truman administration, especially his alliterative charge that Stevenson had graduated from "Dean Acheson's Cowardly College of Communist Containment."[24]

Without a doubt, the corrosive effects of McCarthyism had long since stymied and neutralized the Truman administration's ability to govern proactively and effectively. And the unabashed partisan politicization and exaggeration of alleged internal communist subversion had by now become characteristic trademarks of Republican campaign tactics. Thus, as the 1952 elections approached, Adlai Stevenson became the new target of Republican-McCarthyite smear tactics. Of course, Truman continued to be personally vilified, while Democrats and liberals in general were guilty merely by association. Indeed, to a growing number of Americans, the Democratic party seemed increasingly less able to govern effectively and even less able to retain its tenuous grasp on the majority position in Congress, not to mention the White House.

So it was in this atmosphere that Eisenhower and Stevenson put forth their views on defense and national security issues. Stevenson, generally less liberal than Truman, fundamentally agreed with Eisenhower on many issues, foreign and domestic. In an important way, Eisenhower's leadership of his party narrowed the gap between the Republicans and Democrats by relegating the isolationist and ultraconservative Republicans to a decidedly peripheral status. Robert Taft and his neo-isolationist cabal were largely silenced and the Great Debate of 1951 was settled for good in favor of the progressive internationalists. Thus, like Stevenson and Truman, Eisenhower was committed to multilateral collective security, lower tariffs, free trade, and an honorable peace in Korea. Domestically, Eisenhower vowed to end wage and price controls, reduce taxes, balance the budget, and contain the sprawl of the federal government while at the same time promising to expand Social Security. All of this would be accomplished through increased efficiency in government brought about by state-of-the-art business management techniques. The budget cuts the General envisioned would come mostly from national security programs. "Here," Eisenhower explained, "is where the largest savings can be

24. See Truman, *Memoirs*, vol. 2, 498–505; and William E. Pemberton, *Harry S. Truman: Fair Dealer and Cold Warrior*, 170–71 for the president's reactions to the 1952 campaign. For Nixon's quotation see Ambrose, *Eisenhower*, 553.

made." He blasted the current administration for its on-again, off-again mobilization planning, promising that the Republicans would "plan for the future on something more than yesterday's headlines." Although Eisenhower would later find it difficult to balance the budget—especially through defense cuts alone—at the time his rhetoric greatly appealed to an electorate worn down by high taxes and government controls.[25]

Adlai Stevenson's domestic platform was not drastically different from that of Eisenhower's. He too called for stringent government economy and a balanced budget. Where he diverged from Eisenhower's program was in the area of taxes and economic controls. He did not promise tax breaks nor did he vow to end immediately economic controls. Instead, he urged greater restraints on private credit accumulation and the continuation of wage, price, and material controls as "temporary bridges" between abnormal and normal times. He was confident that such a program would halt inflation without disrupting either the growth of the economy or the ongoing rearmament program.[26]

Sensing the immense public antipathy toward Truman, Stevenson tried to distance himself from the president. Only during the closing weeks of the campaign did the Stevenson camp reluctantly allow Truman to make appearances in the Democratic candidate's behalf. Truman, ever the trooper, embarked on a brief but intense campaign tour of the nation, not unlike that of his famous 1948 whistle-stop tour. He was confident that he could help Stevenson beat the odds and defeat General Eisenhower. Neither Stevenson nor the Democrats were quite as hopeful, however. They turned out to be right. Truman's involvement may indeed have hurt the Democratic ticket. But even that mattered little. On November 4, Dwight D. Eisenhower crushed Stevenson, winning over 55 percent of the popular vote and carrying thirty-nine states. For the first time since 1928, the GOP cracked the solidly Democratic South, capturing Florida, Virginia, Texas, and Tennessee. Eisenhower's victory also shifted the balance of power in both houses of Congress toward the Republicans. Thus for the first time in twenty years, the Republicans controlled Congress and the White House.[27]

25. Ambrose, *Eisenhower*, 568–69 (quotations from p. 568); "The Republican Platform," *U.S. News* 33 (July 18, 1952): 82–87; *Newsweek* 40 (July 21, 1952): 69.

26. OPS Daily News, September 24, 1994, RG 295 Central Files 1952–1953, box 632, file: "Daily News Digest, September," NA; see also "The Democratic Platform," *U.S. News* 33 (August 1, 1952): 83–90.

27. *Congressional Quarterly Almanac*, 1952, 484; Pemberton, *Harry S. Truman*, 170–71.

In the final analysis, the Democrats' loss in the 1952 elections was less a repudiation of Stevenson or of the New Deal and Fair Deal than it was a repudiation of Truman himself. Eisenhower's victory was a personal one, and Americans embraced the messenger as much as they embraced his message. Eisenhower's moderate stance on domestic social programs and his basic agreement with Truman's containment policy did not alter the political-economic trajectory of U.S. policy-making. Instead, Eisenhower tried to change—as best he could—the means by which the ends would be achieved. This meant in principle . that he came to rely more heavily upon indirect government control of the economy, the linchpins of which would be an activist monetary policy combined with a more conservative fiscal policy. To be sure, Eisenhower eschewed the direct economic controls favored by the Truman administration. As a result, the president-elect enjoyed the full support of conservative business groups like the National Association of Manufacturers (NAM) and the U.S. Chamber of Commerce, as well as more moderate, progressive groups like the Council for Economic Development (CED) and the Business Advisory Council (BAC).[28]

If Cold War tensions splintered the New Deal–Fair Deal coalition, so too did they weaken the ideological underpinnings of the Right. After twenty years of economic depression, world war, and Communist containment, the federal government had become a large, centralized, and institutionalized facet of American society. The Left and Right may have debated *why* it should be so, but neither side sought to dismantle it. Moderate conservatives like Eisenhower had little choice but to accept big government. The alternative was, in their minds, far worse: capitulation to Communism. Republicans thus only hoped to stave off further government bloating by relying upon private, corporate initiatives to execute Cold War policies. They also sought to contain government growth by trying to reduce defense expenditures through increased military effectiveness. This meant the further deemphasis of conventional arms and standing armies in favor of high-tech weapons and nuclear deterrence—a trend already begun under Truman. Try as he did, Eisenhower was never able to reduce military spending below $44 billion per year, a far cry from the pre-Korean level of $13 billion. Nor was he able to reduce in any measure the growth or scope of the federal government. And reflecting his now famous ex post

28. McQuaid, *Uneasy Partners,* 62, 64–65; Robert Griffith, "Dwight D. Eisenhower and the Corporate Commonwealth," 87–122.

facto warning about the dangers of a military-industrial complex in his 1961 Farewell Address, the military-industrial sector grew inexorably throughout the 1950s. It was fueled by increasingly high-tech weaponry and fused together by public-private linkages that came to incorporate large sectors of the political economy, including academia.[29]

In the short-term, the Republican victory did little to change the Truman administration's national security and economic stabilization programs. First, the Truman administration sought to continue a policy of limited mobilization for the foreseeable future, maintaining an active and broadbased military production program coupled with a mobilization base designed to swing into action at the first sign of crisis. The defense program and mobilization base were, as they had been since June 1950, predicated upon a maximization of economic growth and stability. The National Security Council, in reviewing the vast scope of the rearmament program, was confident that the United States had made great strides in developing its economic and military power—so much so that it considered a Moscow-inspired all-out war far more unlikely than it had appeared only two years before. Second, the administration continued to pace the rearmament effort in accordance with military needs and economic and political realities. Thus, although the ODM reported industrial production at a record high and materials shortages easing, military schedules continued to be stretched out, particularly for aircraft and tank production. This was a result of design difficulties and procurement backlogs as much as it was a continuation of the policies established a year earlier, ones that more realistically aligned military spending with fiscal realities and allied capabilities.[30]

In the realm of economic stabilization, the same policies held— the administration attempted to maintain the status quo. On November 18, the acting director of the National Production Authority (NPA)

29. McQuaid, *Uneasy Partners*, 73–77. See also Galambos and Pratt, *Rise of the Corporate Commonwealth;* Robert H. Ferrell, ed., *The Eisenhower Diaries;* and Robert Higgs, *Crisis and Leviathan: Critical Episodes in the Growth of American Government,* esp. x–xi, 7–8, 73, 238–42.

30. "Current Problems of the Government of the United States of America Relating to National Security," vol. 1, November 1, 1952, President's Secretary's Files, box 194, file: "Subject File-NSC Misc. Data," HSTL; Report to the President by the Director of Defense Mobilization, November 1, 1952, President's Secretary's Files, Subject Files Agencies A, box 142, file: "Advisory Board on Mobilization Policy, National," HSTL; National Advisory Board on Mobilization Policy Meeting No. 22, December 16, 1952, President's Secretary's Files, box 131, file: "General File: National Advisory Board, Mobilization," HSTL.

Ralph S. Trigg wrote to ODM Director Henry H. Fowler that "preliminary data . . . show that we may be approaching a reasonable balance between supply and (demand) requirements for most of the materials under CMP." Decontrol of critical materials, however, would not occur before Eisenhower took office because "the interregnum between two administrations does not afford the ideal environment for a policy decision of such momentous import," Trigg concluded.[31] The same attitude prevailed when it came to wage and price controls. ESA and OPS officials were convinced that inflationary pressures still presented enough of a danger that they would continue to actively prosecute controls rather than allow them to languish. The decision to continue general price controls was made partly because stabilization officials honestly believed that they were needed, although decontrol of individual commodities was pursued whenever feasible and prudent. But price controls were actively continued for another reason: Mobilization officials wished to give the new administration as much leeway as possible in the prosecution of the military buildup. Thus they left the issue of total decontrol in the hands of President-elect Eisenhower.[32]

Eisenhower's election brought other issues to the fore as well. First, no sooner had Eisenhower been elected than there was talk of an economic downturn in the offing. The Truman administration itself began to talk privately about such a scenario soon after the election. The Treasury Department, in addition to fretting over the possibility of a recession, also warned of a resurgence in the budget deficit as many of the taxes implemented just after Korea were due to lapse. The Treasury attributed the possibility of recession to the successive stretch-outs in defense production, increasing deficits and debt burdens, and the anticipated end of economic controls. It did not take long for the press to realize these implications. In December, *Fortune* magazine stated that "if the U.S. is not yet worrying much about the strength of the economy, it soon will be." Financial guru Sylvia Porter lamented that "our economy is where it is because of our immense spending on rearmament. The fact is that we would have been in trouble before this—had it not been for Korea." These fears, which turned out to be quite prescient, did not

31. Memo to Fowler, December 18, 1952, RG 277, Correspondence with Government Agencies, box 15, NA.

32. Memo to Tighe E. Woods and Roger L. Putnam, November 25, 1952, RG 296, Records Maintained by the Administrator, Classified General Files, box 2, NA; OPS Daily News, November 28 and December 3, 1952, RG 295, Central Files, 1952–1953, box 632, file: "Daily News Digest," NA.

deter the Eisenhower administration from cutting federal spending or ending economic controls. The recurrent but relatively brief economic recessions and slower economic growth during Eisenhower's tenure thus amply demonstrated the countercyclical forces inherent in postwar military Keynesianism.[33]

If the Republican sweep in November sounded the death knell for economic controls, the December wage settlement in the coal industry was the final nail in the coffin. Once again the Wage Stabilization Board (WSB) found itself entangled in an imbroglio with labor and management. And yet again Harry Truman found it necessary to step in and solve the crisis. As a result, the WSB chairman resigned swiftly followed by industry members. OPS Director Woods followed suit as did ESA Administrator Roger Putnam. By the middle of December, Truman found himself with an unworkable wage board and vacancies at the top three stabilization posts. The sudden unraveling of the wage board convinced the incoming administration that controls had to go and go quickly. The public too reached the same conclusion. The best the White House could now hope for was an orderly transition of power; it had no further delusions that its control programs would be continued much beyond the first few months of the new administration.

The coal case had its origins in the September 29 contract agreement signed by the majority of bituminous coal mine operators and the United Mine Workers of America (UMW). The contract provided for an across-the-board wage increase of $1.90 per day. Because the increase would have exceeded by 85 cents the automatically approvable amount set by the WSB, the contract had to be submitted to the wage board for review and approval. The coal case was the first major test of the newly reconstituted WSB. And it turned out to be its last. As a result of the December coal wage settlement, the new board, sworn in on August 5 under the chairmanship of labor attorney and Harvard professor Archibald Cox, virtually disintegrated as a tripartite body.[34]

33. Memo to Tighe E. Woods and Roger L. Putnam, November 25, 1952, RG 296, Records Maintained by the Administrator, Classified General Files, box 2, NA; "Tax Issues in 1953," Treasury Department, Tax Advisory Staff, December 15, 1952, Papers of L. Laszio Ecker-Racz, box 7, file: "Tax Issues in 1953," HSTL; *Nation* (September 29, 1952): 483–85. For quotations and a good review of the concerns at the time see *Fortune* 46 (December 1952): 112–17.

34. Wage Stabilization Program, 1950–1953, vol. 1, xiii, RG 293, Records of the WSB and SSB of the Economic Stabilization Agency, box 1, file: "WSB-ESA 6/30/53," NA; "Background of this Appeal," November 23, 1952, RG 296, Letters and Memos of Roger L. Putnam, box 99, file: "Coal Dispute," NA.

On October 18, the WSB ruled on the coal contract. By a majority ruling of eight to four (labor members dissenting), the board granted only $1.50 of the previously negotiated increase of $1.90 per day. Under OPS guidelines, the coal industry had the right to pass through most, if not all, of the wage costs to the consumer. The inflationary effects would ripple throughout the economy, affecting everything from electricity costs to steel prices. With the steel debacle fresh on their minds, however, mobilization and stabilization officials refused to give the coal case any special treatment. Even the president's Advisory Board on Mobilization Policy remained silent on the issue. All hoped that both sides would abide by the wage board's ultimate decision. That was wishful thinking. The UMW was outraged at the WSB's decision and immediately sought an appeal. Meanwhile, the UMW rank and file walked off the job, curtailing coal production just as the nation headed into the coldest part of the year. And although ESA officials acknowledged that there was a sizable supply of accessible coal on hand, enough so that a stoppage of forty-five to sixty days would not be catastrophic, they did fear the long-term inflationary threats of a lengthy strike.[35]

Predictably, the UMW, led by the fiery John L. Lewis, eviscerated the WSB. Lewis wasted no time in asking the National Coal Operators' Association to join him in his efforts to reverse the WSB decision. In a letter to the Association on October 21, Lewis had this to say about the wage board: "Four agents of the National Association of Manufacturers, aided by a professor from the Harvard Law School and his timid trio of dilettante associates, form a cabal to steal forty cents a day from each mineworker . . . The NAM-Professor Cox cabal ignored the representatives of labor. The procedure invalidates collective bargaining and would make economic serfs of American citizens." Lewis was not much kinder to ESA director Putnam: "Mr. Putnam is an honorable man . . . his only sadistic trait is his penchant for robbing miners' babies of life-giving milk."[36]

35. Memorandum for the Record, October 17, 1952, RG 296 Letters and Memos of Roger L. Putnam, box 99, file: "Coal Dispute," NA; "Background of this Appeal," November 23, 1952, RG 296 Letter and Memos of Putnam, box 99, file: "Coal Dispute," NA; National Advisory Board on Mobilization Policy Meeting No. 20, October 20 and 21, 1952, Papers of Harry S. Truman, White House Central Files, Confidential Files, box 26, file: "National Advisory Board on Mobilization Policy 1951–1952," HSTL; ESA Executive Staff Meeting, October 15, 1952, RG 296 Letters and Memos of Putnam, box 100, file: "Position Papers," NA.

36. Letter to National Bituminous Coal Operators' Association, October 21, 1952, RG 296 Letters and Memos of Roger L. Putnam, box 99, file: "Coal Dispute," NA.

The war of words embarrassed the White House and infuriated Putnam, who by now planned to quit the ESA as soon as the coal dispute could be settled. Nonetheless, Putnam and Woods fully backed the WSB's ruling. Convinced that the $1.50 per day increase was as high as the board could go without risking an inflationary surge, Putnam had no choice but to support Cox's offer. There were, however, other reasons why Putnam felt so obliged to support the wage board's decision. A majority of the WSB along with Archibald Cox made it clear that to approve the full wage increase would in effect mean the end to wage stabilization in general. Further, Cox and industry members made it known that the board would more than likely disband if its decision were overturned. Putnam thus dared not put himself into the position of challenging the WSB by himself.[37]

On October 27, Truman convened a special meeting of the UMW and the coal executives in the Oval Office. He promised to submit a petition for reconsideration of the WSB ruling to stabilization officials. Meanwhile the president secured assurances from John Lewis that the UMW would cooperate by sending its workers back to work until the appeal was settled. The work stoppage was thus ended. But the wage issue was far from settled. Roger Putnam, whose job it now was to settle the dispute, had not fundamentally changed his view toward the coal case. He still backed the WSB's recommendation. But Putnam came under enormous pressure to overrule the board. First, unlike in the steel crisis, the two petitioning parties were on the same side. Both the UMW and the coal companies wanted the matter settled by granting the full $1.90 per day wage increase. Second, other unions joined in the fray by bashing the WSB and stabilization efforts in general. By mid-November, even the CIO, heretofore staunchly pro-controls, went on record requesting that controls end in the spring, asserting that price controls in particular had "been inadequate from the start." With major unions now backing away from their support of the administration's controls policies, the system of stabilization began to come apart. But still Putnam refused to be herded into a hasty decision, not wanting to be known as the stabilization official responsible for killing economic controls.[38]

37. OPS Daily News, November 7, 1952, RG 295 Central Files 1952–53, box 632, file: "Daily News Digest," NA;"Courses of Action Available in the Coal Case," (no date), RG 296 Letters and Memos of Roger L. Putnam, box 99, file: "Coal Dispute," NA.

38. OPS Daily News, October 27 and November 24, 1952, RG 295 Central Files 1952–53, box 632, file: "Daily News Digest," NA; Report to the President by the Director of

In the end, the final decision was not Putnam's to make. After more than a month of careful deliberation, Putnam and other mobilization officials including ODM Director Henry Fowler had decided to uphold the WSB's ruling. Truman did not agree. On December 3, he stepped into the growing crisis and with a stroke of his pen granted the full wage increase to the coal workers. His rationale for the move was to avoid handing the problem to Dwight Eisenhower: "I am not willing to take an action that will create a crisis for my successor." Unwilling to risk a long strike and the further derision of labor, Truman believed that his decision was the best way to preserve the remnants of the stabilization program. But the president's decision, by undermining his own wage board, did just the opposite. Only the UMW was truly mollified. The public and industry officials were outraged by the action, viewing it as yet another unnecessary capitulation to labor's demands. The coal wage decision put a practical end to wage and price controls.[39]

As predicted, on December 4, Archibald Cox resigned his WSB post in protest of Truman's decision. On December 6, all of the industry representatives on the WSB resigned in protest. On December 15, after the NAM and the U.S. Chamber refused to take part in any reconstituted wage board, Roger Putnam appointed an all-public Wage Stabilization Committee. The next day, Putnam resigned in frustration, knowing full well that the effective end of economic stabilization was upon him. Two weeks earlier, OPS Director Tighe Woods had resigned. Like a toothless tiger, Truman's economic stabilization program was now bereft of purpose—not to mention personnel. The effective end of controls had arrived.[40]

On December 22, former OPS director Michael V. DiSalle was sworn in as the new ESA administrator. Having lost his bid to become Ohio's junior senator, DiSalle returned to Washington as a personal favor to Roger Putnam and the president. Highly regarded as the OPS director,

Defense Mobilization, November 1, 1952, p. 20, President's Secretary's Files Agencies A, box 142, file: "Advisory Board on Mobilization Policy, National," HSTL; "Opinion in the Bituminous Coal Case," November 20, 1952, RG 296 Letters and Memos of Roger L. Putnam, box 99, file: "Coal Dispute," NA. For CIO quotation see OPS Daily News, November 26, 1952, RG 295 Central Files 1952–53, box 632, file: "Daily News Digest," NA.
    39. Letter to Mr. Putnam, December 3, 1952, RG 296 Letters and Memos of Putnam, box 99, file: "Coal Dispute," NA.
    40. "Wage Stabilization Program, 1950–1953," vol. 1, RG 293, box 1, file: "WSB-ESA 6/30/53," NA; NAM Press Release, December 10, 1952, RG 296, box 4, NA; OPS Daily News, December 10, 1952, RG 295 Central Files 1952–53, box 632, file: "Daily News Digest," NA.

he was the perfect man to oversee the transition of power to the Eisenhower administration. He was also well suited to petition the Congress to pass a standby controls law, which Truman tried to do one final time. Even his stature, however, proved no match for a Republican-controlled Congress already disgusted with the current controls setup. Congress refused to act on the Truman administration's control recommendations. DiSalle was no luckier in luring industry representatives back to the wage board. The NAM and the U.S. Chamber steadfastly refused to participate in any government controls board. They simply waited with anticipation for the more pro-business Eisenhower administration to strike the final blow at economic controls.[41]

As 1953 began, the Truman administration made a valiant last-ditch effort to convince Congress and Eisenhower of the need for continued controls. As DiSalle continued to beat the controls drum, other administration officials joined in. Secretary of Commerce Charles Sawyer, a self-avowed conservative Democrat and no fan of economic controls, warned against the imminent expiration of controls. "It would be foolhardy," said Sawyer, "for us to abandon all controls so long as there remains a threat of Communist aggression. And stripping the Executive branch of the power to move swiftly to control materials needed for national security would play into the hands of our potential enemies."[42] But neither the incoming Eisenhower administration nor the new Congress would hear any of it. Eisenhower, looking at the great progress made in military production and steadily rising industrial output and capacity, was convinced that ongoing controls were no longer needed. So the best the outgoing administration could do was to persuade the incoming one of the need to draft and pass a standby war powers act that included wage, price, credit, and material controls. This too proved to be an impossible sell.[43]

41. Letter to DiSalle, November 25, 1952, RG 296, box 23, NA; "Wage Stabilization Program, 1950–1953," vol. 1, RG 293, box 1, file: "WSB-ESA 6/30/53," NA; Letter to Laurence F. Lee, December 17, 1952, RG 296 Automotive Equipment-Boards, box 4, NA; Letter to Charles Sligh Jr., December 17, 1952, RG 296 Letters and Memos of Michael V. DiSalle, box 104, file: "ODM (M.V. DiSalle)," NA; Letter to DiSalle, December 22, 1952, RG 296 Automotive Equipment-Boards, box 4, NA; Letter to DiSalle, December 23, 1952, RG 296 Automotive Equipment-Boards, box 4, NA.

42. OPS Daily News, January 3, 4, and 5, 1953, RG 295 Central Files 1952–1953, box 632, file: "Daily News Digest," NA.

43. *Washington Evening Star,* January 4, 1953, 2A; National Advisory Board on Mobilization Policy Meeting No. 22, December 16, 1952, President's Secretary's Files, box 131, file: "General File, National Advisory Board-Mobilization," HSTL; Statement Accompanying Emergency Stabilization Bill," RG 296 General Files of Michael DiSalle, box 104, NA.

There was strong and growing opposition to the enactment of a standby war powers act within the Republican ranks. And most business groups, too, opposed such a move. Neither Jesse Wolcott (R-MI), chairman of the House Banking Committee, nor Homer Capehart (R-IN), chairman of the Senate Banking Committee, favored standby emergency powers. Both committees were charged with the writing of control legislation, and both had led earlier assaults against controls by repeatedly diluting the Defense Production Act. Less than a week before Eisenhower's inauguration, Wolcott launched a stinging invective against economic controls and ruled out any House support for standby controls, asserting that they "would swing like a sword over the heads of business." Meanwhile, Republican Senator John W. Bricker (OH) asked that Eisenhower suspend wage, price, and rent controls on his first day in office. Although Eisenhower intended to end economic controls as quickly as possible, he remained silent on the issue of standby powers prior to his taking office.[44]

When General Eisenhower became President Eisenhower on January 20, 1953, the issue of controls was uppermost on the agenda of the new administration. Although Eisenhower had campaigned vigorously against the continuation of direct controls and had promised fellow Republicans that they would be ended with all due haste, new opinion polls showed a majority of voters favoring their continuation. Of those polled, 61 percent favored the continuation of controls, while only 29 percent wanted them ended. This caused the new president to pause temporarily on the issue of decontrol. Not until two days before his State of the Union Address did he decide to scrap controls, bowing to pressure from business and other Republican-oriented groups that had helped get him elected. It was actually Eisenhower's longtime friend and informal advisor General Lucius Clay who finally tipped the scales in favor of immediate decontrol. Clay, of course, had something of a personal vendetta against the mobilization setup, having been sacked as an ODM advisor by Charles Wilson in 1951 as a sop to disgruntled labor groups. So Clay was all too happy to see Eisenhower do away with the vestiges of Truman's stabilization program. At Eisenhower's direction, Clay discussed the issue with Secretary of Commerce Sinclair Weeks and labor secretary Martin Durkin. Weeks, of course, backed Clay's position, and Durkin believed that organized labor would not protest a decision to end controls. In the end, Clay persuaded Eisenhower that

44. OPS Daily News, January 10, 11, and 12, 1953, RG 295 Central Files 1952–1953, box 632, file: "Daily News Digest," NA; *Journal of Commerce,* January 12, 1953, 1–2.

controls should be liquidated and that standby controls would not be needed.[45]

On February 2, Eisenhower formally announced the end of wage and price controls in his State of the Union Address. "The character of our people," intoned the president, "resists artificial and arbitrary controls of any kind. Direct controls, except those on credit, deal not with the real causes of inflation but only with its symptoms." Accordingly, Eisenhower requested that wage and price controls end no later than April 30, at which time the DPA legislation was due to lapse. He also asked that material and product controls be ended except for those specifically targeted to defense needs and scarce or critical items. Thus, the ESA, OPS, WSB, and SSB and their constituent agencies were liquidated and closed out by the middle of 1953. Eisenhower's decision also terminated the Controlled Materials Plan (CMP) and severed the last of the nation's ties with the waning International Materials Conference. The National Production Authority was also largely eliminated, retaining only its divisions responsible for carrying out the long-term certificates of necessity and tax amortization grants already begun under the Truman administration. So anxious was the Eisenhower administration to kill controls that it managed to end price controls by March 18, some six weeks before they were formally due to expire.[46]

Eisenhower also moved quickly to consolidate mobilization agencies that had not already been liquidated. The major step he took almost immediately after assuming the presidency was the combination of the National Security Resources Board (NSRB) with the Office of Defense Mobilization (ODM) under the ODM banner. Thus the NSRB was wiped out in name as well as function. From that point forward, the ODM was given complete responsibility for future mobilization planning as well as the execution of the current buildup. In 1958, Eisenhower further combined mobilization and readiness functions by

45. OPS Daily News, January 23 and 24, 1953, RG 295 Central Files 1952–1953, box 632, file: "Daily News Digest," NA; The Gallup Poll, by George Gallup, January 22, 1953, Princeton, New Jersey, RG 296 Records Maintained by the Administrator, box 18, file: "General Statistics, 1952–53," NA; Daily News Record, January 22, 1953, 1 and 3.

46. "Excerpts from the State of the Union Message discussing price and wage controls," February 2, 1953, RG 296 Economic Stabilization Agency, box 18, NA; Roderick W. Vawter, Industrial Mobilization: The Relevant History, 36–41; Albert C. Lazure, "Legal and Other Problems of Military Mobilization Base Planning," 155–70; Reynold Bennett, "Tax Relief—An Aid to the Retention of the Mobilization Base," 179–88; OPS Daily News, March 18, 1953 RG 295 Central Files 1952–1953, box 632, file: "Daily News Digest," NA.

consolidating the ODM and the Federal Civil Defense Agency (FCDA) into a single unit under the new banner of the Office of Civil and Defense Mobilization (OCDM). Through the years emergency military and civil defense agencies underwent further changes and consolidations leading to the current setup under which nearly all military and civil defense responsibilities fall under the aegis of the Federal Emergency Management Agency (FEMA), which was established in 1978.[47]

Eisenhower's decision to consolidate the top two civilian defense agencies brought several issues to light. First, the Truman administration made the move far easier by providing the new president with the necessary criteria needed to make such a decision. It was, in fact, the Truman administration itself that had recommended the consolidation. The need to combine and coordinate defense plans in progress with future mobilization goals was one of the greatest motivating factors. Another factor was the need to better coordinate private and public-sponsored defense and weapons research. In November 1952, ODM Director Henry Fowler raised the issue directly with President Truman, arguing that the ODM was far better suited to estimate requirements and implement plans for all-out war than was the isolated and ineffectual NSRB. In principle, the President's National Advisory Board on Mobilization Policy concurred, writing in its last report that "[m]uch remains to be done in the way of coordinating private and government-financed (defense-related) research. The plans which have been initiated to that end should be vigorously developed." The plans of which the board wrote included the consolidation of the ODM and NSRB into a single agency better suited to the overall supervision and coordination of defense production and research.[48]

The NSRB-ODM consolidation also brought to the fore two additional issues. The decision to consolidate was premised partly on the fact that the NSRB, since its inception in 1947, had repeatedly failed to provide the centralized and coordinating function of mobilization planning and policymaking. It was the weak link in the national security

47. Vawter, *Industrial Mobilization*, 79–80; Report to the President by the National Advisory Board on Mobilization Policy, January 12, 1953, 11–12, Papers of Harry S. Truman, OF, box 1737, file: "2855-A," HSTL.

48. OPS Daily News, January 13 and 14, 1953, RG 295 Central Files 1952–1953, box 632, file: "Daily News Digest," NA; Report to the President by the Director of Defense Mobilization, November 1, 1952, President's Secretary's Files, Subject File Agencies A, box 142, file: "Advisory Board on Mobilization Policy, National," HSTL; Report to the President by the National Advisory Board on Mobilization Policy, January 12, 1953 (for quotations see p. 11), Papers of Harry S. Truman, OF, box 1737, file: "2855-A," HSTL.

apparatus from the very beginning. Once war in Korea broke out, the agency's deficiencies became all too evident. Nothing better demonstrated the NSRB's weaknesses than did Truman's December 1950 decision to create the ODM, which effectively relegated the NSRB to the twilight zone of defense and mobilization planning. So in one sense, the final demise of the NSRB was a natural institutional progression. After December 1950, it lost what little credibility and effectiveness it may have had. The consolidation also marked the difference between Truman's and Eisenhower's approach to national security. Eisenhower's concerted effort to move the nation—and the government—toward a more normal "peacetime" stance had to include the liquidation of redundant and ineffective agencies. Indeed, he had already established this pattern by his quick termination of most civilian stabilization agencies. Once again, the NSRB's demise fit into a larger institutional dynamic.

Of course, the change in administrations brought more than just a practical end to mobilization and economic stabilization controls. It also brought an end to the war in Korea. After intense discussions among the combatants, the warring parties finally signed an armistice on July 27, 1953. The fighting was ended, but the Korean peninsula remained divided near the thirty-eighth parallel, and North and South Korea still technically remained in a state of war. At the time of this writing, no permanent state of peace exists between the two countries.

America's first war in the name of containment was something of a mixed bag for the nation and the world. While it is true that U.S. intervention prevented the collapse of South Korea, that goal was met in October of 1950. After that, the United States tried unsuccessfully to reunite Korea under a pro-Western regime. When that failed and China entered the war in November 1950, the war became stalemated. The conflict continued for another two and one-half years. But it did not accomplish the reunification of Korea nor did it push back the Communist menace, at least in the eyes of most policymakers. What Korea did do, however, was kill 34,000 U.S. soldiers and wound another 100,000. And it largely destroyed the Korean society—both in the north and the south. Casualties for all Koreans numbered three million. Moreover, of course, the Korean War in part provided the rationale for America's involvement in yet another Asian debacle: Vietnam. On the other hand, the Korean War had some positive results as well. South Korea became a regional economic dynamo; wartime spending rehabilitated the Japanese economy; NATO was strengthened significantly and West

Germany was admitted to the Alliance. At the same time, the war led to strained Sino-Soviet relations that led ultimately to a Sino-Soviet split later in the 1950s.

At home, the Korean War provided a powerful boost to the American economy. Despite some short-term dislocations, economic growth and employment expanded rapidly between 1950 and 1953. And except for the two periods of high inflation during the early months of the war, the Truman administration successfully held inflation in check while at the same significantly increasing both military and civilian production. To accomplish this feat, however, the administration reluctantly acquiesced to budget deficits and a growing national debt. The Korean rearmament effort also reshaped business-government relations. Ties between the public and private sector grew more numerous and far more complex. Big business, in tandem with the federal government, science, and academia, provided the foundation upon which the United States' postwar national security state was built. In large part a consequence of the decisions made during the Korean War, the political economy of the 1950s and 1960s projected to the rest of the world the entire image of the United States. This image reflected a nation of almost overbearing confidence in international affairs, a polity governed increasingly by public and private sector technocrats singularly driven in their pursuit of managerial and productive efficiency and mesmerized by the possibilities supposedly inherent in technological supremacy.

CONCLUSION

Toward an American Sparta?

Legacies of the Korean Era

> I suppose that history will remember my term in office as the years when the 'cold war' began to overshadow our lives. I have hardly had a day in office that has not been dominated by this all-embracing struggle . . . And always in the back-ground there has been the atomic bomb.
>
> Harry S. Truman, Farewell Address, January 15, 1953.[1]

The seeds of mutual distrust and misunderstanding between the United States and the Soviet Union germinated during World War II, having been sown during World War I. The immense power vacuums left in the wake of the Second World War combined with vague and unenforceable postwar settlements only widened the growing rift between the two nations. Between 1945 and 1950, this deteriorating relationship became known as the Cold War, a time of neither war nor peace, punctuated by a series of crises that only served to heighten tensions between the superpowers. Yet despite the recurrent crises of this period, the Cold War did not seriously challenge the American domestic system or the traditions and beliefs upon which that system was built. The Korean War and the consequences it wrought changed that. Indeed, Truman's decision to intervene in the Korean War and to simultaneously rearm the nation along the lines prescribed in NSC-68 shook the very pillars of American free-market capitalism, not to mention the ideological tenets that undergirded it. After 1950, the

1. *Public Papers of the President: Harry S. Truman* (1952–1953), 1201.

Cold War not only continued to shape to a significant degree political and ideological discourse in the United States, but it also began to reshape aggregate economic policy—both fiscal and monetary—and thus began to alter the nation's industrial and economic contours. Clearly, by the mid-1950s, the consequences of Truman's decisions cast long shadows over the nation's political, economic, and cultural landscapes.

What made the Korean decisions perhaps even more momentous was the fact that the fundamental presumptions upon which those decisions were based never received truly serious scrutiny, much less a serious challenge. It is doubtful, given the tenor of the times and his own political inclinations, that President Truman would have agreed to implement fully NSC-68 prior to June 1950. Once the Korean War broke out, however, alternatives to the prescriptions of NSC-68 were quickly cast aside. And in September 1950 President Truman approved in toto the implementation of NSC-68, thus engaging the nation in a costly and vaguely indefinite rearmament. From that point forward, even after the Korean War had ended in July 1953, the United States' military and national security spending remained at levels unthinkable prior to Korea. Indeed, the decisions made in 1950 stood practically unchallenged for nearly two generations. Not until 1989, when the Berlin Wall was torn down and the Soviet empire began to crumble, did American policymakers seriously consider dismantling the nation's massive military apparatus that was originally designed to contain Soviet expansionism.

Although most policymakers at the time did not challenge the basic assumptions or implementation of NSC-68, they did to a degree sense the enormity of the political and economic changes wrought by the massive rearmament program. As a result, in late 1952, mobilization officials conducted an internal management analysis of the Korean era mobilization program. Their findings explain many of the difficulties and controversies that arose during the period. From a management and operational standpoint, many of the emergency mobilization agencies established in December 1950 were designed for conditions that simply never arose.[2]

2. For a detailed study of the organizational components and related problems of the Korean mobilization program see "An Analysis of the Central Management Elements of the Defense Mobilization Program," October 23, 1952, Papers of David H. Stowe, box 3, file: "Organizational Study: ODM-NSRB-NPA-ESA (1952)," HSTL, which was prepared by mobilization officials.

The Korean rearmament program and its mobilization agencies tended to be modeled after World War II agencies. Quite obviously, however, the Korean War was far from being another world war. And the contexts within which these wars took place were vastly different. The Korean mobilization thus represented a misapplication of policy, not to mention inappropriate historical learning. Unlike World War II, there were no severe labor shortages in defense industries, no significant shortages of critical materials, no consumer rationing, and generally no widespread economic dislocation. In an organizational sense then, one could argue that the Truman administration over-prepared for the Korean mobilization and thus created an unnecessarily large and overlapping bureaucracy. Be that as it may, policymakers in late 1950 acted predictably and relatively prudently. First, they quite naturally based many of their assumptions on the nation's experience during World War II. But unlike that mobilization, the Korean effort was designed to be a limited program of presumably indefinite duration. The rearmament program, like the Korean War itself, had indistinct and changeable objectives. In the end, faced with these ambiguities and with only World Wars I and II as guideposts, mobilization planners started out big and gradually trimmed their objectives to better match the nation's national security needs with its military capabilities. Yet they never seriously engaged in a readjustment of the *organizational* aspects of mobilization and rearmament until late 1952. As a consequence, confusion, duplication, waste, and lack of coordination often resulted.[3]

Interestingly enough, mobilization officials who engaged in the internal evaluation of the rearmament program placed much of the blame for these developments on the Office of Defense Mobilization (ODM). Like other mobilization agencies during Korea, the ODM was set up in anticipation of problems that never materialized. Modeled to an extent after the Office of War Mobilization (OWM) of World War II, the ODM was intended to be a point of conflict settlement short of the Oval Office. But the severe dislocations and attendant conflicts of World War II did not reappear during Korea. As a result, the ODM tended to concentrate exclusively on the production aspects of mobilization. Thus, it came to represent merely another cog in the already fragmented mobilization setup, duplicating and sometimes contradicting the jurisdictions of other agencies—most often the Defense Production Administration (DPA) and the National Production Authority (NPA). This situation

3. Ibid., 1–5, 17.

apparently worsened after the ODM's first director Charles Wilson resigned in April 1952. "The (ODM)," concluded officials, "never got on top of the military or stabilization side of the mobilization program, and the really major stabilization conflicts have been settled outside the (ODM) framework." In other words, not only was the ODM ill-suited for the Korean rearmament, but it was also at times a superfluous detriment to the overall mobilization process.[4]

Assessing the results and ramifications of the Korean mobilization effort yields differing results. Judging it in the short term, the mobilization program accomplished most of the goals set in 1950 and 1951. In this sense, it was a success. In the intermediate and long term, however, the "success" of the Korean rearmament effort became problematic, and the trends and consequences of "perpetual mobilization" became less politically and economically palatable as time went on.

Judging the actual performance of the rearmament program in the short term, however, yields an overwhelmingly positive assessment. When Dwight David Eisenhower took the oath of office in January 1953, the nation's military capabilities and economic strength were far stronger than they had been in June 1950. From a military vantage point, the progress made during the buildup was most impressive. The nation's armed forces were more than doubled; military production of hard goods was seven times the June 1950 rate; the industrial mobilization base was nearly complete; and stockpiles of critical defense materials were substantially larger. Thus, in accordance with the force goals established by the Truman administration in January 1952, the Army now stood at 21 full-strength divisions, compared to 10 divisions and 12 separate regimental-size units in June 1950; more than 400 Navy warships, compared to 200; 16 Navy carrier air groups, compared to 7; and 3 Marine divisions, compared to 2 prior to Korea. Only the Air Force's strength had failed to reach the 1952 goal—143 wings. Still, it boasted 100 wings, compared to only 48 before the war, and mobilization officials predicted that the goal would be met by the end of 1954.[5]

The United States also leapt forward in the development of new technology and weapons, which now included guided missiles, tactical nuclear weapons, and the hydrogen bomb, among many others. During

---

4. Ibid., 42.
5. "The Job Ahead for Defense Mobilization," Eighth Quarterly Report to the President by the Director of Defense Mobilization, January 1, 1953, RG 277, Policy Coordination Bureau, box 2, file: "ODM: The Job Ahead, January 1953," NA, pp. 1–2, 13.

the fourth quarter of 1952, all military deliveries, including defense construction, totaled slightly more than $8 billion per quarter. Aircraft plants turned out nearly 1,000 planes per month, or four times the rate of mid-1950. The production of new military jets was even more impressive—five times the mid-1950 rate. Production of firearms, tanks, trucks, ships, and electronics and avionics showed similar progress. Finally, total military expenditures by European NATO countries reached $11 billion in FY 1953, up from $5 billion in FY 1949. Indeed, the United States and its NATO allies were considerably stronger militarily than they were prior to Korea.[6]

The United States' economy was also far stronger than it had been in June 1950. As the Council of Economic Advisors proudly declared in January 1953, "the rapid growth in productive capacity during the previous 2 years has improved the general ability of the economy to meet increases in spending." In other words, Leon Keyserling's economic growth model and incentives paid handsome dividends: although the nation's consumer and military spending surged forward, inflation and shortages generally did not. The economic "pie" had grown considerably and was thus able to absorb more spending. Average income, adjusted for inflation, grew by 3 percent before taxes. Inflation was largely contained after the imposition of wage and price controls, and the Consumers Price Index (CPI) had risen only about 1 percent from the end of 1951 to the end of 1952. Meanwhile, the Gross National Product (GNP) totaled $345 billion for 1952, a rise of approximately 5 percent over the previous year. In short, the Truman administration remained true to the tenets of NSC-68. The Korea rearmament cum Cold War rearmament was a multifaceted program that provided for a substantial military buildup combined with balanced economic growth and stability in the United States as well as Western Europe.[7]

The economic successes of the Korean rearmament program also permanently laid to rest the outmoded thinking of those who still tended to view the nation's economy as "mature," an economy past its productive prime and incapable of continued long-term growth. Although this idea had been largely discredited by the World War II experience and the resultant economic boom, some still doubted the

6. Ibid., 3, 10, 13–15, 46.
7. Ibid., 7, 38–45; *The Economic Report of the President,* January 14, 1953, Papers of Leon Keyserling, box 5, file: "Economic Report of the President-1953," HSTL (for quotation see p. 36); *Defense Production Act, Progress Report No. 21,* October 1, 1952, Hearing before the Joint Committee on Defense Production, 82d. Cong., 2d sess.

efficacy of economic growth models during peacetime. The nay-sayers who had predicted a depression after World War II were proven wrong. And the Truman administration's successful attempts to construct a postwar national security state predicated upon sustainable economic growth offered proof that Keyserling's growth models could be extended beyond the confines of world war and reconversion. Thus, those who continued to adhere to the idea of a "mature" economy were completely marginalized, and in Alan Brinkley's terms, "the concept of growth (became) the center of liberal hopes." To be sure, the fulfillment of liberal social programs and the construction and maintenance of the national security state through aggregate economic growth became the clarion call of postwar American liberalism.[8]

The Truman administration also demonstrated a remarkable ability to adjust the rearmament effort to the changing goals of the military and the nation's capabilities. At the same time, it kept that effort within the traditional organizational and ideological boundaries of the nation's society and political economy. At the root of the administration's concerns in this regard was that of equity in sacrifice. Policymakers tried desperately to distribute equitably the burdens of the Cold War rearmament among the various economic groups in American society. In doing so, the administration made use of past mobilization experiences and adhered to the principles of decentralization, corporatism, and volunteerism. Government policymakers also borrowed innovative management approaches from the nation's most successful corporations, most notable of which was the Controlled Materials Plan, and many times recruited corporate executives to help them in adapting those approaches to the unique demands of mobilization and national security. Armed with past experience, the willingness to experiment, and the strong desire to retain the integrity of the American system, mobilization officials charted a sometimes perilous middle course between the extremes of totalitarian Communism and dictatorial Fascism.

Of course, Truman cannot take full credit for charting this intermediate course. His administration was pushed and pulled in different directions by a whole host of competing coalitions and interest groups. Reticent at first to vest centralized mobilization control solely in the hands of the Executive branch, Truman quickly reversed course

8. Alan Brinkley, "The New Deal and the Idea of the State," 105–9; Herbert Stein, *The Fiscal Revolution in America*, 175–77; Alan S. Milward, *War, Economy, and Society: 1939–1945*, 330.

upon the Chinese intervention in late 1950. Once the second phase of mobilization was upon him in early 1951, the president tended to favor tighter control over the mobilization and stabilization process by vesting in the Oval Office and the Executive Office of the President sweeping powers to regulate the overall rearmament effort. This was especially the case in the area of price and wage controls. The congressional backlash against this approach, emanating mostly from the Republican and conservative Democratic ranks, checked Truman's moves toward organizational and managerial centralization. And increasingly shrill corporate protests against centralization also blunted the White House's efforts. These coalitions thus played a significant role in preventing the emergence of a Cold War garrison state. Without a doubt, the Korean rearmament program, like the many governmental initiatives that preceded it, reflected the traditional American propensity for experimentation and compromise.

In the final analysis, the Truman administration's rearmament program was a success on any number of fronts. The sheer numbers in military production speak for themselves, as do the economic statistics. The nation's first "peacetime" military mobilization provided both an adequate supply of guns and butter. Criticize the effort as he did while campaigning, President Eisenhower nonetheless inherited a robust economy and a military establishment second to none.

In fact, the relative calm of most of the Eisenhower years was a partial result of the bold steps Harry Truman took during his presidency. First, by providing Dwight Eisenhower with a greatly expanded economy, one that was far more diverse than the one Roosevelt and even Truman himself had inherited, the outgoing president gave to the new president a great deal of latitude in which to make military and fiscal decisions. Second, even though Eisenhower was quite successful in reducing the size of the military and the defense budget throughout most of the 1950s, Truman's policies deserve some credit as well. For instance, Eisenhower's "New Look" defense posture, which sought to reduce manpower requirements and conventional weapons in favor of air power and nuclear deterrence, was actually a strategic policy that had been developed by the Truman administration during the Korean War. What Eisenhower and his advisors did was simply to codify and "market" this concept in order to rationalize defense cuts and production stretch-outs already under way. Third, the series of defense stretch-outs that began in late 1951 meant that *billions* of dollars remained in the military production pipeline well into 1956, making the Eisenhower-era defense "cutbacks" less dramatic than they actually appeared. Thus, Truman's Korean-era rearmament effort made it relatively easier for his successor to implement fully the New Look, to reduce manpower requirements—made far easier with the end of the Korean War—and to reduce defense and national security expenditures. In effect, Truman's decisions to build the hydrogen bomb, to construct a broad industrial mobilization base, and to emphasize air power over the Soviets all paved the way for Eisenhower's success in keeping military spending in check.[9]

Although Eisenhower followed through with his promises to end the Korean War, to dismantle mobilization controls, and to reduce military spending and budget deficits, his efforts by no means put an end to the debates over national security policy or completely abated the fears of an American garrison state. This was never more obvious than during the so-called 1953 Solarium Exercises that considered and formulated a number of varying options for future security policy, and the debates surrounding the 1957 Gaither Report, which was a knee-jerk reaction to the launching of Sputnik that advocated a large increase in conventional forces as well as missile and rocket development. In both cases, and in spite of considerable pressure coming from both the Pentagon and his civilian advisors, Eisenhower distanced himself from those who sought to push for more defense spending. The president considered the Solarium reports only as benchmark beginning points for a new shape to American defense policy, which ultimately took the form of the "New Look" in 1954. In fact, from 1954 to 1958, the number of combat-ready personnel was reduced by about 30 percent from the peak of the Korean War. And defense spending fell by some 20 percent between FY 1953 and FY 1955 before rising slightly later in the 1950s. As far as the Gaither Report was concerned, Eisenhower virtually disowned it, reasoning that "hasty and extraordinary effort under the impetus of sudden fear . . . cannot provide an adequate answer to the (Soviet) threat."[10]

Dwight D. Eisenhower, who one historian has characterized as perhaps the least "militaristic" president ever to occupy the White House,

9. Michael S. Sherry, *In the Shadow of War: The United States since the 1930s*, 192–96; Saki Dockrill, *Eisenhower's New Look National Security Policy, 1953–61*, 29–35; Elmo Richardson, *The Presidency of Dwight D. Eisenhower*, 64–66.
10. Sherry, *Shadow of War*, 196; Douglas Kinnard, *President Eisenhower and Strategy Management: A Study in Defense Politics*, 80–81; Stephen E. Ambrose, *Eisenhower: The President*, vol. 2, 433.

was haunted by the fears of an American Sparta throughout his two terms in office. In both his public and private musings and pronouncements, Eisenhower made plainly known his intentions to keep the Trojan horse of national security tightly bridled. Even his Farewell Address, the last public message he would give as president, took up the themes of caution and prudence in the areas of military preparedness and spending. Of course, part of Eisenhower's anxiety over military spending run amok came from his traditionally conservative, Republican stance toward federal spending and the role of government in a market economy. But as historian Michael Sherry has written, Eisenhower's fears "transcended" traditional Republican conservatism; indeed, a deep-seated antipathy toward militarization affected his thinking as much as did his lengthy military experience. In fact, perhaps only a career soldier like Eisenhower could have sustained such an aversion to the creation of a garrison state—and could have stood steadfast in the way of those who sought to increase American militarization, even amidst the hysteria surrounding Sputnik.[11]

Finally, Eisenhower seemed not to have put a great deal of emphasis on the gospel of Keynesianism as a way to sustain consistently high defense spending *and* high levels of domestic prosperity. To be sure, Eisenhower and his advisors embraced—reluctantly perhaps—the basic tenets of postwar Keynesian economic prescriptions; however, they did not test the limits of these as Truman had done after the outbreak of war in Korea. In Eisenhower's mind, especially, economic decisions and fiscal responsibility meant either more guns or less butter. His thoughts on this theme were especially eloquent in an April 1953 speech in which he stated, "Every gun that is made, every warship launched, every rocket fired, signifies, in the final sense, a theft from those who hunger and are not fed, those who are cold and not clothed. This world in arms is not spending money alone. It is spending the sweat of its laborers, the genius of its scientists, the hopes of its children."[12]

Be that as it may, the Eisenhower years did not in any way result in a major rollback of the American military-industrial establishment. Its growth may have been controlled to an extent, but in 1958 the U. S. Army *still* remained some 50 percent larger than at its low ebb just prior to the Korean War. And the number, effectiveness, and potency of America's nuclear forces—long-range bombers and ICBMs

---

11. Richardson, *The Presidency of Eisenhower*, 43, 63; Sherry, *Shadow of War*, 192–93.
12. Sherry, *Shadow of War*, 195.

in particular—grew significantly. Critics of Eisenhower's reliance on massive retaliation also illuminated the shortsightedness of the New Look, which made the Cold War ever more dangerous and which gave the nation two options in a future crisis: surrender or suicide. Further, these critics pointed out the irony in Eisenhower's ruminations over the fears of a garrison state and the military-industrial complex while his administration actually tightened the ties between the military, industry, and academic science in its continued quest for technological supremacy over the Soviet Union. To be sure, issues concerning rearmament, defense spending, internal and external security, and the garrison state were issues still very much alive throughout the entire decade of the 1950s.[13]

Over the long haul of the Cold War, the Korean rearmament effort and the precedents it set came at a very high price, a price that went far beyond actual military expenditures. The economic, social, and political costs resulting from the decisions made during Korea are perhaps immeasurable, for there was no real "peace dividend" at the end of the Korean War. Defense spending, military preparedness, and the militarization of American foreign and domestic policy remained at levels imponderable prior to June 1950. Thus, like any bureaucratic juggernaut, the Cold War military-industrial-scientific complex developed a momentum all its own during and after Korea, and nobody, not even Dwight Eisenhower, was able to roll it back. The best he and his successors could do was simply to contain its growth. And thus, the best that could be done was to assure simultaneously the containment of the Soviet menace abroad and the containment here at home of the very apparatus designed to check the Soviets. This "dual" containment operated at many different levels during the Cold War, especially during the 1950s and early 1960s. Political debate and discourse, civil rights efforts, gender relations, even labor-management relations were all affected by the very narrow parameters of Cold War thinking and rhetoric. The Korean War, which fully unleashed McCarthyism and the politics of anti-communism, placed strict limits on the number and degree of options available to achieve a more equitable, open, and representative society, and this continued to be the case even after McCarthyism began to fade in the mid-1950s.

The Korean War buildup as well had a profound effect on the evolution of the American democratic process. As Robert H. Wiebe has

---

13. Ibid., 195–96.

recently observed, the Korean conflict resulted in the permanent institutionalization of an ongoing trend in twentieth-century American history: the detachment of the government from the people. Thus NSC-68 and the Korean conflict offered not only a macroeconomic means by which to secure the nation during a seemingly perilous era, but it also simultaneously advocated a fundamentally undemocratic national security apparatus. During and after Korea, legions of unelected "experts," bureaucrats, and resurrected "dollar-a-year" men began to push aside elected politicians and other publicly appointed officials. The result was a national security and foreign policy process that became increasingly enigmatic and unresponsive to the average citizen. Only well-organized, well-funded, functional groups—be they public or private—were allowed access to the inner sanctum of national security decision making. Thus, when Truman-era cold warriors debated policies that affected the citizenry as a whole, popular opinion not associated with these functional groups was rarely measured or considered. Sensing this dilemma, the Truman administration experimented with a whole host of public-private partnerships during Korea. None, however, was terribly successful in extending the scope and diversity of public discourse over foreign and national security policy. For the average American excluded from membership in a functional group, the workings of the national security apparatus were as remote as the machinations of most corporate board rooms.[14]

Of course, the real cost of military spending must surely be quantified in terms of the natural and human resources and productive capital absorbed or diverted for military and defense purposes. For example, the production of a missile, which will either be buried or exploded, may require the same amount of economic activity that is needed to construct a bus or railroad car. Unlike a missile, however, a bus or rail car will actually enhance the productive and economic capacity of the nation, and may continue to do so for many years. A missile once built adds nothing to the nation's economic potential. The same analogy, multiplied by the millions of weapons produced over the long haul, has resulted in monumental lost economic opportunities.[15]

In the same vein, billions of tax dollars spent on defense during the Cold War went to the construction of the nation's long-term mobilization base, a concept that was perfected during Korea. In large part,

14. Robert H. Wiebe, *Self-Rule: A Cultural History of American Democracy*, especially 206–9; Arthur M. Schlesinger Jr., *The Imperial Presidency*, ix; Michael Crozier, Samuel P. Huntington, and Joji Watanuki, *The Crisis of Democracy*, 93.

15. Murray L. Wiedenbaum, *The Economics of Peacetime Defense*, 28–29.

the mobilization base required the creation of an alternate economy, an economy devoted exclusively to the needs of the military and national security establishments. The construction of this de facto defense economy greatly accelerated the shifts already taking place in the nation's traditional industrial base. Thus with the rise of high-tech, defense-oriented industries in the South and West came the decline of America's old industrial heartland in the Northeast and Midwest. As a result, great excess and idled industrial capacity crippled older, traditional industrial areas. This too resulted in lost economic opportunities. The rise of the South and West as new areas of industrial prowess—especially in high-tech defense-related areas—resulted in the gradual decay of the nation's oldest and largest commercial and industrial centers. As these new industrial centers sprang up, reduced tax revenues and a drain of educated and skilled workers left the older cities in a terrible bind. These cities thus became increasingly populated by a large number of permanently displaced blue collar workers and a growing urban underclass and lacked the necessary resources to retrain and educate their citizens.[16]

The Korean experience also solidified and institutionalized the Cold War mentality. Truman and his successors held the "vital center" of American politics by focusing much of the nation's attention and energies on the Soviet Union. Korea turned peripheral areas of national interest into strategic ones. Eisenhower's so-called domino theory originated with the decisions of 1950 and eventually enveloped the United States in the quagmire of Vietnam. As a result of this thinking, many parts of the Developing World became embroiled in proxy wars fought by the Superpowers. More often than not, conflicts of colonial oppression and internal civil wars—like the one in Korea—evolved into huge conflagrations, fanned by one or both of the Superpowers. Other areas of the Developing World, fortunate enough to have escaped such disaster, were simply ignored altogether by the advanced industrial powers.

Most assuredly, the social ills and fiscal crisis that faced America at the end of the Cold War were in part a result of the last forty-five years of Cold War decision making. First, continued economic stimulation by defense spending masked growing structural difficulties in the economy and encouraged technological innovation that was largely limited to military applications. Second, the dialogue and discourse of the Cold War captured the attention of most of the nation's media

16. Markusen et al., *Rise of the Gunbelt*, 6–7.

and political establishments, thus sweeping under the carpet other crucial social and political debates. Only now, with the Cold War presumably over, is the nation fully able to address these problems. Unfortunately, however, they have become far more intractable after nearly two generations have ignored them completely.[17]

Perennial budget deficits and the mounting multitrillion dollar national debt were also legacies handed down to us by early cold warriors. The triumph of the national security managers during the Korean War legitimized military Keynesianism, which over the succeeding decades devolved into a spending formula that was applied to domestic social as well as national security programs. A balanced budget was thus no longer sacrosanct. And as the United States' economy inevitably lost its overwhelming preponderance of power in the late 1960s, reduced growth and accelerating government spending turned a manageable national debt into the intractable behemoth that looms over us today. It is a bitter irony that now when the nation can begin to address its many social and economic ills, it lacks the monetary resources with which to do it.

Over the long term, the United States mortgaged its economic and human resource potential in the name of national security. It blurred the distinction between war and peace and oftentimes used war, sometimes hot and sometimes cold, as a way to preserve peace. Thus, while the Trojan horse of national security may not have unleashed a true garrison state, it did increasingly invoke images of an American Sparta.

17. Gar Alperovitz and Kai Bird, "The Fading of the Cold War—and the Demystification of Twentieth-Century Issues," in Michael J. Hogan, 207–16.

BIBLIOGRAPHY

Primary Sources

Manuscript Collections

Harry S. Truman Library, Independence, MO
    Eben A. Ayers Papers
    Roy Blough Papers
    John D. Clark Papers
    Matthew J. Connelly Papers
    L. Laszio Ecker-Racz Papers
    George M. Elsey Papers
    Harold L. Enarson Papers
    Robert Goodwin Papers
    Leon Keyserling Papers
    Frederick J. Lawton Papers
    Charles S. Murphy Papers
    Edwin M. Nourse Papers
    Charles Sawyer Papers
    John W. Snyder Papers
    Stephen J. Spingarn Papers
    David H. Stowe Papers
    Harry S. Truman Papers
       President's Confidential Files
       President's Official Files
       President's Secretary's Files
       White House Central Files
    James E. Webb Papers
    Leon Keyserling, Oral History Interview
    David H. Stowe, Oral History Interview
    Records of the National Security Council
    Records of the President's Materials Policy Commission

Government Archives

National Archives of the United States, Washington, D.C.
Record Group 51, Records of the Bureau of the Budget Series 47.8A
Record Group 277, Records of the National Production Authority
    Correspondence with Government Agencies
    Miscellaneous Publications, 1950–1953
    Policy Coordination Bureau
    Reference Materials, 1951–1953
Record Group 293, Records of the Wage Stabilization Board
    General Files
    Wage Board Transcripts
Record Group 295, Records of the Office of Price Stabilization
    Central Files, 1951–1953
    Records of Joseph Freehill
    Records and Letters of Ellis G. Arnall
    Records of Michael V. DiSalle
    Records of Tighe E. Woods
Record Group 296, Records of the Economic Stabilization Agency
    Central Files, 1951–1953
    Classified General Files
    Letters and Memoranda of Eric Johnston
    Letters and Memoranda of Roger L. Putnam
    Economics
    General Files of Michael V. DiSalle
    Office of the Director
    Records and Reports of the Secretariat
    Records Maintained by the Administrators
    Secretariat-Classified Files
Record Group 304, Records of the National Security Resources Board
    and the Office of Defense Mobilization
    Classified "Safe" File
    NSRB Name Correspondence Files
    "Safe" File of the Economic Adviser, 1951–1953
    Records of the Office of Program Evaluation, 1951–1953
    Records of the Office of the Chairman
Published Government Documents
U.S. Congress. *Congressional Record*, 1950–1953.
U.S. Congress, House. Subcommittee of the Committee on Education

and Labor. *Disputes Functions of the Wage Stabilization Board*, 82d Cong., 1st sess., 1951.

Committee on Ways and Means. *Revenue Revision of 1951*, Parts 1 and 2, 82d Cong., 1st sess., 1951.

Committee on the Judiciary. *The Mobilization Program, H. Report 1217*, 82d Cong., 1st sess., 1951.

Committee on Banking and Currency. *Defense Production Act of 1950, Hearings*, 81st Cong., 2d sess., 1950.

Joint Committee on Defense Production. *Defense Production Act: Hoarding and Strategic Materials: Restrictions upon Shipments of Strategic Materials*, 81st Cong., 2d sess., 1950.

Joint Committee on Defense Production. *Progress Report No. 1*, 82d Cong., 1st sess., 1951.

Progress Report No. 2, 82d Cong., 1st sess., 1951.

Progress Report No. 7, 82d Cong., 1st sess., 1951.

Progress Report No. 8, 82d Cong., 1st sess., 1951.

Progress Report No. 11, 82d Cong., 1st sess., 1951.

Progress Report No. 21, 82d Cong., 2d sess., 1952.

Progress Report No. 23, 82d Cong., 2d sess., 1952.

Joint Hearings before the Select Committee on Small Business, United States House and United States Senate. *Participation of Small Businesses in Military Procurement*, 82d Cong., 1st sess., 1951.

U.S. Congress, Senate. Committee on Banking and Currency. *Nomination of Roy Blough*, 81st Cong., 2d sess., 1950.

Committee on Banking and Currency. *Confirmation of Dr. Alan Valentine*, 81st Cong., 2d sess., 1950.

Committee on Banking and Currency. *Confirmation of Michael V. DiSalle*, 81st Cong., 2d sess., 1950.

Committee on Banking and Currency. *Defense Production Amendments of 1951*, Parts 1–3, 82d Cong., 1st sess., 1951.

Subcommittee on Labor and Labor-Management Relations of the Committee on Labor and Public Welfare. *Operations of the Wage Stabilization Board and Dispute Settlement Functions*, 82d Cong., 1st sess., 1951.

Committee on Banking and Currency. *Nomination of Ellis G. Arnall*, 82d Cong., 2d sess., 1952.

U.S. Council of Economic Advisors. *The Economic Report of the President, Together with a Report to the President: The Annual Economic Review by the Council of Economic Advisors, 1950*. Washington, D.C.: Government Printing Office, 1950.

The Economic Report of the President, Together with a Report to the President: The Annual Economic Review by the Council of Economic Advisors, 1951. Washington, D.C.: Government Printing Office, 1951.

U.S. Department of State. *Foreign Relations of the United States, 1949.* Vol. 1. Washington, D.C.: Government Printing Office, 1976.

Foreign Relations of the United States, 1950. Vol. 1. Washington, D.C.: Government Printing Office, 1977.

U.S. Office of Defense Mobilization. *Building America's Might: A Report to the President.* No. 1. Washington, D.C.: Government Printing Office, 1951.

Eighth Quarterly Report to the President. Washington, D.C.: Government Printing Office, 1953.

U.S. Office of the Federal Register. *Public Papers of the Presidents of the United States: Harry S Truman, 1949–1953.* Washington, D.C.: Government Printing Office, 1965.

Federal Register 16. Washington, D.C.: Government Printing Office, 1951.

Contemporary Periodicals

Business Week
Colliers
Congressional Quarterly Alamanac, 1950–1952
Daily News Record
Fortune
The Journal of Commerce
Life
Nation
New Leader
Newsweek
New York Herald Tribune
New York Post
New York Times
New York Times Magazine
U.S. News and World Report
Wall Street Journal
Washington Daily News
Washington Post
Washington Star

Secondary Sources

Articles

Belair, Felix, Jr. "The Amiable 'Mike'—Policeman of Prices." *New York Times Magazine* (February 18, 1951): 13–15

Bennett, Reynold. "Tax Relief—An Aid to the Retention of the Mobilization Base." *Federal Bar Journal* 13 (April–June 1953): 179–88.

Bissell, Richard M., Jr. "The Impact of Rearmament on the Free World Economy." *Foreign Affairs* 29 (April 1951): 385–405.

Brune, Lester H. "Guns and Butter: The Pre-Korean War Dispute over Budget Allocations: Nourse's Conservative Keynesianism Loses Favor over Keyserling's Economic Expansion Plan." *American Journal of Economics and Sociology* 48 (July 1989): 357–71.

Correa, Rodolfo A. "The Organization for Defense Mobilization." *Federal Bar Journal* 13 (September 1952): 1–18.

Cuff, Robert D. "An Organizational Perspective on the Military-Industrial Complex." *Business History Review* 52 (summer 1978): 250–67.

———. "Ferdinand Eberstadt, the National Security Resources Board, and the Search for Integrated Mobilization Planning, 1947–1948." *Public Historian* 7 (fall 1985): 37–52.

Ferguson, Thomas. "From Normalcy to New Deal: Industrial Structure, Party Competition, and American Public Policy in the Great Depression." *International Organization* 38 (winter 1984): 41–93.

Fleischmann, Manly. "Policies and Procedures for Limited Mobilization." *Annals of the American Academy of Political and Social Science* (November 1951): 110–18.

Foot, Rosemary, "Making Known the Unknown War: Policy Analysis of the Korean Conflict in the Last Decade." *Diplomatic History* 15 (summer 1991): 411–31.

Friedberg, Aaron L. "Why Didn't the United States Become a Garrison State?" *International Security* 16 (spring 1992): 109–42.

Galambos, Louis. "The Emerging Organizational Synthesis in Modern American History." *Business History Review* 44 (autumn 1970): 279–90.

———. "Technology, Political Economy, and Professionalization: Central Themes of the Organizational Synthesis." *Business History Review* (winter 1983): 471–93.

Galbraith, John Kenneth. "The Disequilibrium System." *American Economic Review* 37 (June 1947): 287–302.

Ginsburg, David. "Price Stabilization, 1950–52: Retrospect and Prospect." *University of Pennsylvania Law Review* 100 (January 1952): 520–36.

Griffith, Robert. "Dwight D. Eisenhower and the Corporate Commonwealth." *American Historical Review* 87 (February 1982): 87–122.

Gross, Bertram M., and John P. Lewis. "The President's Economic Staff during the Truman Administration." *American Political Science Review* 48 (March 1954): 14–130.

Hamby, Alonzo L. "The Vital Center, the Fair Deal, and the Quest for a Liberal Political Economy." *American Historical Review* 77 (June 1972): 653–78.

Hawley, Ellis W. "The Discovery and Study of a 'Corporate Liberalism.'" *Business History Review* 52 (autumn 1978): 309–30.

———. "Herbert Hoover, The Commerce Secretariat, and the Vision of an 'Associative State,' 1921–1928." *Journal of American History* 61 (June 1974): 116–40

Hogan, Michael J. "Revival and Reform: America's Search for a New Economic Order Abroad." *Diplomatic History* 8 (fall 1984): 287–310.

———. "Corporatism: A Positive Appraisal." *Diplomatic History* 10 (fall 1986): 363–72.

Huntington, Samuel P. "Conservatism as an Ideology." *American Political Science Review* 51 (June 1957): 454–73.

Jacobs, Meg. "'How About Some Meat?': The Office of Price Administration, Consumption Politics, and State Building from the Bottom Up, 1941–1946." *Journal of American History* 84 (December 1997): 910–41.

Jervis, Robert. "The Impact of the Korean War on the Cold War." *Journal of Conflict Resolution* 24 (December 1980): 555–72.

Kaskell, Peter H. "Production under the CMP." *Federal Bar Journal* 13 (September 1952): 16–36.

Koistinen, Paul A. C. "Mobilizing the World War II Economy: Labor and the Industrial-Military Alliance." *Pacific Historical Review* 42 (March 1973): 443–78.

Lasswell, Harold D. "Sino-Soviet Crisis: The Garrison State versus the Civilian State." *China Quarterly* 11 (fall 1937): 643–49.

———. "The Garrison State." *American Journal of Sociology* 46 (January 1941): 455–68.

Lazure, Albert C. "Legal and Other Problems of Military Mobilization Base Planning." *Federal Bar Journal* 13 (April–June 1953): 155–70.

Lee, Kendrick. "Labor in Government." *Editorial Research Reports* 1 (April 29, 1943): 275–89.

Leventhal, Harold. "The Organization for Defense Mobilization, Part 2: Price Controls under the Defense Production Act as Amended." *Federal Bar Journal* 13 (December 1952 #2): 99–116.

Lo, Clarence Y. H. "Military Spending as Crisis Management: The U.S. Response to the Berlin Blockade and the Korean War." *Berkeley Journal of Sociology* 20 (1975–1976): 165–88.

Lunn, George R., Jr. "Voluntary Cooperative Action between Industry and Government under the Defense Production Act of 1950." *Federal Bar Journal* 13 (September 1952): 35–42.

Markusen, Ann R. "Defense Spending: A Successful Industrial Policy?" *International Journal of Urban and Regional Research* 10 (March 1986): 105–21.

McCormick, Thomas J. "Drift or Mastery?: A Corporatist Synthesis for American Diplomatic History." *Reviews in American History* 10 (December 1982): 318–30.

McQuaid, Kim. "Corporate Liberalism in the American Business Community, 1920–1940." *Business History Review* 52 (autumn 1978): 342–68.

Meyerowitz, Joanne. "Beyond the Feminine Mystique: A Reassessment of Postwar Mass Culture, 1946–1958." *Journal of American History* 79 (March 1993): 1455–82.

Nelson, Anna Kasten. "President Truman and the Evolution of the National Security Council." *Journal of American History* 72 (September 1985): 360–78.

Pierpaoli, Paul G., Jr. "Corporatist and Voluntarist Approaches to Cold War Rearmament: The Private Side of Industrial and Economic Mobilization." *Essays in Economic and Business History* 15 (April 1997): 263–75.

Ramsett, David E., and Tom R. Heck, "Wage and Price Controls: A Historical Survey." *North Dakota Quarterly* 45 (autumn 1977): 5–22.

Roberts, B. C. "Wage Stabilization in the United States." *Oxford Economic Papers* 4 (1952): 149–52.

Sandler, Alfred D. "Truman and the National Security Council: 1945–1947." *Journal of American History* 59 (September 1972): 369–88.

Schilling, Warren R. "The H-Bomb Decision: How to Decide without Actually Choosing." *Political Science Quarterly* 76 (March 1961): 24–46.

Steelman, John R., and DeWayne H. Kreager. "The Executive Office as Administrative Coordinator." *Law and Contemporary Politics* 21 (autumn 1956): 688–709.

Steinberg, Fritz. "Why Our Allies Complain." *Nation* 172 (May 12, 1951): 443–44.

Truman, Harry S. "Our Amed Forces Must Be Unified." *Colliers* (August 26, 1944): 63–64.

Wells, Samuel F., Jr. "Sounding the Tocsin: NSC-68 and the Soviet Threat." *International Security* 4 (fall 1979): 116–58.

Books

Acheson, Dean. *Present at the Creation: My Years in the State Department.* New York: Norton, 1969.

Alexander, Bevin. *Korea: The First War We Lost.* New York: Hippocrene Press, 1986.

Allison, Graham. *Essence of Decision: Explaining the Cuban Missile Crisis.* Boston: Little, Brown, 1971.

Ambrose, Stephen E. *Eisenhower: Soldier, General of the Army, President-Elect, 1890–1952.* Vol. 1. New York: Simon & Schuster, 1983.

———. *Eisenhower: The President.* Vol. 2. New York: Simon & Schuster, 1984.

Anderson, Patrick. *The Presidents' Men: White House Assistants of Franklin D. Roosevelt, Harry S. Truman, Dwight D. Eisenhower, John F. Kennedy, and Lyndon B. Johnson.* Garden City, N.Y.: Doubleday and Company, 1968.

Arnall, Ellis G. *The Shore Dimly Seen.* Philadelphia: J.B. Lippincott, 1946.

Baldwin, Hanson. *The Price of Power.* New York: Council on Foreign Relations, 1948.

Becker, William H. *The Dynamics of Business-Government Relations: Industry and Exports, 1893–1921.* Chicago: University of Chicago Press, 1982.

Bernstein, Irving. *Turbulent Years: A History of the American Worker, 1933–1941.* Boston: Houghton Mifflin, 1970.

Black, Charles L., Jr. *The People and the Court: Judicial Review in a Democracy.* New York: MacMillan, 1960.

———. *Perspectives in Constitutional Law.* Englewood Cliffs, N.J.: Prentice-Hall, 1970.

Blackford, Mansel G. *A History of Small Business in America.* New York: Twayne, 1992.

Blair, Clay. *The Forgotten War: America in Korea, 1950–1953.* New York: Times Books, 1987.

Blinder, Alan S. and Robert M. Solow, eds. *The Economics of Public Finance.* Washington, D.C.: Brookings Institute, 1974.

Blum, John Morton. *V Was for Victory: Politics and American Culture during World War II.* New York: Harcourt, Brace, Jovanovich, 1976.

Bohlen, Charles E. *Witness to History, 1929–1969.* New York: Norton, 1973.

Braeman, John, Robert H. Bremner, and Everett Walters, eds., *Change and Continuity in Twentieth-Century America.* New York: Harper & Row, 1966.

Bright, Charles, and Susan Harding. *Statemaking and Social Movements: Essays in History and Theory.* Ann Arbor: University of Michigan Press, 1984.

Brown, Seyom. *The Faces of Power: Constancy and Change in United States Foreign Policy from Truman to Clinton.* 2d ed. New York: Columbia University Press, 1994.

Bruchey, Stuart, ed., *Small Business in American Life.* New York: Columbia University Press, 1980.

Calleo, David P. *The Bankrupting of America: How the Federal Budget Is Impoverishing the Nation.* New York: W. Morrow, 1992.

———. *Beyond American Hegemony: The Future of the Western Alliance.* New York: Basic Books, 1987.

Caridi, Ronald J. *The Korean War and American Politics: The Republican Party as a Case Study.* Philadelphia: University of Pennsylvania Press, 1968.

Carter, Paul A. *Another Part of the Fifties.* New York: Columbia University Press, 1983.

Cebula, Richard J. *The Deficit Problem in Perspective.* Lexington, Mass.: Lexington Books, 1987.

Chafe, William H. *The American Woman: Her Changing Social, Economic, and Political Roles, 1920–1970.* New York: Oxford University Press, 1972.

Chandler, Alfred D. *Strategy and Structure: Chapters in the History of Industrial Enterprise.* Cambridge: Harvard University Press, 1962.

———. *The Visible Hand: The Managerial Revolution in American Business.* Cambridge: Harvard University Press, 1977.

Ching, Cyrus Stuart. *Review and Reflection: A Half-Century of Labor Relations*. New York: B. C. Forbes, 1953.

Collins, J. Lawton. *War in Peacetime: The History and Lessons of Korea*. Boston: Houghton Mifflin, 1969.

Collins, Robert M. *The Business Response to Keynes, 1929–1964*. New York: Columbia University Press, 1981.

Crozier, Michael, et al. *The Crisis of Democracy*. New York: Columbia University Press, 1975.

Cuff, Robert D. *The War Industries Board: Business-Government Relations during World War I*. Baltimore: Johns Hopkins University Press, 1973.

Cumings, Bruce. *The Origins of the Korean War: Liberation and the Emergence of Separate Regimes, 1945–1947*. Vol. 1. Princeton: Princeton University Press, 1981.

———. *The Origins of the Korean War: The Roaring of the Cataract, 1947–1950*. Vol. 2. Princeton: Princeton University Press, 1990.

———. *Child of Conflict: The Korean-American Relationship, 1943–1953*. Seattle: University of Washington Press, 1983.

Dawson, Joseph G. III, ed. *Commander in Chief: Presidential Leadership in Modern Wars*. Lawrence: Regents Press of Kansas, 1993.

Degler, Carl N. *Out of Our Past: The Forces That Shaped Modern America*. New York: Harper & Row, 1970.

Derber, Milton, and Edwin Young, eds., *Labor and the New Deal*. Madison: University of Wisconsin Press, 1961.

Dockrill, Saki. *Eisenhower's New-Look National Security Policy, 1953–1961*. New York: St. Martin's Press, 1996.

Donovan, Robert J. *Conflict and Crisis: The Presidency of Harry S. Truman, 1945–1948*. New York: W. W. Norton, 1977.

———. *Tumultuous Years: The Presidency of Harry S. Truman, 1949–1953*. New York: W. W. Norton, 1982.

Drucker, Peter F. *Big Business: A Study of the Political Problems of American Capitalism*. New York: Harper & Row, 1949.

Eckes, Alfred E. *The United States and the Global Struggle for Minerals*. Austin: University of Texas Press, 1979.

First, Edythe W. *Industry and Labor Advisory Committees in the National Defense Advisory Commission and the Office of Production Management*. Washington, D.C.: Civilian Production Administration, 1946.

Foot, Rosemary. *The Wrong War: American Policy and the Dimensions of the Korean Conflict, 1950–1953*. Ithaca, N.Y.: Cornell University Press, 1985.

Ferrell, Robert H., ed. *The Eisenhower Diaries.* New York: Norton, 1981.

Fraser, Ronald, and Gary Gerstle, eds. *The Rise and Fall of the New Deal Order, 1930–1980.* Princeton: Princeton University Press, 1988.

Fried, Richard M. *Nightmare in Red: The McCarthy Era in Perspective.* New York: Oxford University Press, 1990.

Gaddis, John Lewis. *Strategies of Containment: A Critical Appraisal of Postwar National Security Policy.* New York: Oxford University Press, 1982.

Galambos, Louis, and Joseph Pratt. *The Rise of the Corporate Commonwealth: U.S. Business and Public Policy in the Twentieth Century.* New York: Basic Books, 1988.

Gallup, George H. *The Gallup Poll: Public Opinion 1935–1971.* Vols. 1–3. New York: Random House, 1972.

Halperin, Morton H. *Bureaucratic Politics and Foreign Policy.* Washington, D.C.: Brookings Institute, 1974.

Hamby, Alonzo L. *Beyond the New Deal: Harry S. Truman and American Liberalism.* New York: Columbia University Press, 1973.

Hammond, Paul Y. *Organizing for Defense: The American Military Establishment in the Twentieth Century.* Princeton: Princeton University Press, 1961.

Hartmann, Susan M. *The Home Front and Beyond, American Women in the 1940s.* Boston: Twayne Publishers, 1982.

Hastings, Max. *The Korean War.* New York: Simon & Schuster, 1987.

Hawley, Ellis W. *The Great War and the Search for a Modern Order: A History of the American People and Their Institutions, 1917–1933.* New York: St. Martin's Press, 1979.

Hayek, Freidrich von. *The Road to Serfdom.* Chicago: University of Chicago Press, 1944.

Hays, Samuel P. *Conservation and the Gospel of Efficiency: The Progressive Conservation Movement, 1890–1920.* Cambridge: Harvard University Press, 1959.

Heller, Francis H., ed. *The Korean War: A 25-Year Perspective.* Lawrence: Regents Press of Kansas, 1977.

Henkin, Louis. *Foreign Affairs and the Constitution.* Mineola, N.Y.: Foundation Press, 1972.

Hickman, Bert G. *Growth and Stability of the Postwar Economy.* Washington, D.C.: Brookings Institute, 1960.

Higgs, Robert. *Crisis and Leviathan: Critical Episodes in the Growth of American Government.* New York: Oxford University Press, 1987.

Hoff-Wilson, Joan. *Herbert Hoover: Forgotten Progressive.* Boston: Little, Brown, 1975.

Hogan, Michael J. and Thomas Paterson, eds. *Explaining the History of American Foreign Relations.* New York: Cambridge University Press, 1991.

Hogan, Michael J., ed. *The End of the Cold War: Its Meanings and Implications.* New York: Cambridge University Press, 1992.

Hogan, Michael J. *Informal Entente: The Private Structure of Cooperation in Anglo-American Economic Diplomacy, 1918–1928.* Columbia: University of Missouri Press, 1977.

———. *The Marshall Plan: America, Britain, and the Reconstruction of Western Europe, 1947–1952.* New York: Cambridge University Press, 1987.

Hooks, Gregory D. *Forging the Military-Industrial Complex: World War II's Battle of the Potomac.* Urbana: University of Illinois Press, 1991.

Hoover, Herbert. *Addresses upon the American Road, 1950–1955.* Stanford: Stanford University Press, 1955.

Huntington, Samuel P. *The Promise of Disharmony.* Cambridge: Harvard University Press, 1981.

Industrial College of the Armed Forces. *Emergency Management of the National Economy: Reconversion and Partial Mobilization.* Washington, D.C.: Industrial College of the Armed Forces, 1954.

Johnston, Eric. *America Unlimited.* Garden City, N.J.: Doubleday, Doran, 1944.

Kaledin, Eugenia. *Mothers and More: American Women in the 1950s.* Boston: Twayne Publishers, 1984.

Kaplan, Lawrence S. *The United States and NATO: The Formative Years.* Lexington: University of Kentucky Press, 1984.

Katzenstein, Peter, ed. *Between Power and Plenty: Foreign Economic Policies of Advanced Industrial States.* Madison: University of Wisconsin Press, 1978.

Kaufman, Burton I. *The Korean War: Challenges in Crisis, Credibility, and Command.* Philadelphia: Temple University Press, 1986.

Kinnard, Douglas. *President Eisenhower and Strategy Management: A Study in Defense Politics.* Lexington: University Press of Kentucky, 1977.

Kolko, Gabriel. *The Triumph of Conservatism: A Reinterpretation of American History, 1900–1916.* New York: Free Press, 1963.

Krasner, Stephen. *Defending the National Interest: Raw Materials Investments and U.S. Foreign Policy.* Princeton: Princeton University Press, 1978.

Lacey, Michael J., ed. *The Truman Presidency.* Cambridge, England: Cambridge University Press, 1989.

Lacey, Robert. *Ford, the Men and the Machine.* London: Heinemann, 1976.

LaFeber, Walter. *America, Russia, and the Cold War, 1945–1984.* 5th ed. New York: Alfred A. Knopf, 1985.

Lasswell, Harold D., ed. *The Analysis of Political Behavior: An Empirical Approach.* Hamden, Conn.: Archon Books, 1966.

———. *National Security and Individual Freedom.* New York: McGraw-Hill, 1950.

Lee, Alton R. *Truman and Taft-Hartley: A Question of Mandate.* Lexington: University of Kentucky Press, 1966.

Leffler, Melvyn P. *A Preponderance of Power: National Security, the Truman Administration, and the Cold War.* Stanford: Stanford University Press, 1992.

———. *The Elusive Quest: America's Pursuit of European Stability and French Security, 1919–1933.* Chapel Hill: University of North Carolina Press, 1979.

Lincoln, George A. *Economics of National Security: Managing America's Resources for Defense.* New York: Prentice-Hall, 1954.

Lipsett, Charles H. *Price and Wage Controls.* New York: Atlas Publishing, 1970.

Lotchin, Roger W. *Fortress California, 1910–1961: From Warfare to Welfare.* New York: Oxford University Press, 1992.

Marcus, Maeva. *Truman and the Steel Seizure Case: The Limits of Presidential Power.* New York: Columbia University Press, 1977.

Markusen, Ann et al. *The Rise of the Gunbelt: The Military Remapping of Industrial America.* New York: Oxford University Press, 1991.

Matray, James. *The Reluctant Crusade: American Foreign Policy in Korea, 1941–1950.* Honolulu: University of Hawaii Press, 1985.

May, Elaine Tyler. *Homeward Bound: American Families in the Cold War Era.* New York: Basic Books, 1988.

McClure, Arthur F. *The Truman Administration and the Problems of Post-War Labor, 1945–1948.* Rutherford, N.J.: Fairleigh Dickinson University Press, 1969.

McCoy, Donald R. *The Presidency of Harry S. Truman.* Lawrence: University Press of Kansas, 1984.

McCraw, Thomas K., ed. *The Essential Alfred Chandler: Essays toward a Historical Theory of Big Business.* Boston: Harvard Business School Press, 1988.

McCullough, David. *Truman.* New York: Simon & Schuster, 1992.

McDonald, Callum A. *Korea: The War before Vietnam*. London: MacMillan, 1986.

McQuaid, Kim. *Uneasy Partners: Big Business in American Politics, 1945–1990*. Baltimore: Johns Hopkins University Press, 1994.

———. *Big Business and Presidential Power: From FDR to Reagan*. New York: William Morrow, 1982.

Meyerowitz, Joanne, ed. *Not June Cleaver: Women and Gender in Postwar America*. Philadelphia: Temple University Press, 1994.

Millis, Walter et al. *Arms and the State: Civil-Military Elements in National Policy*. New York: The 20th Century Fund, 1958.

Millis, Walter, ed. *The Forrestal Diaries*. New York: Viking, 1951.

Milward, Alan S. *War, Economy, and Society: 1939–1945*. Berkeley: University of California Press, 1977.

Mucciaroni, Gary. *The Political Failure of Employment Policy, 1945–1982*. Pittsburgh: University of Pittsburgh Press, 1990.

Mueller, John E. *War, Presidents, and Public Opinion*. New York: Wiley, 1973.

———. *Retreat from Doomsday: The Obsolescence of Major War*. New York: Harper & Row, 1989.

Nash, George H. *The Conservative Intellectual Movement in America since 1945*. New York: Basic Books, 1976.

Nelson, Donald M. *Arsenal of Democracy: The Story of American War Production*. New York: Harcourt Brace, 1946.

Neustadt, Richard. *Presidential Power: The Politics of Leadership*. New York: Wiley Publishing, 1960.

Novick, David et al. *Wartime Production Controls*. New York: Columbia University Press, 1949.

O'Neill, William L. *American High: The Years of Confidence, 1945–1960*. New York: Free Press, 1986.

Patterson, James T. *Mr. Republican: A Biography of Robert A. Taft*. Boston: Houghton Mifflin, 1972.

Pells, Richard H. *The Liberal Mind in a Conservative Age: American Intellectuals in the 1940s and 1950s*. New York: Harper & Row, 1985.

Pemberton, William E. *Harry S. Truman: Fair Dealer and Cold Warrior*. Boston: Twayne Publishers, 1989.

Pollard, Robert A. *Economic Security and the Origins of the Cold War, 1945–1950*. New York: Columbia University Press, 1985.

Poole, Walter S. *The History of the Joint Chiefs of Staff, The Joint Chiefs of Staff and National Policy. Volume 4*. Wilmington, Del.: Glazier, 1980.

Porter, Bruce D. *War and the Rise of the State.* New York: Free Press, 1994.

Radosh, Ronald, and Murray N. Rothbard, eds. *A New History of Leviathan: Essays on the Rise of the American Corporate State.* New York: Dutton, 1972.

Rankin, Robert S., and Winfried R. Dallmayr. *Freedom and Emergency Powers in the Cold War.* New York: Appleton, Century, Crofts, 1964.

Rees, David. *Korea: The Limited War.* Baltimore: Penguin Books, 1964.

Reeves, Thomas C. *The Life and Times of Joe McCarthy.* Lanham, Md.: Madison Books, 1997.

Reichard, Gary. *Politics as Usual: The Age of Truman and Eisenhower.* Arlington Heights, Ill.: Greenwood Press, 1987.

Richardson, Elmo. *The Presidency of Dwight D. Eisenhower.* Lawrence: Regents Press of Kansas, 1979.

Rockoff, Hugh. *Drastic Measures: A History of Wage and Price Controls in the United States.* New York: Cambridge University Press, 1984.

Rosecrance, Richard, and Arthur A. Stein, eds. *The Domestic Bases of Grand Strategy.* Ithaca, N.Y.: Cornell University Press, 1993.

Ryan, Halford R. *Harry S. Truman: Presidential Rhetoric.* Westport, Conn.: Greenwood Press, 1993.

Sawyer, Charles. *Concerns of a Conservative Democrat.* Edwardsville: Southern Illinois University Press, 1968.

Schlesinger, Arthur M., Jr. *The Imperial Presidency.* Boston: Houghton Mifflin, 1973.

Schriftgiesser, Karl. *Business and Public Policy: The Role of the Committee for Economic Development, 1942–1967.* Englewood Cliffs, N.J.: Prentice Hall, 1967.

Scitovsky, Tibor et al. *Mobilizing Resources for War: The Economic Alternatives.* New York: McGraw-Hill, 1951.

Sherry, Michael S. *In The Shadow of War: United States since the 1930s.* New Haven: Yale University Press, 1995.

———. *The Rise of American Air Power: The Creation of Armageddon.* New Haven: Yale University Press, 1987.

Skocpol, Theda et al., eds. *Bringing the State Back In.* New York: Cambridge University Press, 1985.

Skowronek, Stephen. *Building a New American State: The Expansion of National Administrative Capacities, 1877–1920.* New York: Cambridge University Press, 1982.

Sloan, Alfred P. *My Years with General Motors.* Garden City, N.J.: Doubleday, 1972.

Soloman, William S., and Robert McChesney. *Ruthless Criticism: New Perspectives in U.S. Communications History.* Minneapolis: University of Minnesota Press, 1993.

Stebbins, Richard P. *The United States in World Affairs, 1951.* New York: Harper & Brothers (for the Council on Foreign Relations), 1952.

Stein, Herbert. *The Fiscal Revolution in America.* Chicago: University of Chicago Press, 1969.

Stokesbury, James L. *A Short History of the Korean War.* New York: William Morrow, 1988.

Summers, Harry G., Jr. *Korean War Almanac.* New York: Facts on File, 1990.

Truman, Harry S. *Memoirs: Years of Trial and Hope.* Vol. 2. New York: Da Capo, 1956.

Tucker, Nancy B. *Patterns in the Dust: Chinese-American Relations and the Recognition Controversy, 1949–1950.* New York: Columbia University Press, 1983.

Vawter, Roderick W. *Industrial Mobilization: The Relevant History.* Washington, D.C.: National Defense University Press, 1983.

Weinstein, James. *The Corporate Ideal in the Liberal State.* Boston: Beacon Press, 1968.

Whitfield, Stephen J. *The Culture of the Cold War.* Baltimore: Johns Hopkins University Press, 1991.

Wiebe, Robert H. *Businessmen and Reform: A Study of the Progressive Movement.* Cambridge: Harvard University Press, 1962.

———. *The Search for Order, 1877–1920.* New York: Hill and Wang, 1967.

———. *The Segmented Society: An Introduction to the Meaning of America.* New York: Oxford University Press, 1975.

———. *Self-Rule: A Cultural History of American Democracy.* Chicago: University of Chicago Press, 1995.

Wiedenbaum, Murray L. *The Economics of Peacetime Defense.* New York: Praeger Publishers, 1974.

Wilkins, Mira. *The Maturing of Multinational Enterprise: American Business Abroad from 1914 to 1970.* Cambridge: Harvard University Press, 1974.

Williams, William Appleman. *The Contours of American History.* Chicago: University of Chicago Press, 1968.

Yoshpe, Harry. *The National Security Resources Board 1947–1953: A Case Study in Peacetime Mobilization.* Washington, D.C.: Government Printing Office, 1953.

Unpublished Materials

Cuff, Robert D. "Organizational Capabilities and U.S. War Production: The Controlled Materials Plan of World War II." Paper presented at the Business History Conference, Johns Hopkins University, Baltimore, March 1990.

Koistinen, Paul A. C. "The Hammer and the Sword: Labor, the Military, and Industrial Mobilization, 1920–1945." Ph.D. diss., University of California–Berkeley, 1964.

Index